Diagnosis and Management of Learning Disabilities

Diagnosis and Management of Learning Disabilities:

An Interdisciplinary Approach

By

Frank R. Brown, III, Ph.D., M.D.
Associate Professor of Pediatrics
Medical University of South Carolina
Director, Division of Developmental Disabilities and
  Vince Moseley Center for Handicapped Children
Charleston, South Carolina

Elizabeth H. Aylward, Ph.D.
Instructor in Medical Psychology
Department of Psychiatry and Behavioral Sciences
The Johns Hopkins University School of Medicine
Licensed Psychologist, Pediatric Consultants—A Professional
  Affiliate of The Johns Hopkins University School of Medicine
Baltimore, Maryland

A College-Hill Publication
Little, Brown and Company
Boston/Toronto/San Diego

College-Hill Press
A Division of
Little, Brown and Company (Inc.)
34 Beacon Street
Boston, Massachusetts 02108

Library of Congress Cataloging-in-Publication Data
Brown, Frank R., III, 1943–
  Diagnosis and management of learning disabilities.

  "A College-Hill publication."
  Bibliography.
  Includes index.
  1. Learning disabilities—Treatment. 2. Learning
disabled children—Rehabilitation. 3. Learning disabled
children—Education. I. Aylward, Elizabeth H.,
1954–   . II. Title. [DNLM: 1. Learning Disorders—
diagnosis. 2. Learning Disorders—therapy. 3. Remedial
Teaching. LC 4704 B877d]
RJ506.L4B76   1987   616.89   87–3133

ISBN 0-316-11189-9

Printed in the United States of America

Contents

Chapter 1   **Introduction**

Learning Disability: What Is it? • Prevalence of
Learning Disabilities • Etiology of Learning
Disabilities • The Interdisciplinary Process in
Diagnosis and Treatment • Conclusion

Frank R. Brown, III, and Elizabeth H. Aylward

PART I: ESTABLISHING THE DIAGNOSIS

Chapter 2   **Neurodevelopmental Evaluation**
                      (The Physician's Role in Learning Disabilities)

Identification of Learning Disabilities in Preschool-
Aged Children • Neurodevelopmental History and
Examination for the School-Aged Child •
Conclusion

Frank R. Brown, III

Chapter 3   **Psychological Evaluation**

History Taking • Psychological Testing • Conclusion

Elizabeth H. Aylward

Chapter 4   **Educational Evaluation**

The Educational History • Educational Testing •
Conclusion

*Elizabeth H. Aylward, Frank R. Brown, III,
M. E. B. Lewis, and Carol R. Savage*

Chapter 5   **Speech-Language, Occupational Therapy, and**
                      Physical Therapy Evaluation

Language Evaluation • Occupational Therapy
Evaluation • Physical Therapy Evaluation

*Barbara L. Armstrong, Jean A. Lewis,
and Beverly D. Cusick*

GLOSSARY, APPENDICES, REFERENCES, AND REFERENCE LIST OF TESTS

Acknowledgment

The authors are indebted to Dennis Whitehouse, M.D., Director of the Diagnostic and Evaluation Center, The Kennedy Institute, Inc., The Johns Hopkins University. Dr. Whitehouse's leadership, sensitivity, and respect for others in implementing the interdisciplinary process serve as a continuing model for our approach to the diagnosis and management of learning disabilities.

Foreword

There have been numerous books written about learning disabilities and their associated lifelong problems. This pervasive disorder has been treated in ways that leave very little to the imagination. These have included pharmacological approaches, educational therapies, perceptual exercises, and psychotherapies. It often appears that the method preferred depends to a great extent upon which professionals presently have center stage and on what is in vogue in the literature.

Doctors Brown and Aylward, highly respected clinicians who are involved with learning disabled individuals on a regular basis, have developed in this text what I feel has long been needed by those of us who work with learning disabled populations. They have managed to take a complex area—with its academic, emotional, social, behavioral, and familial overtones—and present the reader with a concise picture of what practitioners are faced with as they are asked for their professional judgment in defining areas of education, medical, and psychological concern.

Throughout the text, the importance of an interdisciplinary approach rings clear. The authors honestly and unequivocally express their desire to maximize teamwork in planning and sharing evaluation results. Practitioners such as Brown and Aylward speak from experience when they say they want to present information that is brief and direct and not bogged down in the jargon and rhetoric that often accompany comprehensive reports in this area. It is this philosophy and approach that I believe will make this book a sought-after resource—a resource that takes the reader from the first "suspect" of a learning disability to the reporting of evaluation results, and finally to realistic and objectively stated recommendations.

A final word about the authors. This material is written primarily by a pediatrician and a psychologist, who work with learning disabled populations and who are both very much *educators*, in a true sense: they understand the complexities of educational placement and school programs. They have also been ever so cautious to include the expertise of educators and speech-language pathologists throughout the book, as well as that of physical and occupational therapists whenever appropriate. This is especially evident in the section "Planning for Treatment," which provides help to the practitioner who has established a diagnosis but needs to go further in developing a treatment plan.

Parents may also find a great amount of this information useful, as they begin, more and more, to interact with professionals to help develop their child's Individualized Educational Plan. The Glossary will be especially useful to parents, as some new terminology cannot be avoided when developing a common language.

On a personal note, I have known the authors for many years, as well as the work they do as part of interdisciplinary teams. Their willingness to share their experience and insights in a concise manner bodes well for the future of interdisciplinary diagnosis and treatment, at a time when anything less will not be helpful to those with learning disorders.

Michael Bender, Ed.D.
Vice President of Educational Programs, The Kennedy Institute
Professor of Education, The Johns Hopkins University

Preface

Of all childhood disorders, learning disabilities and its concomitant condition, attention deficit disorder, are by far the most prevalent, occurring in approximately 10 to 15 percent of school-aged children. It is important, therefore, that all professionals who work with children understand basic concepts in the identification and treatment of these disorders. Although this book is written at a level that can be understood by parents or professionals who have little familiarity with learning disorders, it is designed primarily for practitioners who are involved to some degree with diagnosis and treatment of learning-disabled children.

Children with learning disabilities often have a multitude of problems that span many facets of their lives, including academic, social, emotional, behavioral, and familial. It is imperative, therefore, to consider the total child from several points of view. Practitioners must consider the difficulties encountered in each sphere, as well as the *interactions* among the various problem areas. In the case of the learning-disabled child, the whole is greater than the sum of the parts.

We believe that an *interdisciplinary* approach allows for the most thorough understanding of the child's problems and needs. When an interdisciplinary approach is used, professionals from many disciplines come together to plan the evaluation, to share results of the assessments they have conducted individually, to discuss how results from evaluation in one discipline relate to results from another discipline, to formulate diagnoses, to plan for treatment and follow-up.

The purpose of this book is to facilitate an interdisciplinary approach to the diagnosis and treatment of learning disabilities. As a developmental pediatrician and developmental psychologist, we have attempted to convey in a simple, straightforward manner what we do when we evaluate and plan treatment for a child with learning disabilities. We have asked colleagues in the areas of special education, speech-language therapy, occupational therapy, and physical therapy to do the same. We present the methods we have found most useful in integrating the data from the various disciplines to arrive at diagnoses. We discuss what types of treatments are available for various aspects of the disorder, and try to objectively assess the effectiveness of these intervention techniques. Finally, we discuss ways to convey information to parents and to plan for follow-up.

We have intentionally tried to be brief and direct. Our plan in writing this book was to answer the question "What do you, as a practitioner, do from the moment you first suspect that a child might have a learning disability?" We intend for this book to become a part of the practitioner's working library, as a guide to be used on a day-to-day basis.

Contributors

Barbara L. Armstrong, M.S., CCC
Instructor of Pediatrics
Medical University of South Carolina
Director of Speech and Language
Vince Moseley Center for Handicapped Children
Charleston, South Carolina

Beverly D. Cusick, B.S., RPT
Instructor of Pediatrics
Associate, College of Health-Related Professions
Medical University of South Carolina
Director of Physical Therapy
Vince Moseley Center for Handicapped Children
Charleston, South Carolina

Jean A. Lewis, M.S., OTR
Instructor of Pediatrics
Assistant Professor, College of Health-Related Professions
Medical University of South Carolina
Director of Occupational Therapy
Vince Moseley Center for Handicapped Children
Charleston, South Carolina

M. E. B. Lewis, Ed.D.
Principal, The Kennedy School
The Kennedy Institute, Inc.
The Johns Hopkins University
Instructor, Division of Continuing Studies
The Johns Hopkins University
Baltimore, Maryland

Carol R. Savage, Ph.D.
Assistant Professor of Pediatrics
Medical University of South Carolina
Director of Special Education
Vince Moseley Center for Handicapped Children
Charleston, South Carolina

CHAPTER 1

Introduction

Frank R. Brown, III
Elizabeth H. Aylward

LEARNING DISABILITY: WHAT IS IT?

Since the term *learning disabilities* was first used by Samuel Kirk in 1962, there has been a great deal of confusion and controversy regarding the nature of this disorder. Special educators, other school personnel, psychologists, physicians, and researchers have proposed many definitions and descriptions of the disorder, a myriad of terms used interchangeably with *learning disabilities*, many theories regarding the etiology of the disorder, and many programs for its remediation.

In 1975 the United States Congress recognized learning disabilities as a handicapping condition and assured free and appropriate education for all learning-disabled children. At this time it became imperative that schools devise a system for making decisions about the eligibility of individual students for participation in the required special education programs. The federal government's definition of *specific learning disabilities* was included in the Education for All Handicapped Children Act as part of Public Law 94-142. The definition cited in the act is as follows:

Specific learning disability means a disorder in one or more of the basic psychological processes involved in the understanding or in using language, spoken or written, which may manifest itself in an imperfect ability to listen, think, speak, read, write, spell, or to do mathematical calculations. The term includes such conditions as perceptual handicaps, brain injury, minimal brain dysfunction, dyslexia, and developmental aphasia. The term does not apply to children who have learning problems which are primarily the result of visual, hearing, or motor handicaps, of mental retardation, or emotional disturbance, or of environmental, cultural or economic disadvantages (Public Law 94-142, 34 C.F.R. 300.5 [b] [9]).

To clarify further the term *learning disabilities*, the government provided educators with a separate set of federal regulations for the implementation of Public Law 94-142. These regulations are the "Procedures for Evaluation of Specific Learning Disabilities" (U.S. Office of Education, 1977). According to these regulations, a child has a specific learning disability if:

1. The child does not achieve commensurate with his or her age and ability levels in one or more of seven specific areas when provided with learning experiences appropriate for the child's age and ability level.
2. The team finds that a child has a severe discrepancy between achievement and intellectual ability in one or more of the following areas:
    (a) oral expression
    (b) listening comprehension
    (c) written expression
    (d) basic reading skills
    (e) reading comprehension
    (f) mathematics calculation
    (g) mathematics reasoning. (p. 65083)

Despite federal efforts to clarify the definition of learning disabilities, many professionals launched criticisms based on the definition's ambiguity, redundancy, and unnecessary restrictions. (See Berk, 1984, for further discussion). In order to address these criticisms, the National Joint Committee for Learning Disabilities (NJCLD), composed of representatives from six professional organizations, proposed a new definition, which was presented as follows in 1981:

Learning disabilities is a generic term that refers to a heterogeneous group of disorders manifested by significant difficulties in the acquisition and use of listening, speaking, reading, writing, reasoning, or mathematical abilities. These disorders are intrinsic to the individual and presumed to be due to central nervous system dysfunction.

Even though a learning disability may occur concomitantly with other handicapping conditions (e.g., sensory impairment, mental retardation, social and emotional disturbance) or environmental influences (e.g., cultural differences, insufficient/inappropriate instruction, psychogenic factors), it is not the direct result of those conditions or influences. (National Joint Committee for Learning Disabilities, 1981, p. 5).

Most school systems have used a combination of these definitions and regulations as the basis for establishing procedures to identify learning-disabled children. In doing so, the attempt has been made to determine the existence of "severe discrepancy" between achievement and intellectual ability in the individual. Because no federal guidelines have been established for defining "severe discrepancy," state and local education agencies have been forced to establish their own procedures for measuring achievement and intellectual ability, and for identifying "severe discrepancy." Even within states or regions where procedures have been established, many different approaches are used by various professionals to identify learning-disabled students. Especially for parents and professionals not specializing in the identification of learning disabilities on a day-to-day basis, there continues to be a great deal of confusion in determining whether or not any particular child is or is not learning disabled.

It is our opinion that much of the confusion regarding learning disabilities reflects a lack of understanding of the underlying basis and natural history of this disorder. This lack of understanding is reflected in the large number of terms that are often used imprecisely and inappropriately to suggest more understanding of the disorder than is justified. These include terms such as *specific learning disability, minimal brain dysfunction, attention deficit disorder, hyperactivity,* and *dyslexia.* In this book the use of terms reflects our philosophy regarding the neurological basis of learning disabilities. These definitions are presented in a format that, it is hoped, will clarify a distinction that we wish to make between *primary* (neurologically based) and *secondary* (derivative of primary) disorders.

Primary (Neurologically Based) Handicapping Conditions

The primary handicapping conditions for learning-disabled children are assumed to reflect brain "damage," albeit often of subtle degree and undetectable given current medical technologies. Like all disorders, mild degrees of brain damage are far more common than more serious degrees. This is reflected in the high incidence of learning disabilities and associated primary handicapping conditions, in comparison to more serious neurological dysfunctions, such as mental retardation and cerebral palsy.

The brain damage assumed in learning-disabled children is typically diffuse, meaning that multiple brain functions are affected. Two important areas of neurological functioning for the learning-disabled child are cognitive and motor skills. Diffuse cognitive dysfunction might involve expressive or receptive language, visual-spatial perceptual abilities, or the ability to focus and maintain attention. Diffuse motor dysfunction might include weaknesses in gross motor, fine motor, or oral motor skills.

The typical learning-disabled child will show some mixture of difficulties in cognitive and motor function. Because the motor and cognitive difficulties in learning-disabled children are frequently very subtle, parents and professionals may sometimes not appreciate their impact on the child. It is especially important to look not just at the "tip of the iceberg" (i.e., see the obvious and most major handicapping condition), but to also be alert to less obvious associated difficulties.

The primary handicapping conditions most often seen in learning-disabled children (and requiring careful definition) are defined as follows.

Learning Disability

The definition of learning disability that we use is based on the 1975 federal definition included as part of Public Law 94-142, the 1977 U.S. Office of Education (U.S.O.E.) regulations, and the 1981 NJCLD definitions. We limit the use of the term *learning disability* to a condition whereby an individual's academic achievement level is significantly below the level that would be predicted from the level of intellectual ability. The cause for the discrepancy between academic achievement and intellectual ability is presumed to be neurologically based. Although learning disabilities can occur concomitantly with other handicapping conditions or environmental influences, they are not the direct result of these conditions or influences. Learning disabilities can occur in the areas of listening, speaking, reading, writing, reasoning, or mathematical abilities. Primary focus, however, is placed on learning disabilities in three areas:

READING. A reading disability (also termed *dyslexia*) occurs when individual reading skills (e.g., word attack, reading comprehension) or general reading ability are significantly below the level that would be predicted from the individual's level of intellectual ability, assuming other handicapping conditions or environmental influences have been ruled out. If the reading disability is thought to be caused by an overall weakness in language skills, it may be referred to as a "language-based" learning disability.

MATHEMATICS. A mathematics disability (also termed *dyscalculia*) occurs when individual math skills (e.g., acquisition of number facts, written calculations, mathematical reasoning) or general mathematical ability are significantly below the level that would be predicted from the individual's level of intellectual ability, assuming other handicapping conditions or environmental influences have been ruled out.

WRITTEN LANGUAGE. A written language disability (also termed *dysgraphia*) occurs when individual written language skills (e.g., spelling, application of grammar, punctuation, usage skills, organization of thoughts in writing) or general written language ability are significantly below the level that would be predicted from the individual's level of intellectual ability, assuming other handicapping conditions or environmental influences have been ruled out. Although it may be considered a learning disability in itself, poor handwriting is not included in the term *dysgraphia*, as we use it.

Attention Deficit Disorder (ADD)

The definition that we use is based on the criteria set in the *Diagnostic and Statistical Manual III* of the American Psychiatric Association (1980). In order to be diagnosed as having ADD, a child must meet criteria for inattention (e.g., failure to finish things he or she starts, failure to listen, easy distractibility, difficulty in concentrating or sticking to a play activity) and criteria for impulsivity (e.g., acting before thinking, shifting from one activity to another, difficulty in organization, need for supervision, frequent calling out in class, and difficulty awaiting turns). For a diagnosis of ADD with hyperactivity, the child must also run or climb excessively, have difficulty sitting still or staying seated, move excessively during sleep, or act as if "driven by a motor" (American Psychiatric Association, 1980, p. 44).

We attempt to clearly distinguish between a child who has ADD with hyperactivity and a child who has ADD without hyperactivity. We also wish to make clear that many children have ADD without learning disabilities, and many learning-disabled children do not have ADD. The two disorders are, however, often seen concomitantly.

Minimal Brain Dysfunction (MBD)

We use this term to refer to the child who has a mixture of some or all of the subtle cognitive and motor dysfunctions described previously. Components of MBD may include learning disabilities, language disabilities, other inconsistencies among various cognitive functions, ADD, gross-, fine-, and oral-motor dyscoordinations. What is clear from this listing is that ADD is part of a larger syndrome that was originally termed MBD. Developmentalists and educators have, with the term ADD, focused on that part of this larger MBD syndrome that they felt was most significant in terms of school dysfunction. Clearly, there are a number of children who exhibit a much wider spectrum of symptoms than are accounted for by the term ADD, and for these children the term MBD may still be an appropriate description.

Secondary (Derivative of Primary) Handicapping Conditions

Unlike the primary handicapping conditions described previously, secondary handicapping conditions do not have a direct neurological basis. They are instead the *result* of the primary handicapping conditions, especially when the primary handicapping conditions have not been properly managed. The most common secondary handicapping conditions are poor self-concept and inappropriate attention-seeking behaviors. Poor self-concept is often the result of academic failure, especially when the child is blamed or told that the failure is due to lack of motivation. When learning-disabled children are unable to receive recognition for positive achievements (e.g., academic success) they sometimes resort to inappropriate behaviors in order to obtain recognition, despite the fact that the recognition is often negative. In addition to these two common secondary handicapping conditions, learning-disabled children may also exhibit such secondary characteristics as poor peer relationships, compliance problems, oppositional behaviors, depression, school phobia, and other problems of adjustment.

Slow Learner

Although learning-disabled children demonstrate slow achievement in some or all academic areas, their cognitive functioning is usually average or better. We wish to distinguish between children with learning disabilities and children labeled "slow learners." *Slow learner* is a term used to describe the child whose learning ability in all areas is delayed in comparison to children of the same chronological age. These children are characterized by low-normal to borderline intelligence, with corresponding slow academic progress. These children are not considered learning disabled because there is no discrepancy between cognitive expectations and academic achievement. Although generally not eligible for special education services, these children are often in need of a modified curriculum and more individual attention than their nonaffected peers. We will not address this population except to point out that the number of slow learners is as great as the number of learning-disabled students, and to express an opinion that these students need and deserve special education services as much as learning-disabled students.

PREVALENCE OF LEARNING DISABILITIES

Failure to define terms precisely has led to confusion over prevalence rates. Prevalence rates for learning disabilities are generally quoted between 3 and 15 percent of the school age population (Phye and Reschly, 1979). Boys are diagnosed as being learning disabled four to eight times as often as girls (Marsh, Gearhart, and Gearhart, 1978). Although there are no definite figures regarding the prevalence of ADD within the learning-disabled population, Meier (1971) reported a 20 percent incidence of learning disabilities and a 4 percent incidence of "hyperactivity." Safer and Allen (1976) estimate that approximately 30 percent of hyperactive children are learning disabled, whereas approximately 40 percent of learning-disabled children are hyperactive.

ETIOLOGY OF LEARNING DISABILITIES

In discussing learning disabilities, many parents ask, "Why is my child learning disabled?" In most cases, professionals must answer "I don't know," as the etiology of learning disabilities can rarely be determined for certain. However, it is known that the incidence of learning disabilities is increased among family members of children with the disorder, suggesting a genetic link. Parents (especially fathers) will sometimes remark that their child's difficulties are similar to problems they experienced themselves as children. Children who have experienced certain types of birth trauma (e.g., lack of sufficient oxygen at or around the time of birth, difficult delivery, prematurity) also have a higher incidence of learning disabilities, as well as other developmental delays. However, it must be kept in mind that causality cannot be presumed from the fact that two conditions frequently occur together. It is, therefore, rarely possible to pinpoint for certain the exact "cause" of the problem within an individual child.

As the term *learning disabilities* is usually defined, the assumption is made that the disorder is due, at least in part, to some type of neurological irregularity. The nature of the irregularity has, however, been much debated. One general view presumes that the neurological abnormalities are a consequence of aberrant organization or dysfunction of the central nervous system Critchley, 1970; Hinshelwood, 1917; and others). The neurological "deficits" referred to in this "deficit" model are very subtle and cannot be recognized or localized using present technologies. An alternative view is the "no defect" or maturational lag hypothesis (Bender, 1957; Kinsbourne, 1975; and others). This hypothesis suggests that learning-disabled children merely possess a slower rate of normal development of neural processes relevant to the acquisition of academic skills. It implies that learning-disabled children will eventually develop the requisite neural processes and will then learn with normal or near-normal facility (McKeever and VanDeventer, 1975).

Witelson (1977) points out that there is no empirical support for the hypothesis implied by the "developmental lag" model that learning-disabled children eventually "catch up" and become normal. We agree that most learning-disabled children, especially those with a concomitant ADD, continue to demonstrate weaknesses in academic achievement, despite all remedial efforts, well into adolescence and beyond. As Witelson (1977) notes, a "deficit model" does not preclude the manifestation of a lag in development of cognitive skills. Most disorders, she states, result in test performance that is at least superficially comparable to that of normal children at some earlier chronological age.

Parents will occasionally ask if their child is learning disabled or merely suffering from some type of developmental lag or delay. We would generally answer these parents by agreeing that the child does, indeed, have a delay that makes him or her appear "immature" or poorly developed in certain areas. Parents would, however, be discouraged from believing that the child will "catch up" (with or without intervention) and eventually appear normal. Of course, children with mild delays, especially if they are bright, may learn ways to circumvent their weaknesses. However, it would be a mistake to say that the neurological abnormalities underlying these weaknesses do not continue to exist. It should also be noted that learning-disabled individuals often experience few difficulties once they have finished school because they can avoid situations that demand those skills that caused problems for them in the school setting.

It may be inappropriate to assume that all symptomatology related to learning disabilities, and especially ADD, will necessarily prove ultimately to be so maladaptive. Levine, Brooks, and Shonkoff (1980) have suggested that many of the symptoms of ADD may have some positive facets and potential for good prognosis. The child with disabling distractibility in school may prove to make interesting observations with less confined associations as an adult. The child with ADD and fast paced cognitive tempo may prove to be an extremely productive adult. In essence, when the child with ADD is permitted as an adult to develop his own strengths (and opportunity to bypass areas of weakness), the "disorder" may evolve into some areas of strength.

Finally, in discussing the etiology of learning disabilities, it must be mentioned that investigators over the years have proposed many theories to explain what is "wrong" in the brains of learning-disabled children. For example, it has been proposed that these children suffer from inadequate lateralization of the brain hemispheres, from language processing deficits, from deficits in visual discrimination, from poor auditory-visual integration, from poor visual closure, or from poor auditory sequential memory. (See Johnson, 1981, for a thorough history of these theories.) We will not add to this list of theories by attempting to identify *the* underlying problem that leads to learning disabilities. We assume, however, that learning-disabled children are not a homogeneous group. Learning disabilities are not the result of one etiology (e.g., genetics or birth trauma) and are not caused by one type of deficit (e.g., language-processing or lack of cerebral lateralization). The diagnostic process is designed primarily to identify which children are actually experiencing learning disabilities, not to theorize about possible underlying causes.

THE INTERDISCIPLINARY PROCESS IN DIAGNOSIS AND TREATMENT

What Is the Interdisciplinary Process?

We wish to distinguish between a *multi-disciplinary* and an *interdisciplinary* process. The former involves a series of individual evaluations and treatment plans by several disciplines (e.g., special education, medicine, psychology). The latter involves a comprehensive integrated and systematic approach, whereby professionals from several disciplines come together to plan the diagnostic procedures to be used, carry out a variety of evaluative procedures, meet again to share the results of the evaluations, formulate diagnoses based on these evaluations, work together to devise appropriate treatment procedures, and assign responsibility to individual team members for carrying out various parts of the plan.

Who Is Involved?

The interdisciplinary process can be carried out in a variety of settings. One common setting would be a diagnostic and evaluation clinic, whose staff would probably include physicians, psychologists, and special educators, as well as professionals in allied fields such as speech-language therapy and occupational and physical therapy. In this case, outside professionals who are familiar with the child, especially school personnel, would be asked to participate. Alternatively, the interdisciplinary process could be initiated by the school, with participation solicited from the child's physician and any other outside professionals familiar with the child. An individual professional working privately with the child, such as a physician, private language therapist, tutor, or psychologist, might initiate and coordinate the process. On rare occasions, the procedure might even be initiated by parents, who would make arrangements for all of the professionals working with their child to meet for interdisciplinary diagnosis and development of therapeutic recommendations.

Regardless of the setting, the interdisciplinary process should minimally consist of a physician, psychologist, and educator. Other professionals who may be very beneficial in the process would include any other school personnel familiar with the child (school principal, special education teacher, school psychologist, school nurse, speech-language therapist, occupational or physical therapist, guidance counselor, social worker, regular classroom teachers), as well as nonschool personnel (physician, psychologists who may have been enlisted independently by the family for evaluation, therapists, social workers from outside agencies, nursery school teachers, community health nurses, and private tutors).

Nonschool professionals must, of course, respect the fact that the school, as the primary service-provider, has regulations and procedures that must be followed. These professionals should assist school personnel in determining whether or not the child meets criteria for diagnosis of learning disability by providing information about the child to which the school may not have immediate access (assuming, of course, that the child's parents have agreed to such disclosure). They should assist in the development of appropriate in-school interventions, again by providing additional information about the child that may be relevant in deciding which strategies will be most effective. Nonschool professionals can play a major role in devising out-of-school interventions that may augment the program provided by the school (e.g., instructing parents in behavior management strategies, providing extracurricular activities that might build the child's self-concept, or suggesting counseling for parents whose expectations are unrealistic). Of course, the physician is a vital member of the team when decisions are being made regarding the need for medication to control ADD.

Certain nonschool professionals, especially the child's physician, may be in an excellent position to ensure continuity of appropriate services, even if the child moves from school to school. Because most children have regular contact with their physician and because parents are usually willing to share information freely with the physician, he or she can monitor the child's treatment and progress. Children who might otherwise "fall through the cracks" of the educational system can be assured appropriate ongoing services.

Finally, nonschool personnel should, when necessary, monitor the school's approach to diagnosis and treatment. Unfortunately, some schools are still using outdated methods for identifying learning-disabled children. Nonschool personnel may need to make certain that the children they represent are not disqualified from service because they do not meet certain inappropriate criteria (e.g., large subtest scatter on the intelligence test). Nonschool personnel may need to monitor the type and amount of special education service the school is planning to provide. For example, if a child needs speech therapy but the school does not employ a speech therapist, the school may not be willing to include the therapy as part of the treatment plan. Nonschool personnel may need to intervene on behalf of the child.

Of course, the primary goal of the interdisciplinary team is to serve the child. Team members, both school and nonschool personnel, should view the interdisciplinary process as an opportunity to educate one another regarding their individual disciplines, as well as an opportunity to provide optimal service to both child and family.

How Does the Interdisciplinary Process Work?

The first step in the interdisciplinary process is generally some type of *prescreening*. This may be done by the case manager or by a committee, and involves determining whether or not the child is experiencing difficulty that warrants thorough evaluation. This determination is generally made by talking with the person who initiated the referral (e.g., parents, teacher, physician) to obtain a description of the nature and history of the problems the child is experiencing. When possible, it is beneficial for those conducting the prescreening process to review records or talk briefly with individuals other than the referral source.

The most important aspect of the prescreening process is to determine what types of evaluation are most appropriate and will probably lead to the most fruitful results. Just as a physician determines what types of lab tests to conduct on the basis of the patient's symptoms, the individual(s) conducting the prescreening must determine from a description of the child's problems whether it would be more productive to explore the possibility of learning disabilities rather than other disorders (e.g., serious emotional disturbance). More specifically, the prescreening process will allow the case manager to make arrangements, when necessary, for evaluations from allied professionals (e.g., speech-language therapist, occupational therapist, physical therapist).

Finally, the individual(s) conducting the prescreening process should determine whether any evaluations have already been conducted that will be relevant in the formulation of the diagnoses and therapeutic recommendations. Although it is not necessary that the case manager determine precisely what evaluations will be carried out before the diagnostic process is initiated, some preplanning may reduce the number of visits the family must make to the clinic, reduce redundancy among the evaluations, and ensure that the concerns of the referring party are thoroughly addressed.

After the prescreening team or case manager has determined which evaluations will probably be most productive, individual professionals conduct the appropriate evaluations. These evaluations generally consist of a thorough history (obtained through review of records and interviews with the parents, teachers, and child), as well as assessment with specific tests. The types of evaluation procedures employed by the physician, psychologist, educator, and allied professionals are described thoroughly in Chapters 2, 3, 4, and 5.

After the individual professionals have conducted their evaluations, a case conference is held during which each professional shares the results of his or her evaluation. By reviewing Chapters 2, 3, 4, and 5, individual team members will have the necessary background to understand the evaluation techniques employed by each of the various disciplines. It is important, for example, for the special educator to understand how the physician arrived at a diagnosis of ADD. It is equally important for the physician to understand the nature of the tests used by the psychologist to determine the level of the child's cognitive abilities. By understanding each discipline's evaluative procedures, team members can better understand the data presented and its relationship to their own data, suggest alternative interpretations to the data, monitor the appropriateness of the evaluation procedures for individual children, and identify areas in which information is incomplete.

After the data have been presented, the case manager will need to summarize the data presented and formulate tentative diagnoses to be discussed by the team. (Chapter 6 describes how the information gathered by each of the team members can be integrated to arrive at appropriate diagnoses.) Following discussion of the data presented, team members should be able to agree upon a list of the primary and secondary handicapping conditions that are interfering with successful performance. On occasion, however, team members may decide that further evaluation is necessary before the diagnoses can be formulated. In this case, final diagnoses are postponed until a later meeting.

After diagnoses have been established, the interdisciplinary team should formulate a general treatment plan. For example, it might be determined that the child should receive special education services in math and written language, that a trial on medication for ADD should be initiated, and that the parents should be provided with some training in behavior management strategies. Just as individual team members need to understand the evaluation procedures employed by professionals from other disciplines, it is important that they understand the various treatment strategies used. The special education teacher, for example, needs to understand what should be expected from a child treated with medication for ADD. Similarly, the psychologist needs to understand what types of reading programs are used by special educators to deal with a child who demonstrates language processing difficulties. By understanding the various treatment modalities available to the child, team members can better determine which treatments should be used, when and how they should be employed (e.g., all treatments started simultaneously or various treatments added in increments), how to evaluate their effectiveness, and how to determine when they are no longer needed. Strategies for management of primary and secondary handicapping conditions are discussed in Chapters 7, 8, and 9.

The team should not attempt at the time of the initial interdisciplinary conference to develop specific goals and objectives, timelines for accomplishing their aims, or criteria for success. Instead, individual team members should be assigned responsibility for ensuring that the general areas of the treatment plan are further refined and implemented. The team should determine, however, what procedures will be used to coordinate and monitor the implementation of the general treatment plan. Procedures for follow-up and reevaluation should also be addressed.

Following this interdisciplinary case conference, the case manager (or other person appointed by the team) will be responsible for sharing the results of the evaluation, the diagnostic formulation, and the general therapeutic recommendations with the parents. Strategies for parent counseling are discussed in Chapter 10. This step is necessary in order to promote the parents' understanding and acceptance of their child's disorders and to elicit their cooperation in treatment. Parents are often encouraged to participate in the development of the Individualized Educational Program (IEP) at the child's school (see Chapter 7). Their contribution to this process will be greatly enhanced if they have previously been presented with information regarding their child's disorders, been given the opportunity to ask the questions necessary to clarify their understanding of the situation, and had a chance to discuss treatment options.

CONCLUSIONS

The field of learning disabilities has matured tremendously since the term was first introduced in 1962. However, there is still a great deal of confusion and misunderstanding, even among professionals who diagnose and treat learning-disabled children on a regular basis. Part of the reason for misunderstanding involves the interdisciplinary nature of the disorder. Because the learning-disabled child often exhibits problems that are generally treated by professionals in different disciplines, it has been difficult for individual professionals to be able to deal effectively with the total child. For this reason, an interdisciplinary approach is vitally important. By understanding better the diagnostic and treatment tools available to each discipline involved with the child, individual professionals can work together more effectively for the child's *total* well-being.

PART I

ESTABLISHING THE DIAGNOSIS

CHAPTER 2

Neurodevelopmental Evaluation (The Physician's Diagnostic Role in Learning Disabilities)

Frank R. Brown, III

The diagnosis of a learning disability depends upon measurement of, and establishment of a discrepancy between, academic achievement and cognitive functioning levels. There is no single characteristic sign that clearly indicates a learning disability. The diagnostic process is a team effort, recognizing that no particular discipline, in and of itself, has the capacity to adequately diagnose and develop prescriptive (remediation) programs. The physician should be a vital member of this team process because he or she may be the first professional resource contacted for developmental questions, especially with preschool children who are at risk for subsequent learning disabilities based on developmental and behavioral aberrancies. The physician is uniquely positioned in regard to certain highly sensitive areas, especially the family history. Other professionals often cannot ask some of the intimate and charged questions about the family that the physician is permitted to ask. With school age children, the physician can contribute both in the diagnostic process and in ensuring a balance of professional perspectives when establishing a remediation program.

In order to make these contributions to the diagnostic and prescriptive process, the physician must expand the traditional role of medical history-taking and examination to include a neurodevelopmental history and neurodevelopmental examination. The physician embarks in these areas, traditionally the purview of psychology and education, not because he or she doesn't trust these professionals in their ability to perform their tasks, but rather to ensure the physician's well-considered input in the evaluation process. Components of the physician's expanded neurodevelopmental history and examination process for the preschool and school-age child are the focus of this chapter.

IDENTIFICATION OF LEARNING DISABILITIES IN PRESCHOOL-AGED CHILDREN

Learning disabilities in children have typically been detected late—in second to third grade. This stems from a tendency in many schools to define learning disabilities on the basis of a lag (typically at least two grade equivalents) in learning skills, and from the fact that this represents an age at which children become more demonstrative in asserting their frustrations in not being able to keep up with their classmates. These frustrations may take the form of pseudohyperactivity or pseudo-attention deficit disorder, for example, running in the classroom and in general disrupting other students and classroom activities. At this point the school is forced to address the situation.

There are several problems with detection of learning disabilities by a two grade level school lag and associated secondary behavioral manifestations. First, it would be desirable to develop more sensitive indicators of learning disabilities that would permit detection at the earliest possible moment, reasoning that our ability to remediate would be dependent upon providing appropriate services at the earliest conceivable stage of the education process. Second, it is not appropriate to rely solely on indirect measures of learning disabilities such as the behavioral manifestations of frustration with the education process. Recognizing this, there has been a recent push to identify learning disabilities at the earliest point, and the physician is in a unique position to participate in this early identification process.

Neurodevelopmental History

The physician, by virtue of early (frequently pre- and perinatal) involvement with the child and family, is in a position to recognize preschool children at risk for learning disabilities. Through a carefully elicited pregnancy, labor, and birth history the physician can identify pregnancies that represent high risks and deserve careful developmental monitoring. It is important to remember that some of the risk factors elicited in the pre- and perinatal history (Table 2-1) may manifest in subtle, sometimes undetectable fashion. For example, although the effects of high maternal alcohol consumption on the fetus and fetal alcohol syndrome are obvious

TABLE 2-1

Prenatal and Perinatal History—Risk Factors Associated with Learning Disabilities

Pregnancy	Labor and Delivery (cont'd)
Maternal age	Problems:
Paternal age	premature rupture of membranes
Parity	maternal fever
Length of gestation	toxemia
Maternal weight gain	abnormal bleeding
Fetal activity	fetal monitoring
Previous maternal obstetrical	failure of labor to progress
problems	labor induced
Problems:	Caesarian section
bleeding/spotting	forceps/instrumentation
medications	resuscitation
trauma	abnormalities at birth
toxemia	abnormal placenta
radiation	
rash/infection	*Neonatal*
fluid retention	Duration of hospitalization
abnormal fetal movements	Problems:
alcohol	respiratory distress syndrome
tobacco	cyanosis
	seizures
Labor and Delivery	oxygen therapy
Hospital	feeding problems
Duration of labor	infections
Birth weight	jaundice
Apgars	metabolic
Analgesia/sedation	congenital abnormalities
Presentation	apnea

(intrauterine and postnatal growth retardation, physical abnormalities, and impaired cognitive development), one must wonder about the effects of lesser degrees of alcohol and cigarette consumption, and other factors, such as subclinical maternal viral infections, on the developing fetus. Suffice it to say that the outcomes of these more subtle (and more frequently occurring) situations are just beginning to be appreciated.

In addition to the historical questions used to identify high risk pregnancies, the physician should elicit a careful neurodevelopmental history, that is, a history of the temporal patterns of development. Children's neurodevelopment can be assessed along four major lines: motor (gross/fine), visual problem solving, language (expressive/receptive), and social-adaptive.

A major purpose of obtaining the developmental history is to permit a comparison of the rate of present development with what has been historically true. Such a comparison will tell the physician whether an observed developmental delay has always been true or may represent an evolving process of neurodegeneration that would demand careful medical workup.

Of the four areas of development listed, the physician does not typically ask the parents questions about the child's historical visual problem-solving abilities, in major part because most parents do not think about their child's development in these terms. Likewise, the physician does not dwell very long on social-adaptive skills, as acquisition of these skills is so dependent upon willingness of the parents to permit the child to do things for himself. The focus of the neurodevelopmental history then becomes the child's motor (gross/fine) and cognitive development.

Gross motor milestones (Table 2-2) are typically the best noted and remembered by parents and health care professionals. They have, however, the poorest correlation with ultimate function in life. That is, a child's ultimate well being depends more on cognitive aspects of development such as visual problem solving and language. Despite this, a careful review of gross and fine motor development is important because gross motor skills affect in a major way how children, especially younger children, relate to

TABLE 2-2
Gross Motor Developmental Milestones

Approximate Age	Skill Attained
4 mo	Roll over, face down to face up
5 mo	Roll over, face up to face down
6 mo	Sit without support
9 mo	Pull to standing
12 mo	Walk independently
18 mo	Run
27 mo	Walk up stairs ("marking time")
36 mo	Walk up stairs alternating feet and down stairs "marking time"
	Pedal tricycle
3.5 yr	Walk up and down stairs alternating feet
5 yr	Skip
7 yr	Ride two-wheel bicycle without training wheels

each other in play and because fine motor skills are important when hand-written work becomes a determinant in school performance.

The most important area of development for children, and the one that most developmentalists feel is the most informative of ultimate function in life, is receptive language development (Table 2-3). Therefore, a great deal of emphasis should be given to this part of the developmental history and a considerable amount of time may be required to elicit this history, as this is an area where the parents may not be good observers.

TABLE 2-3
Language—Expressive and Receptive

Approximate Age	Skill Attained
6 mo	Babbling (playful repetition of consonant-vowel syllables—should consist of at least four different consonants repeated in a string)
9 mo	Gesture language (child either spontaneously or imitatively engages in gestures to communicate wants; waves bye-bye or plays pat-a-cake)
12 mo	Ma-Ma/Da-Da, used appropriately to mean mother or father First word other than ma-ma, da-da, or name of family member
18 mo	Follow one-step command without gestures, e.g., "Give me _____"
2 yr	Two word phrases, 20 word vocabulary
2.5 yr	Follows two-step command without gestures, e.g., "Put the ball on the table and give the pencil to me"
3 yr	Vocabulary 250 words, three and four word sentences Answers appropriately, "What do you do when you are hungry?"
4 yr	Tells stories about experiences using complex syntax Answers appropriately, "What is a house made of?"
5 yr	Vocabulary too numerous to count Follows three-step command in the correct order

Neurodevelopmental Examination

By the time the physician begins the neurodevelopmental examination of the preschool child, he or she should have, based on the neurodevelopmental history obtained from the parents, a good idea of where present development is and at what level to begin developmental testing. The neurodevelopmental examination typically focuses on three of the four major areas discussed previously: motor (gross/fine), visual problem solving, and language (expressive/receptive). The physician will screen, or hopefully, assess the child's level of development in these three areas and will then refer the child for additional, more detailed evaluations as required.

Physicians have typically made these referral decisions on the basis of results of developmental screening instruments such as the Denver Developmental Screening Test (Frankenburg and Dodds, 1967). The problem with all screening instruments is that they necessarily have a number of false positives and negatives. We feel that children are best assessed and referred for additional testing on the basis of clinical judgment. Development of this judgment necessitates that the physician make an effort to learn what represents normal and abnormal development. The neurodevelopmental assessment tools described in this chapter are not intended to replace more detailed evaluations by allied professionals, but they can provide a basis for the physician to think about normal and abnormal development and to make subsequent referrals based on his or her clinical judgment.

Assessment of Gross/Fine Motor Abilities

Table 2-2 describes some major gross motor developmental milestones for preschool and school-age children. One obvious conclusion from this table is that the majority of gross motor skills required for adult life are attained, in the course of normal gross motor development, by approximately 5 to 6 years of age. By this developmental age a child is able to run, hop, skip, and balance. When evaluating the gross motor developmental level of preschool children, it is especially valuable to observe their performance with stair ascension and descension. Performance on this task, as shown in Table 2-2, identifies gross motor abilities in an approximate 27 month (ascension of stairs "marking time," i.e., placing a foot up onto a stair and bringing the other foot up to the same level) to 42 month (ascension and descension of stairs with alternating feet) range.

Fine motor skills are normally inferred from observation of a child's performance on the visual problem solving tasks employing manipulations of one-inch cubes and pencil and paper described subsequently and in

Table 2-4. Most of the visual problem solving tasks described in Table 2-4 represent a combination of the cognitive task of conceptualizing the drawing or block assembly, together with the fine motor ability to appropriately manipulate the objects. An exact level of fine motor functioning is not derived from this process, but rather a determination is made of whether fine motor abilities significantly interfere with completion of the visual problem solving task.

TABLE 2-4
Assessment of Visual Problem Solving Abilities

One-Inch Cubes (18 months-7 years)

18 mo	Vertical tower of 3 cubes (a)		(a)
24 mo	Train of 3 cubes (b)		(b)
27 mo	Train of 4 cubes with smoke stack (c)		(c)
36 mo	3 block bridge (d)		(d)
4 yr	5 block gate (e)		(e)
5 yr	6 block staircase (f)		(f)
7 yr	10 block staircase (g)		(g)

Pencil and Paper (3 years-12 years)

3 yr	Copies circle
3.5 yr	Copies cross
4 yr	Copies square
5 yr	Copies triangle
6 yr	Copies "Union Jack"
7 yr	Copies diamond
8 yr	Copies Maltese cross
9 yr	Copies cylinder
12 yr	Copies cube

Gesell Drawings
(see Figure 2-1)

Assessment of Visual Problem Solving Abilities

In the developmental assessment of preschool children, primary focus is on those aspects of development that are most predictive of ultimate function, including success in school. These are the cognitive areas of problem solving and expressive/receptive language development.

Assessment of visual problem solving for preschool children involves analysis of their play skills with simple toy items (Table 2-4) such as one-inch cubes and pencil and paper. The one-inch cubes cover an approximate 18 month to 7 year range and pencil and paper an approximate 3 year to 12 year visual perceptual developmental age range. When testing a child's visual problem solving abilities with one-inch cubes, the examiner first builds the test item (Table 2-4, a-e) out of sight of the child (typically by covering the assembly process with their hand). The child is then given the appropriate number of blocks and is asked to duplicate the model construct built by the examiner. The two exceptions to this procedure are the staircase assemblies (Table 2-4, f and g), where the model, once built and shown to the child, is destroyed and the child is asked to build the assembly from visual memory.

The drawing tasks listed in Table 2-4 are suitable for testing visual perceptual development for both preschool and school-age children. These drawings are presented to the child in a completed format and the child is asked to replicate the figures. These drawings and their interpretations are described in detail later and are included in Figure 2-1.

The visual problem solving tasks presented here for one-inch cubes and pencil and paper represent only two of a wide range of such test items that might be included in a battery for testing visual problem solving abilities of preschool children. These two test items do have particular value in terms of the breadth of developmental age range covered (also useful for assessment of school-age children) and because they represent very simple test procedures that the physician may incorporate in the neurodevelopmental assessment battery. They will not interfere with subsequent more detailed psychological assessments of visual problem solving abilities.

Assessment of Language Functioning

Assessment of language (especially receptive language) for the preschool child does not depend on specific test items of the type described previously for assessment of abilities in visual problem solving. Language development can be assessed through an awareness of the normal sequence of language development described in Table 2-3. When assessing language development, the physician should be most concerned with what might be termed *connected language understanding and usage*, that is, the practical everyday language required for communicating and following directions.

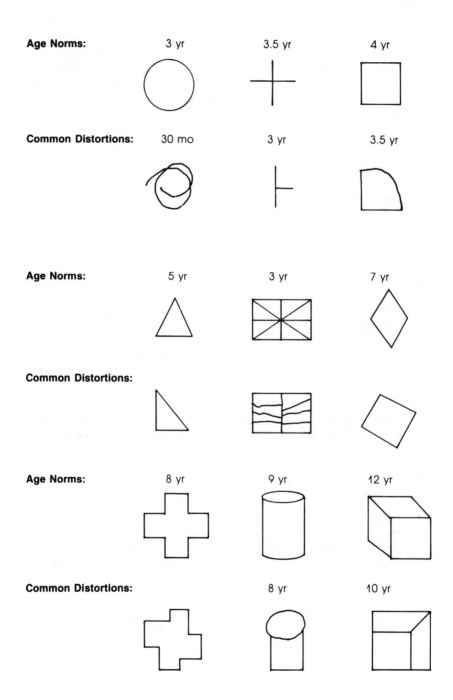

FIGURE 2-1. *Assessment of Visual Problem Solving Abilities (Gesell Drawings)*

This connected language is best assessed by comparison of observed language output, ability to answer comprehension questions, and to follow directions with the developmental norms described in Table 2-3. Instruments such as the Peabody Picture Vocabulary Test (see Chapter 3) may assess more limited aspects of language development (picture identification), but should not be construed as describing connected language understanding and usage.

It is unrealistic to expect a child to exhibit his or her full expressive language repertoire in the physician's office. Frequently, one has to rely on the parents' reporting of expressive language capabilities, and it is not unusual for a child to appear more advanced in receptive than expressive language development. It is for these reasons that a child's receptive language is usually considered to be a truer indicator of inherent language capabilities. When in doubt about expressive or receptive language capabilities, the physician should refer the child for more detailed language assessment by a speech-language pathologist.

NEURODEVELOPMENTAL HISTORY AND EXAMINATION FOR THE SCHOOL-AGED CHILD

The neurodevelopmental history and examination process described previously serves well for children under five years of age and permits identification of preschool children at possible risk for subsequent learning disabilities based on delays in neurodevelopment. When the physician is asked to evaluate school-age children for possible learning disabilities the evaluative task will be different. Definition of a learning disability depends upon establishment of a discrepancy between cognitive functioning and academic achievement levels, and therefore, one of the physician's responsibilities is to perform a neurodevelopmental evaluation that will at least screen whether such a discrepancy exists. The physician has some tools available to assess developmental functioning and academic achievement levels for these older, school-age children. More typically he or she will ask that precise levels of cognitive functioning be established on the basis of more detailed psychological and special education assessments as described in Chapters 3 and 4. The physician evaluating the school-age child is looking for neurodevelopmental findings that, although not pathognomonic for identification of a learning disability, nevertheless correlate quite highly with and are risk factors for subsequent development of a learning disability.

Neurodevelopmental History

The physician's history for the school-age child with learning difficulties begins in the same format for the preschool child; that is, the history will begin with a review of the pregnancy, labor, and birth history to identify pregnancies that represent high risks for subsequent developmental problems (Table 2-1). The physician will next elicit a neurodevelopmental history, that is, a history of temporal patterns of development. Historical questions will be asked in the developmental areas discussed previously for the preschool child, especially detailing the parents' conception of the preschool developmental course in motor (gross/fine) and language (expressive/receptive) areas. The history to this point then identifies risk factors in the pregnancy, labor and delivery, and slowness in early (preschool) development for the child.

The remainder of the history will be somewhat similar to that elicited by the psychologist and educational specialist. Questions will typically be asked regarding present educational placement (including the current type of class and present attempts at remediation), past educational placements and attempts at remediation, the parents' conception of present levels of academic achievement and developmental (cognitive) functioning, presence of attention deficits and behavioral problems (and whether these are occurring more at home or in school), family history of learning disabilities and related developmental problems, and psychosocial circumstances of the family. A flow sheet for this history-taking process is shown in Table 2-5.

The history described previously is obtained in major part directly from the parents. Supplementary information can be obtained through phone conversations with school personnel and review of materials submitted by the school, as well as through the team staffing conference (Chapter 6). Comparison of the school's information with the parents' history can be very instructive of the depth and accuracy of the parents' understanding of issues relevant to their child's learning difficulties. This insight will be of great value in subsequent counseling with the family.

Neurodevelopmental Examination

The physician's examination of the school-age child with learning difficulties should focus on establishment of an understanding of present levels of cognitive functioning and academic achievement, along with identification of some problem areas of neurodevelopment that, although not pathognomonic for learning disabilities, correlate quite highly with the presence of same. The remainder of this chapter focuses on the physician's individual role in this examination process.

Assessment of Visual Perceptual Development—Gesell Figures

There are a variety of drawing tests that may be appropriately used by the physician or allied personnel to assess visual perceptual/motor development. The Gesell figures, a series of increasingly complex figures

TABLE 2-5
History Taking—School Age Child

EDUCATION—CURRENT PLACEMENT
School
Grade
Type of class
Description of specific remedial assistance
Problems:
  Academic—present academic achievement levels
  Behavior—problems occurring in school setting

BEHAVIOR
Disposition
Interpersonal relationships
Group activities
Hobbies/interests
Behavior problems:
  Short attention span
  Attention seeking
  Distractibility
  Impulsivity
  Hyperactivity
  Noncompliance
  Oppositionalism
  Avoidance
  Truancy
  Fire Setting
  Cruelty to animals
  Lying
  Stealing
Parental management of behavior

FAMILY/PSYCHOSOCIAL HISTORY
Family History (for both mother and father)
  Age
  Education
  Academic problems—including family history of learning disability
  Illness
  Occupation
  Marital Status
Social History
  Marital problems
  Caretakers
  Financial problems
  Medical insurance

that the child is asked to replicate, represent the most generally useful. These drawings (Figure 2-1) are presented to the child in a completed, predrawn fashion and the child is asked to draw a likeness of the figures. It is mandatory that the physician observe the child in the drawing process, as satisfactory completion of the drawings is not the only information to be gleaned. For example, the child with attention deficit disorder (ADD) may execute the figures in driven fashion, omitting key elements of the drawings (e.g., omission of component lines in the "Union Jack" figure). The child who does not understand the gestalt of the figures may, although producing a satisfactory final representation of the figures, assemble the drawings in an abnormal fashion (e.g., composing the "Union Jack" figure from a series of small triangles). Quite often these errors of approach or assembly of drawings would be missed if the drawing process were not observed and only the completed figure inspected.

Common distortions of the Gesell drawings are shown under each of the drawings in Figure 2-1 and include the following:

1. Circle—at an approximate 30 month level, a child will imitate circular motions, but will not stop with satisfactory completion of a circle.
2. Intersecting lines—at an approximate 27 month level, a child will imitate horizontal and vertical strokes. The most common distortion in copying intersecting lines is shown in Figure 2-1.
3. Square—the most common distortion of a square includes partial replication of a square with the remainder of the figure completed with a circular motion as shown in Figure 2-1. This distorted figure represents a synthesis of the circle and square and is at an approximate 3.5 year level.
4. Triangle—the most common distortion of the triangle includes a right angle with the remainder of the figure completed with a sloping line. The resultant drawing looks more like a right triangle.
5. "Union Jack"—the most common distortion is drawing the figure in a fragmented fashion (as a series of pie slices or with spokes radiating out from a central focus). Another common distortion is shown in Figure 2-1.
6. Vertical diamond—the most common distortion is drawing the figure as a square tipped on its side rather than as a diamond.
7. Maltese Cross—distortions include unequal arm heights and widths.
8. Cylinder—this is the first figure in the series that is three-dimensional. The most common distortion of the figure is a drawing with a circular top or flat bottom, missing the concept that the figure has depth into the page.
9. Opaque three-dimensional cube—this again is a three-dimensional figure, and the most common distortion is to draw it as a series

of flat squares or with poor perspective. Quite often, when one observes a child who has extreme difficulty in copying this last figure, comparable difficulty may be observed in the parent's replication of this same figure. If this process can be conducted in a tactful fashion it may help the parents better understand their child's visual perceptual difficulties. The parents may have learned to rationalize their own perceptual difficulties by defenses of the type, "I never liked art." In effect what they may well share with their child is an unrecognized visual perceptual deficit.

Assessment of Visual Perceptual Development—Block Performance

Earlier in this chapter, the use of one-inch cubes was discussed in the assessment of visual perceptual abilities for preschool children. Two of the block constructs presented in Table 2-4 (staircase assemblies f and g) may be useful for assessing visual problem solving for early school-age (5 to 7 years) children.

The relationships among visual perceptual deficits, the type of learning disabilities encountered, and the most effective modes of remediation are quite unclear. It is still taken on faith that children with visual perceptual deficits will have more substantial difficulties with letter and shape recognition and will have more difficulty perceiving whole words visually as gestalts. Intuitively, it seems reasonable to suppose that a careful evaluation of a child's strengths and weaknesses would be useful in remediation planning, although sadly this has not been a very straightforward process.

Short-Term Memory Assessment

Short-term memory is tested with digits forward, digits reversed, and sentence memory (Table 2-6). Qualitative deviance may be noted when a child remembers the digits, but does not get them in the correct order (sequential memory deficit rather than a rote auditory memory deficit). Additionally, the child with ADD frequently exhibits an inconsistent performance with digit recall, doing somewhat better when attention is carefully focused and distractions minimized. The child with ADD may also exhibit better ability to reverse digits than to perform them forward.

Handedness, Laterality, and Dominance

A number of authors have observed developmentally inappropriate right–left confusion, failure to establish hand preference at an appropriate age, and problems with laterality (child's awareness of the two sides of his body and ability to identify them as left and right) in dyslexic

TABLE 2-6

Auditory Memory

Digits Forward—Digits spaced approximately 1 second apart

2.5	yr	47 _____	63 _____	58 _____
3	yr	641 _____	352 _____	837 _____
4.5	yr	4729 _____	3852 _____	7261 _____
7	yr	31589 _____	48372 _____	96183 _____
10	yr	473859 _____	429746 _____	728394 _____
Adult		72594836 _____	47153962 _____	41935826 _____

Digits Reversed

7	yr	295 _____	816 _____	473 _____
9	yr	8526 _____	4937 _____	3629 _____
12	yr	81379 _____	69582 _____	52618 _____
Adult		471952 _____	583694 _____	752618 _____

Sentences—Read at a normal rate

4 yr
We are going to buy some candy for mother.
Jack likes to feed the little puppies in the barn.

5 yr
Jane wants to build a big castle in her playhouse.
Tom has lots of fun playing ball with his sister.

8 yr
Fred asked his father to take him to see the clowns in the circus.
Billy made a beautiful boat out of wood with his sharp knife.

11 yr
At the summer camp the children get up early in the morning and go swimming.
Yesterday we went for a ride in our car along the road that crosses the bridge.

13 yr
The airplane made a careful landing in the space which had been prepared for it.
Tom Brown's dog ran quickly down the road with a huge bone in his mouth.

Adult
The red headed woodpecker made a terrible fuss as they tried to drive the young away from the nest.
The early settlers had little idea of the great changes that were to take place in this country.

TABLE 2-7
Left-Right Discrimination Testing

Show me your *left* hand ⎱ Show me your *right* eye ⎰	4.5 yr
Put your *left* hand on your *left* eye ⎱ Put your *right* hand on your *right* ear ⎰	4.5 yr
Put your *left* hand on your *right* eye ⎱ Put your *right* hand on your *left* ear ⎰	5.5 yr
Touch my *right* hand ⎱ Touch my *left* knee ⎰	7.5 yr
Put your *left* hand on my *right* hand ⎱ Put your *right* hand on my *left* knee ⎰	7.5 yr
Put your *left* hand on my *left* knee ⎱ Put your *right* hand on my *right* hand ⎰	7.5 yr

children. Tests of right–left discrimination and laterality are included in Table 2-7. There is, however, no conclusive evidence to support the proposition that these developmental problems are related to a failure to establish asymmetrical functions of the two brain hemispheres. Furthermore, neither mixed dominance (e.g., preference for the right hand but the left eye) nor left-handedness per se seem to be related to learning disabilities in children.

There are several "red flags" of underlying significant pathology related to the issue of handedness with preschool children:

1. Establishment of handedness below 1 year of age is an abnormal finding, and until proven otherwise should be construed as equivalent to a hemiparesis (relative motor disability on one side of the body).
2. Failure to develop hand preference by 2 years of age should be considered equally suspect.

Soft Neurological Signs

The classical neurological examination looks at what are termed *hard neurological signs*, that is, neurological findings that are either present or absent and do not appear to be modified by maturation of the child's nervous system. In this context the presence or absence of neurological findings is used to identify the presence of and permit localization of pathology in the nervous system. In the child's developing nervous system, however, things are not so simple. The physician performing a neurological examination with a child's developing nervous system is faced with neurological findings that are themselves on a developmental continuum, that is, they appear and disappear with development and maturation of the nervous system. Pathology here does not equate simply with the presence or absence of physical findings, but rather will depend on the extent of their presence and the timing of their appearance and disappearance. This fact has led to a great deal of confusion in interpreting the significance of these *soft neurological signs*. It has been demonstrated that, despite some variability on serial examination, soft signs can have a reasonably high interexaminer reliability and their presence may correlate significantly with a learning disability.

Between one-third and one-half of children with learning problems demonstrate significant soft neurological signs. Mirror movements and synkinesias (associated movements) are the most commonly encountered soft neurological signs. Mirror movements are associated movements of the opposite extremity that arise when a specific request is made for isolated movements of one of the extremities. Synkinesias represent an overflow or overshooting of muscle movements into other surrounding muscle groups when a request is made for performance with an isolated muscle group. Both mirror movements and synkinesias are commonly encountered in children with learning disabilities, but their presence is not pathognomonic.

CONCLUSIONS

The physician, because of early and ongoing contact with the child, is in an opportune position to identify early delays that may portend subsequent learning difficulties. This chapter has described how the physician, through an expanded neurodevelopmental history and neurodevelopmental examination, can make an individual contribution in this early identification process. With older children, and with further progression of the learning disability, the physician can be a valuable participant in the interdisciplinary diagnostic and therapeutic process. The role of the physician in the interdisciplinary process will be discussed in subsequent chapters.

CHAPTER 3

Psychological Evaluation

Elizabeth H. Aylward

A s mentioned previously, the diagnosis of learning disabilities is based on evidence of a discrepancy between the child's cognitive abilities and academic achievement, when other handicapping conditions (e.g., sensory impairment, mental retardation, social and emotional disturbance) or environmental influences (e.g., cultural differences, insufficient or inappropriate instruction, psychogenic factors) have been ruled out as primary reasons for the discrepancy. The psychologist plays an important role in making the diagnosis by providing information regarding the child's cognitive functioning, as well as by providing information that helps rule out other conditions, and information that helps to explain the nature of the disabilities.

HISTORY TAKING

Like the physician, the psychologist is in an excellent position to gather important information from the parents that may assist in understanding the child's school difficulties. Some of the questions will necessarily overlap those included in the physician's interview and in the special educator's information gathering process. It is not a waste of time to have questions repeated by various professionals, as it will provide each professional with a clearer understanding of the parents' perception of the problems. Furthermore, parents are bound to share different bits and pieces of the puzzle with different professionals, even if the questions asked are identical. This will allow for a clearer view of the total picture when the team gets together to share information.

The psychologist will want to gather information from the parents either before or after testing the child. He or she may want to ask about the child's school history, if this information is not already available from the special educator's report. (See Chapter 4.) The psychologist will want to ask parents about their perceptions of current behavior problems at school and perceptions of strengths and weaknesses in the various subject areas. The psychologist will also want to explore issues that relate to the child's success and satisfaction with school, including ability to interact with peers (both at home and at school), involvement in extracurricular activities, and self-concept.

In order to determine if problems observed in school are unique to the school situation or more pervasive, the psychologist should ask about behavior problems at home (e.g., excessive activity level, tantrums, inability to listen to and follow instructions, lying, stealing, refusal to do what is asked). The psychologist should ask about homework: how much is assigned (in the parents' estimation), how long it actually takes the child to complete the work, whether parental supervision is required, and particular problems with completion of homework (e.g., procrastination, whining, distractibility, need for assistance). The child's ability to carry out other responsibilities (e.g., regular daily chores) should also be discussed.

The psychologist should question the parents regarding the presence of symptoms of depression or other emotional disturbance in the child (e.g., unusual fears, sleeping problems, eating problems, mood swings, difficulty separating from parents). The psychologist may want to ask questions regarding any learning, emotional, or behavior problems in other family members. Finally, the psychologist should ask whether the child is currently taking any medication that might affect testing.

An interview form that the psychologist might want to use with parents is included in Appendix A. Of course, the psychologist will want to modify the form to suit the individual case.

PSYCHOLOGICAL TESTING

The basis for a diagnosis of learning disability is performance on individually administered tests of intelligence and academic achievement. A learning disability exists when academic achievement in one or more areas is significantly lower than the level that would be predicted from the child's cognitive profile, assuming that other conditions (e.g., emotional disturbance, excessive school absences, vision or hearing problems, inappropriate educational techniques) are not present. It is clear, then, that accurate assessments of both academic achievement and intellectual abilities are essential for accurate diagnosis. The psychologist is generally responsible for the assessment of intellectual abilities, whereas the educator is responsible for assessment of academic achievement.

Test Selection

Because an accurate assessment of intelligence is essential to the diagnosis of learning disabilities, it is imperative that the psychologist select a valid and reliable instrument to measure the child's intellectual abilities in a way that is not biased by the child's lack of academic achievement. There is, of course, no single, correct definition of *intelligence*. Therefore, there is no single, correct way of measuring this concept. The examiner must be aware of the types of cognitive abilities tapped by the various intelligence tests in order to select the test(s) that will provide the most valid results for his or her population of students.

Although most school systems now have adopted programs of testing at regular intervals throughout the elementary and secondary school years, these tests are typically administered to students in large groups (20 or more students). Although these tests provide fairly accurate evaluations of academic skills (and sometimes overall intellectual ability) for many students, they may be especially inappropriate for children suspected of having learning disabilities. First, many children with learning disabilities have concomitant attention deficits, and they are at particular disadvantage in a group testing situation, especially if the tests are administered with a time limit. A group testing situation is a perfect environment for daydreaming and other off-task behaviors for the child with attention deficit disorder. Second, most group tests require the student to read the items. Although poor reading abilities will be more or less accurately reflected in reading subtest scores on group tests, they will provide a serious confounding variable in the measurement of other academic abilities (e.g., social studies, applied math) and overall cognitive abilities. Third, group testing does not provide the examiner with an opportunity to closely observe many of the behaviors that interfere with testing and similarly interfere with classroom learning (e.g., limited attention span, impulsivity, excessive frustration). For these reasons, individual testing is essential for correct diagnosis of learning disabilities.

In diagnosing learning disabilities, the minimum information necessary is an accurate assessment of intelligence (often in the form of an IQ score) and an accurate assessment of academic achievement. Although many tests on the market claim to provide an IQ or other score reflecting overall cognitive ability, few are appropriate in making the learning disability diagnosis.

In a 1984 report of the United States Department of Education, Special Education Programs Work Group on Management Issues in the Assessment of Learning Disabilities (Reynolds, 1984-1985), eleven considerations were presented for selection of instruments used in the diagnosis of learning disabilities (see Table 3-1). Basically, these standards require tests used for the diagnosis of learning disabilities to meet generally accepted criteria for reliability (i.e., ability of a test to consistently measure what it measures) and validity (i.e., ability of a test to actually measure what it purports to measure). Furthermore, the test norms must be based on a sufficiently large sample that reflects the demographic characteristics of the national population. The test norms should allow the examiner to compare the child with other children of the same age. The degree to which different ethnic and cultural populations perform differently on the test should have been studied and reported. The test of cognitive abilities should measure general intelligence. Another primary consideration, which will be discussed in Chapter 6, is the need for the test of cognitive ability and the test of academic achievement to be normed on the same or similar populations.

TABLE 3-1
Essential Characteristics of Tests Used in Making the Diagnosis of Learning Disabilities

1. Tests should meet all requirements stated for assessment devices in the rules and regulations implementing Public Law 94-142.
2. Normative data should meet contemporary standards of practice and be provided for a sufficiently large, nationally stratified random sample of children.
3. Standardization samples for tests whose scores are being compared must be the same or highly comparable.
4. For the purpose of arriving at a diagnosis, individually administered tests should be used.
5. In the measurement of aptitude, an individually administered test of general intellectual ability should be used.
6. Age-based standard scores should be used for all measures and all should be scaled to a common metric.
7. The measures employed should demonstrate a high level of reliability and have appropriate studies for this determination in the technical manual accompanying the test.
8. The validity coefficient, r_{xy}, representing the relationship between the measures of aptitude and achievement, should be based on an appropriate sample.
9. Validity of test score interpretations should be clearly established.
10. Special technical considerations should be addressed when using performance-based measures of achievement (e.g., writing skill).
11. Bias studies on the instruments in use should have been conducted and reported.

Adapted from Reynolds, C. (1984-1985). Critical measurement issues in learning disabilities. *Journal of Special Education, 18*, 451–476.

In addition to these important criteria, it is desirable to use an intelligence test that allows the examiner to observe the child over a range of response modes (e.g., single word responses, elaborated oral responses, paper-and-pencil tasks, manipulation of materials, identification by pointing, imitation of the examiner, timed and untimed responses). The test should also tap various aspects of intelligence.

THE WECHSLER INTELLIGENCE SCALE FOR CHILDREN-REVISED (WISC-R) AND THE KAUFMAN ASSESSMENT BATTERY FOR CHILDREN (K-ABC). Two intelligence tests that meet the technical criteria described (validity, reliability, adequate norming samples, etc.) and that are most commonly used are the WISC-R and the K-ABC. (See Appendix B and Appendix C for a description of each of these tests.) There is, of course, much debate regarding the nature of intelligence and much debate over the types of tasks that should be used to measure intelligence. The K-ABC and WISC-R differ considerably in their approach to defining and measuring intelligence. Neither test can be considered "right" or "wrong" in its approach. The examiner will have to consider the nature of the individual tasks used within each of these tests of intelligence to determine which is the better choice for each child being evaluated.

The two major aspects of intelligence measured by the WISC-R are verbal (language) and nonverbal (primarily visual-spatial) skills. The K-ABC has been designed to measure two different general aspects of intelligence, simultaneous and sequential mental processing. On tasks measuring sequential mental processing, stimuli are manipulated in serial order to solve problems. On tasks measuring simultaneous mental processing, stimuli are integrated in a holistic, gestalt, or parallel fashion to solve problems. Intelligence, as measured by the K-ABC, is considered to be "an individual's style of solving problems and processing information" (Kaufman and Kaufman, 1983, p. 2). The K-ABC attempts to "minimize the role of language and acquired facts and skills" (Kaufman, 1983, p. 206). Although many of the subtests on the WISC-R are similar to K-ABC subtests in measuring problem-solving and information-processing styles, others are included that definitely rely on learned material for good performance. The type of learning required on these subtests is, however, the type that is generally picked up in day-to-day living (e.g., vocabulary, understanding of social situations, general information), rather than that which relies on direct school learning.

Because the K-ABC is a relatively new test (published in 1983), it is less widely used than the WISC-R, and its advantages and disadvantages are less widely understood. It is recommended that the psychologist on the interdisciplinary team be familiar with both of these intelligence tests. He or she will find it more appropriate to use one or the other in various situations. Although it is impossible to identify the K-ABC or the WISC-R as the "best" test for measuring intelligence as part of the diagnostic process, there are certain factors that the psychologist should consider in each individual case:

1. One of the major advantages of using the K-ABC instead of the WISC-R is the availability of the K-ABC Achievement Subtests, which were normed on the same sample as the K-ABC Mental Processing subtests. This allows the examiner to confidently compare results of the intelligence measure and the academic achievement measure in making the diagnosis of learning disabilities. Unfortunately, many examiners think the Achievement subtests do not adequately test several important academic skills (e.g., spelling, written calculations) that are commonly measured by achievement tests. This issue will be discussed further in Chapter 4.

2. The K-ABC, unlike the WISC-R, includes in its norming sample exceptional children (e.g., learning disabled, mentally retarded, gifted children) in the same proportion as occurs in the national population. Thus, the K-ABC can be considered to be a more valid measure of intelligence for the learning disabled population.

3. Because the K-ABC is a newer test than the WISC-R, the children in its norming sample are probably more similar to children currently being evaluated than the children in the WISC-R norming sample. Thus, scores derived from the K-ABC norms will be somewhat more valid than scores derived from the WISC-R norms.

Also, as outlined in Table 3-1, one of the essential characteristics of tests used in making the diagnosis of learning disabilities is the high comparability of standardization samples for tests whose scores are being compared. That is, when the scores from two tests (e.g., an intelligence test and an achievement test) are to be compared, the samples on which those two tests were normed should be highly similar. The most widely used tests of academic achievement have been standardized within the past ten years. Because the WISC-R was normed in the early 1970s, its standardization sample may be less similar to the standardization samples used in norming the widely used tests of academic achievement than is the K-ABC's standardization sample. Thus, comparisons between scores from a test of intelligence and scores from tests of academic achievement may be more valid if the K-ABC is used.

4. Racial and ethnic differences are less pronounced on the K-ABC than on the WISC-R. For example, Kaufman (1983) reports a 7-point average difference between the scores of black children and white children on the K-ABC, whereas an average difference of 16 points is reported for the WISC-R (Kaufman and Doppelt, 1976). A similar trend is reported for the differences between scores of Hispanic and white children.

5. All K-ABC Mental Processing subtests include teaching or training items. These allow the examiner to use various means to make certain that the child understands the task. Although the WISC-R provides sample

items for most subtests (which allow the examiner to correct mistakes, using a clearly prescribed protocol), these sample items do not always ensure that the child understands what is expected. This is a more serious problem with younger or less intelligent children. The K-ABC teaching items allow the examiner to be more certain that a low score reflects a true weakness in a skill area rather than an inability to understand directions.

6. The K-ABC provides a Nonverbal Scale, made up of subtests that can be administered in pantomime and responded to motorically. This is designed for children who are hearing impaired, who have serious speech or language disorders, or who use English as a second language. Although many of the WISC-R Performance subtests require no verbal response, it might be difficult to communicate the instructions to a hearing-impaired child. Furthermore, this would definitely be considered nonstandard procedure for administration of the WISC-R subtests, thus invalidating norms.

7. The K-ABC provides a variety of supplementary norms, including sociocultural norms (based on a cross-tabulation by race and by parental education). Thus, when desired, children can be compared with peers from similar sociocultural backgrounds.

8. The K-ABC provides specific strategies for teaching reading, math, and spelling, based on the child's profile of strengths and weaknesses on the Simultaneous versus Sequential Mental Processing tasks. (The effectiveness of these strategies, however, has not yet been proven.)

9. On average, WISC-R IQs are approximately 3 to 4 points higher than K-ABC IQs. Kaufman and Kaufman (1983) attribute this to the recency of the K-ABC norms in comparison to the WISC-R norms. (About 10 years passed between the time of WISC-R norming and K-ABC norming).

10. Although the K-ABC intentionally omitted tasks that require extensive verbal expression, it cannot be denied that this is an ability that contributes greatly to school success. The examiner may want information comparing verbal and nonverbal skills, which can be obtained much more directly and thoroughly from the WISC-R than from the K-ABC.

11. Just as the K-ABC may be useful for testing children who are hearing impaired or who have serious speech or language disorders, the WISC-R Verbal subtests may be useful for assessing cognitive abilities of children who are visually impaired. These children would be seriously disadvantaged on the K-ABC tests.

12. Because the WISC-R is more heavily reliant on verbal skills, children from relatively high socioeconomic groups (who often score higher on the WISC-R Verbal tests than on the Performance tests) may obtain lower scores on the K-ABC than on the WISC-R. A lower score on the intelligence test would reduce the amount of discrepancy between academic achievement and intellectual ability for a child suspected of being learning disabled and might prevent him or her from qualifying for special education services.

13. The WISC-R allows the examiner to observe the child over a greater range of response modes than the K-ABC. Manipulation of objects, paper-and-pencil skills, single-word responses, elaborated oral responses, identification by pointing, and imitation of the examiner are all required by the various WISC-R tasks. Although individual scores are not obtained for each of these response modes, the experienced examiner can use his or her observation to formulate some fairly sophisticated hypotheses regarding certain factors that will interfere with the child's learning. Most of the responses on the K-ABC require identification by pointing, although a few require single word responses, manipulation of objects, or imitation of the examiner.

14. The WISC-R, compared to the K-ABC, employs more materials that require the child's manipulation. Although this makes administration of the WISC-R somewhat more cumbersome, it may be more effective in keeping the child's attention (especially at the younger ages).

15. The WISC-R is generally considered to be a more difficult test to learn to administer than the K-ABC. Also, because scoring on several of the WISC-R subtests is somewhat subjective, examiners with less testing experience may have more difficulty scoring the WISC-R as accurately as the K-ABC.

16. The WISC-R is designed to cover a different age range (ages 6 to 16) than the K-ABC (ages 2.5 to 12.5). Obviously, then, the WISC-R would be the test of choice for adolescents. For younger children, the Wechsler Preschool and Primary Scale of Intelligence (WPPSI) or the K-ABC would be appropriate tests to use. (The WPPSI is described in Appendix B.)

17. Because the WISC-R has been available much longer, it is better known and better understood by most professionals. The psychologist who chooses to use the K-ABC will probably have to spend more time explaining the scales and their meaning. This consideration will, of course, become less valid as the K-ABC becomes more widely used.

THE STANFORD-BINET INTELLIGENCE SCALE. One other intelligence test that meets the criteria outlined in Table 3-1 is the Stanford-Binet Intelligence Scale: Fourth Edition. Unlike its predecessor (Form L-M, published in 1960), the new Stanford-Binet provides scores in four broad areas (Verbal Reasoning, Abstract/Visual Reasoning, Quantitative Reasoning, and Short-Term Memory), as well as a composite score that presumes to measure general reasoning ability. This revision allows the psychologist to identify relative strengths and weaknesses within the cognitive profile, which may assist in determining the nature of any learning disabilities that might exist. Because of its recent publication (1986), practitioners have had less experience using the new Stanford-Binet than the WISC-R or K-ABC in the diagnosis of learning disabilities. The new Stanford-Binet does, however, appear to be a promising instrument and deserves consideration from the psychologist when choosing a test of intelligence for use in diagnosing learning disabilities.

THE WOODCOCK-JOHNSON PSYCHO-EDUCATIONAL BATTERY (WJPEB). The WJPEB consists of three sections: Tests of Cognitive Ability, Tests of Academic Achievement, and Tests of Interest Level. The Tests of Cognitive Ability section is sometimes used as a measure of intellectual functioning for the diagnosis of learning disabilities. Although there are several advantages to using the WJPEB Tests of Cognitive Ability as a measure of intelligence, the disadvantages prevent it from being the test of choice for the purpose of diagnosing learning disabilities.

The rationale underlying the Tests of Cognitive Ability was "to develop measures of cognition (i.e., intellectual performance) that accurately predict academic achievement specifically. Therefore, the Tests of Cognitive Ability were not designed as measures of general intellectual functioning, as is the case with, for example, the WISC-R" (Hessler, 1982, p. 384). Thus, the Tests of Cognitive Ability fail to meet one of the important criteria set forth by the U.S. Department of Education, Special Education Programs Work Group on Management Issues in the Assessment of Learning Disabilities. (See Table 3-1.)

Because the Tests of Cognitive Ability measure "verbal cognition that specifically relates to academic achievement," most research has found that scores from this test are lower than the WISC-R IQs for learning-disabled children. In fact, the Tests of Cognitive Ability have been found to yield overall standard scores ½ to 1 standard deviation below the WISC-R Full Scale IQ (Kaufman, 1985). It can be assumed, therefore, that the WJPEB Tests of Cognitive Ability will often underestimate to some degree the learning-disabled child's cognitive abilities, which may in turn diminish the amount of discrepancy between the child's measured cognitive skills and academic abilities. If the discrepancy is diminished, criteria for the diagnosis of learning disability may not be met, and the child with a true learning disability may not qualify for services.

The WJPEB has many valuable applications, one of which is the measurement of academic achievement (through Part II: Tests of Academic Achievement). This section of the Battery is discussed more fully in Chapter 4. Unfortunately, the Tests of Cognitive Ability (Part I) is not as appropriate for the measurement of intelligence in the learning-disabled population. Assuming that the examiner has access to the WISC-R, K-ABC, or Stanford-Binet, the selection of the WJPEB Tests of Cognitive Ability would appear to be a poorer choice.

Appropriate Tests of Intelligence for Preschool Children

Although it is not possible to make a certain diagnosis of learning disabilities before a child has had at least several months of structured, formalized instruction in the various academic areas (usually at least the middle of first grade), some parents and teachers may be interested in identifying the child who is at risk for learning disabilities. In order to do this, the examiner needs to obtain a measure of cognitive abilities (IQ) and a measure of preacademic abilities (e.g., counting, identifying letters, understanding such concepts as "bigger than," "same as," or "less than"). The K-ABC can provide measures of cognitive abilities for preschool children. As noted earlier, the WISC-R is designed for children who are at least 6 years old. The Wechsler Preschool and Primary Scale of Intelligence (WPPSI) is similar to the WISC-R and is designed for children between the ages of 4 and 6.5 years.

Appropriate Tests of Intelligence for Older Children

The K-ABC cannot be used with children over 12.5 years, and the WISC-R cannot be used with children over 16 years, 11 months. The Wechsler Adult Intelligence Scale-Revised (WAIS-R) is similar to the WISC-R and WPPSI in areas tapped, and is designed for individuals who are 16 years or older. It contains the same six Verbal subtests as the WISC-R; the Mazes subtest is omitted from the Performance subtests. Of course, items are more difficult.

Inappropriate Tests of Intelligence for the Diagnosis of Learning Disabilities

As mentioned previously, it is important that the intelligence test selected for use in making the diagnosis of learning disabilities be individually administered, have adequate validity and reliability, include tasks that tap a variety of aspects of intelligence, and provide the examiner an opportunity to observe the student over a range of response modes. There are several commonly used intelligence tests that do not meet these criteria and are, therefore, inappropriate for making the diagnosis of learning disabilities. Among this group of inappropriate, but commonly used, tests is the Slosson Intelligence Test (SIT), which is inappropriate because it is inadequately normed on an unrepresentative sample and contains too few items at each age level. The Peabody Picture Vocabulary Test-Revised (PPVT-R), the Full Range Picture Vocabulary Test, and the Quick Test are inappropriate because they measure only limited aspects of receptive vocabulary skills. The Progressive Matrices test is equally inappropriate for making the diagnosis of learning disabilities because it measures only limited aspects of visual-spatial reasoning. As described previously, the diagnosis of learning disabilities requires scores based on individually administered tests that allow the examiner to closely monitor the child's test behavior and to ensure maximum attention. For this reason, group administered tests of intelligence (e.g., the Otis-Lennon Mental Ability Test, the Cognitive Abilities Test) are inappropriate. Although some of these inappropriate tests may be useful as screening tools for identifying children with possible learning disabilities, they should certainly not be used as the measure of intelligence for making a final diagnosis. Similarly, a child who does not show a significant discrepancy between academic achievement and intellectual ability, as measured by one of these tests, should not be necessarily assumed to be free of learning disabilities if other indications of the disorder are observed.

Test Administration

Appropriate Test Conditions

As outlined in any introductory text of cognitive assessment or any manual for an individually administered test, a proper test environment is essential for accurate assessment. This is especially true for the learning-disabled child who is often easily distracted. The testing room must, of course, be quiet, free from excessive visual distractions, properly ventilated, of comfortable temperature, and equipped with furniture that allows the child to be seated comfortably at a table or desk. Several of the tests most useful in diagnosing learning disabilities will not provide reliable results if such conditions are not maintained.

If possible, the child should be tested in the morning, well-rested and alert. Tests should be administered in sessions no longer than two hours (or shorter for younger children). If tests must be administered in one session, the student should be allowed a short break in the middle of the session.

The examiner should make a special attempt to build rapport with the child being evaluated for possible learning disabilities. Many of these children, after years of poor academic achievement, have poor self-concept, are easily frustrated, poorly motivated, or overly anxious. In order to obtain an accurate assessment of the student's abilities, the examiner must take into account these emotional interferences and must attempt to overcome them.

Behaviors To Be Observed During Intelligence Testing

Critical observation of the child's test behavior may provide as much important information relevant to academic difficulties as the test results themselves. Some of the behaviors that should receive special attention from the examiner are listed:

Distractibility
- [ ] Did the child have difficulty paying attention and staying on task? Did the child appear to be daydreaming, or off in his or her own world?
- [ ] Did the child often ask to have items repeated?
- [ ] Did the child often comment about or seem attuned to unavoidable visual or auditory distractions (e.g., the squeaking of a chair, the examiner's clothing)?
- [ ] Did the child make irrelevant comments or attempt to relate personal experiences that were brought to mind by the various test stimuli? Did he or she often talk to himself or herself, especially on tasks that required manipulation of materials rather than a verbal response?
- [ ] Did the child seem to "lose track" of the task presented? For example, on the "digits reversed" section of the WISC-R Digit Span subtest, did he or she begin to repeat digits forward after several successful trials of repeating digits in reversed order? On the WISC-R Coding subtest did the child stop in the middle of the test, seeming to have forgotten instructions to work as quickly as possible? Did the child frequently lose his or her place on the Coding subtest?

Restlessness, Fidgetiness
- [ ] Did the child have difficulty staying seated, especially on the subtests that did not require manipulation of materials?
- [ ] Did restlessness increase as testing proceeded, or stay at a constant level?
- [ ] Did the child engage in excessive purposeless movement (e.g., squirming, tapping fingers, swinging feet, kicking the table leg?) Were his or her hands overly "busy" (e.g., twirling the pencil, picking at himself or herself)?
- [ ] Did the child chew on his or her pencil, shirt collar, cuffs, or other objects?

Rushed, Careless, Impulsive Approach
- [ ] Did the child appear to give the first answer that came to mind?
- [ ] Did the child attempt to begin tasks before instructions were complete?
- [ ] Did the child attempt to flip pages (e.g., on K-ABC items presented in the Easel-Kits or on the WISC-R Picture Completion subtest) before adequately attending to the material on the current page?

☐ Did the child grab for materials before the examiner was ready to present them?

☐ Did the child appear totally oblivious to obviously incorrect responses (e.g., on the WISC-R Object Assembly or Block Design subtests or on the K-ABC Triangles subtest)?

☐ Did the child noticeably increase his or her speed of responding when he or she was aware that performance was being timed? Did this result in careless errors?

Slow, Obsessive Approach

☐ Did the child take excessive time before responding?

☐ Did the child meticulously check and recheck work (e.g., on WISC-R Picture Arrangement and Block Design or on K-ABC Triangles), resulting in penalties for slow performance?

☐ Were the child's verbal responses more complete than necessary (especially on WISC-R Vocabulary and Comprehension)?

☐ Did the child often come up with correct responses *after* time was up (especially on WISC-R Arithmetic, Picture Completion, Picture Arrangement, Block Design, and Object Assembly subtests, or on K-ABC Triangles)?

☐ Did the child spend excessive time "planning" before responding (especially on WISC-R Mazes or K-ABC Photo Series)?

☐ Were tasks done with excessive precision (e.g., were blocks on the WISC-R Block Design or triangles on the K-ABC Triangles subtests lined up exactly, or were lines drawn extremely neatly or overworked on WISC-R Mazes)?

Anxiety

☐ Did the child have difficulty separating from his or her parent or teacher?

☐ Did the child appear nervous? Did this subside or increase as testing proceeded? Did it diminish with positive reinforcement and reassurance?

☐ Did anxiety appear to increase when tasks were timed?

☐ Was more anxiety observed on certain types of tasks (e.g., those requiring a verbal response, those that were timed) than on other types of tasks?

Confidence

☐ Did the child ask often if his or her responses were correct?

☐ Was the child reluctant to guess at an item he or she did not know?

☐ Could the child be encouraged to take a guess, and, if so, were guesses often correct?

☐ Did the child start to give answers and then change his or her mind and refuse to respond?

☐ Did the child qualify many responses (e.g., by saying, "I don't know, but..." or "This is just a guess")?

☐ Did the child often comment on the difficulty of items (e.g., "These are so easy" or "I'll never get this one")? Were these opinions of difficulty congruent with the child's performance?

☐ Did the child often say "I can't" or "I don't know" without putting forth good effort?

☐ Did the child often ask for assistance on items or look to the examiner for reassurance that he or she was "on the right track"?

Frustration—Perseverance

☐ Did the child often stop working on a task before time was called, claiming an item was too difficult (especially on WISC-R Arithmetic, Picture Arrangement, Block Design, Object Assembly, and Mazes subtests or on the K-ABC Triangles)? Could the child be encouraged to continue and, if so, was he or she able to successfully complete the item?

☐ If unable to succeed on an item within the time limit, did the child request "just a little longer" to complete the task?

☐ Did the child ever scatter materials in frustration (especially on WISC-R Block Design or Object Assembly subtests or on K-ABC Triangles)?

☐ Did the child act disgusted with himself or herself or make disparaging comments when he or she could not succeed on an item?

☐ Did the child ever ask to complete remaining items after failing the prescribed number of items for discontinuing the testing (e.g., on WISC-R Picture Completion, Picture Arrangement, Block Design, Mazes)?

Distortions in Spatial Orientation

☐ Did the child have many rotations on WISC-R Block Design or K-ABC Triangles?

☐ Did the child work from right to left when sequencing WISC-R Picture Arrangement cards or completing the WISC-R Coding task?

Pencil Grasp

☐ Did the child exhibit an immature or awkward pencil grasp on the WISC-R Coding and Mazes subtests?

Avoidance Behavior

☐ Did the child ask for excessive breaks (e.g., for bathroom visits, drinks)?

☐ Did the child complain of stomach aches or other ailments in an apparent attempt to discontinue the session?

☐ Did the child complain of being tired?
☐ Did the child often ask how much longer the testing would last?
☐ Did the child complain about the testing?

Hearing and Vision
☐ Were there any indications that the child had difficulty seeing materials or hearing questions (e.g., squinting, holding materials close to his or her face, often saying "huh?" or asking to have questions repeated)?

Speech and Language
☐ Did the child often ask to have verbal items repeated?
☐ Was the child slow to begin giving verbal responses?
☐ Did the child often appear to not understand verbal directions, but catch on quickly after a few demonstration items?
☐ Did the child have "word finding" problems? For example, did the child often refer to objects on the WISC-R Picture Completion subtest as "those things" or "what-cha-ma-call-its"? Did he or she often give a long verbal explanation to describe something for which more concise terminology would have been more appropriate?
☐ Were verbal responses extremely limited? Did the child resist encouragement to elaborate on verbal responses?
☐ Did the child give totally inappropriate responses to verbal questions and then, upon repetition of the question, provide an accurate response?
☐ Did the child give responses that were related only to a portion of the question?
☐ Did the child have any observable speech impediments (e.g., stuttering, lisping, poor articulation)? Did they interfere with testing?

Personality Characteristics
☐ Was the child friendly, pleasant, well-mannered, cooperative?
☐ Did the child appear well-motivated?
☐ Did the child appear to enjoy the testing and the individual attention of the examiner?
☐ Did the child offer spontaneous conversation?
☐ Did the child make eye-contact with the examiner?
☐ Did the child appear to take pride in his or her successes? Did he or she respond to praise?
☐ Did the child respond to the examiner's attempts to build rapport?
☐ Was the child overly affectionate with the examiner?

Health
☐ Was the child on any type of medication that might have affected performance (e.g., Ritalin, antihistamines)?

☐ Were there any other health conditions that might have affected performance?

Although this list of behavioral observations may seem quite lengthy and detailed, it is important that each area be considered. The psychologist may even want to make a checklist to use during testing to facilitate reporting of these characteristics. Some of the child's major difficulties may be reflected more in these behavioral traits than in any test score. Recommendations for remediation of school difficulties will certainly need to take these traits into account.

Test Interpretation

WISC-R VIQ-PIQ Discrepancy and Subtest Scatter

Many attempts have been made to identify the learning disability profile of subtest scores on the WISC-R. Despite the fact that no consistent profile has been found, some professionals may attempt to diagnose learning disabilities based on the WISC-R profile alone. This is not appropriate. Most commonly, these inappropriate diagnoses are based on an extreme amount of subtest scatter or on a significant discrepancy between Verbal IQ (VIQ) and Performance IQ (PIQ). Although learning-disabled students may show great subtest scatter (i.e., differences in performance among the various subtests) and VIQ-PIQ discrepancies, there are many children without learning disabilities who also show these abnormal patterns, and there are many learning-disabled students who do not show these patterns.

Compounding the problem, many professionals who work primarily with children exhibiting school difficulties are unaware of the amount of subtest scatter and VIQ-PIQ discrepancy found in the profile of the nondisabled child. In examining the standardization data for the WISC-R, Kaufman (1976b) discovered that the average VIQ-PIQ discrepancy (regardless of direction) was 9.7 points. The values for determining whether a particular VIQ-PIQ discrepancy is "real" (i.e., not due to chance) are 9 points ($p < .15$ level), 12 points ($p < .05$ level), and 15 points ($p < .01$ level). Kaufman considers a VIQ-PIQ discrepancy of 12 points or more (regardless or direction) worthy of explanation. It is important to note, however, that a discrepancy of this size is, by no means abnormal, as it is observed in approximately 34 percent of the normal population. Table 3-2 reports the percent of nondisabled children who have VIQ-PIQ discrepancies of various magnitudes. Substantial scatter among the 12 WISC-R subtests is also not unusual. Two-thirds of children have scaled score ranges (the difference between the highest and lowest subtest score) of 7 ± 2 points. An abnormal amount of scatter (that which occurs in less than 15 percent

TABLE 3-2
Percent of Nondisabled Children with WISC-R VIQ-PIQ Discrepancies of a Given Magnitude

Size of V–P Discrepancy (Regardless of Direction)	Parental Occupation					Total Sample
	Professional & Technical	Managerial, Clerical, Sales	Skilled Workers	Semi-skilled Workers	Unskilled Workers	
9	52	48	48	46	43	48
10	48	44	43	41	37	43
11	43	40	39	36	34	39
12	40	35	34	31	29	34
13	36	33	31	28	26	31
14	32	29	29	25	24	28
15	29	25	26	21	22	24
16	26	22	22	19	22	22
17	24	19	18	19	19	18
18	20	16	16	15	16	16
19	16	15	13	14	15	14
20	13	13	12	12	14	12
21	11	11	8	10	13	10
22	10	9	7	9	10	8
23	8	8	6	7	9	7
24	7	7	6	6	8	6
25	6	6	5	5	6	5
26	5	5	3	4	5	4
27	4	4	2	3	4	3
28–30	3	3	1	2	3	2
31–33	2	2	<1	<1	2	1
34+	1	1	<1	<1	1	<1

From Kaufman, A. (1979). *Intelligent testing with the WISC-R.* Copyright © by John Wiley & Sons, Inc. Reprinted by permission of John Wiley & Sons, Inc.

of nondisabled children) is present when there is a spread of 8 points or more between the highest and lowest of the six Verbal subtest scores, or when there is a spread of 9 points or more between the highest and lowest of the six Performance subtest scores (based on a study by Kaufman, 1976a, which examined WISC-R profiles of 2200 nondisabled children). (See Table 3-3.)

Because VIQ-PIQ discrepancies and the amount of subtest scatter in nondisabled populations is larger than many professionals would suspect, and because these intra-test comparisons cannot accurately identify

TABLE 3-3
Percent of Nondisabled Children Obtaining Scaled-Score Ranges of a Given Magnitude

Scaled-Score Range	Regular WISC-R (10 Subtests)			Entire WISC-R (12 Subtests)		
	Verbal (Five Subtests)	Performance (Five Subtests)	Full Scale (10 Subtests)	Verbal (Six Subtests)	Performance (Six Subtests)	Full Scale (12 Subtests)
0	100.0	100.0		100.0		
1	99.9	99.9	100.0	99.9	100.0	
2	97.5	98.6	99.9	99.0	99.6	100.0
3	86.2	92.3	99.6	94.0	97.0	99.9
4	66.7	81.1	97.0	82.1	88.5	99.3
5	45.6	64.1	89.8	62.2	74.9	95.8
6	27.3	45.6	74.7	43.2	57.0	85.9
7	14.3	29.1	56.4	25.9	39.9	70.4
8	6.4	18.0	38.6	13.7	25.9	56.8
9	2.7	10.1	22.6	6.4	14.6	32.9
10	1.2	5.2	12.3	3.0	8.1	19.6
11	0.3	2.6	5.9	1.4	4.1	10.8
12	0.2	1.4	2.9	0.4	2.1	5.3
13	0.0	0.6	1.4	0.1	0.8	2.1
14		0.4	0.5	0.1	0.4	0.6
15		0.1	0.2	0.0	0.1	0.2
16		0.0	0.0		0.0	0.0
Median	4	5	7	5	6	8
Mean	4.5	5.5	7.0	5.3	6.1	7.7
SD	1.9	2.3	2.1	2.0	2.3	2.1

Note: Scaled-score ranges equal children's highest scaled score minus their lowest scaled score on the Verbal, Performance, or Full Scales. Since scores can range from 1 to 19, the maximum possible range equals 18 points.

From Kaufman, A. (1979). *Intelligent testing with the WISC-R.* Copyright © by John Wiley & Sons, Inc. Reprinted by permission of John Wiley & Sons, Inc.

learning-disabled children, care should be taken not to overinterpret WISC-R profiles.

K-ABC Simultaneous-Sequential
Processing Differences and Subtest Scatter

There is less history of misuse of the K-ABC than of the WISC-R in the diagnosis of learning disabilities. This is, of course, due in part to the relatively recent introduction of the K-ABC. In addition, because the K-ABC contains both a measure of intellectual ability (represented by the Sequential Processing, Simultaneous Processing, and Mental Processing Composite scores) and a measure of academic achievement (represented by the Achievement subtests scores), examiners using the test are more likely to correctly rely on a discrepancy between abilities in these two areas to establish a diagnosis of learning disabilities. They are less likely to mistakenly rely solely on cognitive subtest profiles or on the discrepancy between Simultaneous and Sequential Processing scores.

Examiners using the K-ABC should, of course, be aware of the amount of difference needed between the Simultaneous and Sequential Processing scores to reach statistical significance (i.e., the level needed to be confident that differences are not due to chance). A table in the K-ABC manual provides standard score differences required for significance at each age level. The average difference required for significance for children between 2.5 and 5 years is 14 points ($p < .05$), whereas an average difference of 12 points is required for children between 5 and 12.5 years. As with the WISC-R VIQ-PIQ discrepancy, a statistically significant discrepancy is not necessarily an abnormal one. The average difference between Simultaneous and Sequential Processing scores is 12.3 points. Kaufman and Kaufman (1983) suggest that a 22-point discrepancy between Simultaneous and Sequential Processing "is unusual and denotes marked scatter" (p. 194).

As described earlier, research has provided inconsistent data regarding the size and direction of VIQ-PIQ discrepancies for learning-disabled children. Research conducted so far with the K-ABC has been more consistent in demonstrating a difference between the Sequential and Simultaneous Scales for learning-disabled children, with Sequential Processing standard scores averaging 2 to 5 points higher than the Simultaneous Processing scores. Further analysis has shown that learning-disabled children "performed consistently well on Gestalt Closure, one of the purest measures of Simultaneous Processing" and "tended to score most poorly on the Sequential Processing subtests" (Kaufman and Kaufman, 1983, p. 139).

Subtest scatter (i.e., the amount of discrepancy among individual subtest scores) was explored on the K-ABC by Kaufman and his colleagues.

The data from these studies were not available, however, at the time the manual was written.

Common Subtest Patterns Among Learning-Disabled Children

As described earlier, data obtained from cognitive profiles alone are not sufficient to make the diagnosis of learning disabilities. There are several patterns that often show up in test protocols of learning-disabled students. These patterns are not, however, sufficient to make a diagnosis of learning disability, attention deficit disorder, or other developmental disabilities. They are described here simply to help professionals understand possible difficulties that may underlie or exacerbate learning disabilities.

In looking for patterns within the subtest profile, one must keep in mind that, because of error of measurement, a subtest score that is one or two points below another subtest score may not represent a meaningful difference in abilities on the two tasks. Kaufman (1979) suggests an easy method for determining significant strengths and weaknesses within an individual's WISC-R profile. (A similar method for determining significant strengths and weaknesses within the K-ABC profile is described thoroughly in the K-ABC Manual. Examiners using the K-ABC should rely on this method for interpreting K-ABC results.) In reviewing the WISC-R profile, the examiner should first find the mean of the Verbal subtest scores. Next, any Verbal subtest scores that are 3 or more points above this mean should be identified (these are the relative strengths) as well as any subtest scores that are 3 or more points below the mean (these are the relative weaknesses). This procedure should be repeated for the Performance subtest scores. In using this approach, it is clear that, for example, a subtest score of 10 may indicate a relative strength for one child, but may indicate a relative weakness for another child. It is only the relative position of the subtest scores, not their absolute value, that is of interest in determining profile strengths and weaknesses.

In discussing patterns of strengths and weaknesses, Kaufman (1979) suggests that significant strengths and weaknesses be examined in combination with the other scores that are relatively high or low for the individual. For example, the first pattern to be discussed, Excessive Distractibility, is dependent on three subtest scores: Arithmetic, Digit Span, and Coding. In order to say that this pattern exists for a particular child, it would be necessary for the score on one of these subtests to be identified as a significant weakness, and for the score on each of the other two subtests to be below the mean for its respective group of subtests (i.e., Coding would have to be below the mean of the Performance subtests and Arithmetic or Digit Span would have to be below the mean of the Verbal subtests).

Kaufman emphasizes that the patterns thus identified simply provide hypotheses for understanding the child's actual strengths and weaknesses.

The examiner uses the identified patterns in conjunction with other information known about the child (e.g., from observation during testing, interviews with parents and teachers, results from other evaluations). It is recommended that psychologists responsible for interpreting the WISC-R data familiarize themselves with Kaufman's (1979) approach for identifying patterns of strengths and weaknesses.

As noted earlier, several patterns appear frequently in the subtest profiles of learning-disabled students. Again, it must be stressed that these patterns are not to be used to determine whether or not a learning disability exists, but simply to help the examiner better understand the nature of the learning disability once it has been properly identified. The patterns described in the following paragraphs are ones we have seen frequently in learning-disabled children. They are by no means unique, however, to the learning-disabled child.

EXCESSIVE DISTRACTIBILITY. The WISC-R subtests contributing to a pattern that suggests excessive distractibility are Arithmetic, Digit Span, and Coding. The K-ABC subtests that are useful in diagnosing distractibility or short attention span are Magic Window, Face Recognition, Hand Movements, Number Recall, Word Order, and Spatial Memory. When this pattern of weaknesses is seen, the examiner should make certain to question parents and teachers about possible evidence of attention deficits at home and in the classroom. The examiner should also take special care to report any observation of distractibility or short attention span noted within the testing situation. It is not unusual, however, for students who appear to be attentive in the testing situation to have serious attention problems in the classroom. These children often demonstrate weaknesses on the subtest profiles for excessive distractibility, even when they do not exhibit attention problems in the one-on-one testing situation.

PLANNING ABILITY. A pattern of weakness on the WISC-R Picture Arrangement and Mazes subtests suggests that the student works somewhat impulsively, not taking time to plan before approaching a task. Especially on the Mazes subtest, a child who approaches a task impulsively will make many errors that, on this task, cannot be corrected after the student recognizes them. Although Kaufman does not list planning ability as one of the subtest patterns to be observed on the K-ABC, the examiner might observe signs of poor planning ability in the child's approach to the Photo Series subtest.

VERBAL EXPRESSION, VERBAL CONCEPT FORMATION, ABSTRACT THINKING. Many learning-disabled children, especially those from upper socioeconomic groups, have relatively good verbal skills, as measured by the WISC-R Comprehension, Vocabulary, and Similarities subtests. Skills measured by these tests can be practiced in the context of everyday experiences (e.g., listening to adult conversations, asking and answering questions, discussing), and do not rely heavily on school learning, especially in the younger grades. As the learning-disabled child gets older, however, there is sometimes an observed drop in Vocabulary skills, because more of one's vocabulary is derived from reading as one gets older. (Similarly, a drop in the Information subtest score is often seen as the learning-disabled child grows older.)

On the K-ABC, the verbal expression pattern involves the Magic Window and Gestalt Closure subtests of the Mental Processing Scale, plus the Expressive Vocabulary, Faces & Places, Riddles, and Reading/Decoding subtests of the Achievement Scale.

PERCEPTUAL ORGANIZATION. A pattern of relative strengths on those subtests that measure visual-spatial perception and organization (WISC-R Picture Completion, Picture Arrangement, Block Design, Object Assembly, and Mazes; or K-ABC Hand Movements, Gestalt Closure, Triangles, Matrix Analogies, Spatial Memory, and Photo Series) is often seen in learning-disabled children. It should be noted, however, that this pattern is also often observed on the WISC-R for non-learning-disabled children from impoverished environments. As discussed previously, many of the skills measured on the WISC-R Verbal subtests are those which are encouraged by discussion with adults, listening to adult conversation, asking and answering questions, and so forth. In environments where the amount and quality of language stimulation is limited, Verbal subtest scores may be artificially deflated, thus causing many of the Performance subtest scores (which are less influenced by environmental stimulation) to appear as relative strengths.

VISUAL PERCEPTION OF ABSTRACT STIMULI. A pattern of weakness on the WISC-R Block Design and Coding subtests or on the K-ABC Triangles and Matrix Analogies is often seen in learning-disabled children, especially those whose disability appears to be due to weaknesses in spatial perception, not auditory processing. It is speculated that these are the children who often continue to reverse letters and words long after their peers have stopped, and have difficulty recognizing visual configurations of words that cannot be "sounded out" (e.g., often confusing *though*, *through*, and *tough*).

ABILITY TO REPRODUCE A MODEL. A pattern of weakness on the WISC-R Block Design and Coding subtests can also indicate inability to reproduce a model. This can be due to poor fine-motor skills rather than to poor ability to correctly process visual perception of stimuli. The K-ABC Reproduction of a Model pattern includes the Hand Movements, Number

Recall, Triangles, and Spatial Memory subtests. These subtests measure ability to reproduce a model in a variety of modalities—orally, motorically, by pointing, and with manipulative materials. Fine-motor skills are less important in the K-ABC pattern than in the WISC-R pattern. Attention and memory factors are, however, somewhat more heavily tapped by the K-ABC pattern, as several of the subtests require the child to reproduce a model from memory.

Individual learning-disabled students will, of course, exhibit many other patterns of strength and weakness, depending on their individual abilities, backgrounds, and educational experiences. The patterns listed are presented merely to remind the examiner of some of the most common patterns observed in learning-disabled students so that he or she can be on the lookout for them.

Supplemental Psychological Tests That May Be Useful In the Diagnosis of Learning Disabilities

As mentioned previously, measures of both intelligence and academic achievement are essential for diagnosing learning disabilities. There are, however, other tests that can be added to the psychologist's battery that may help in understanding the learning disability after it has been identified. Tests that are often used to supplement the battery include those which purport to measure skills related to visual and auditory processing. Members of the diagnostic team must be cautioned, however, that many of these tests lack sufficient reliability or are inadequately normed. For this reason it may be inappropriate to attempt to use the profiles generated from these tests to subtype the dyslexic child or to plan remedial approaches to be used with the child. Harrington (1984) claims that psychologists wishing to assess sensory process deficits will have to collect data informally. The tests mentioned in the following paragraphs can be used in that informal collection of data. Members of the diagnostic team must simply be cautious not to blindly accept scores and profiles generated by these tests.

Tests to Assess Auditory Processing Skills

Among the tests commonly used to assess auditory processing skills are the Goldman-Fristoe-Woodcock Test of Auditory Discrimination and the Auditory Discrimination Test. It is generally assumed that the child who shows deficits on these auditory processing tests will have difficulty making sound-symbol associations, blending sounds, and sequencing phonemes. These tests will be discussed in more detail in Chapter 5.

Tests to Assess Visual Processing Skills

Among the tests that purport to measure visual processing skills are those that require the child to reproduce the drawing of a figure, either with the model present (the Developmental Test of Visual-Motor Integration, the Bender Visual Motor Gestalt Test) or from memory (the Benton Visual Retention Test and the Memory for Designs Test). Of course, these tests necessarily evaluate fine-motor coordination in conjunction with visual processing skills. The Motor Free Visual Perception Test can be used to identify deficits in visual perception of spatial stimuli in a manner that is not confounded by fine-motor skills. The Frostig Developmental Test of Visual Perception contains items that assess skills in five visual-perceptual areas: Eye-Motor Coordination, Figure-Ground, Constancy of Shape, Positions in Space, and Spatial Relationships. It is generally assumed that a child who shows deficits on these visual processing tests will have difficulty in distinguishing one letter from another and remembering visual configurations of nonphonetic words, will show reversals in letters and words, and will have problems with handwriting. For students whose performance on these visual processing tests is poor, the examiner should be certain to inquire about handwriting quality, speed, and efficiency.

ITPA and Detroit Tests of Learning Aptitude

Two tests that are commonly used inappropriately to make a diagnosis of learning disabilities or are used to supplement the battery of intelligence and academic tests are the Illinois Test of Psycholinguistic Abilities (ITPA) and the Detroit Tests of Learning Aptitude. Each of these tests includes multiple subtests to assess various skills presumed to be associated with academic achievement. The ITPA, for example, includes 12 subtests (Auditory Reception, Visual Reception, Auditory Association, Visual Association, Verbal Expression, Manual Expression, Grammatic Closure, Visual Closure, Auditory Sequential Memory, Visual Sequential Memory, Auditory Closure, and Sound Blending). The Detroit Tests of Learning Aptitude measures skills in 19 categories. Although these tests can be used informally to gather information about the child's approach to tasks, the subtest reliabilities are insufficient to justify using test scores to profile the child's strengths and weaknesses or to prescribe remedial approaches.

Projective Tests

If there is a suspicion of emotional disturbance as a contributory factor in the learning problem, or as a condition resulting from the learning disability, additional tests should be administered by the experienced psychologist. These might include the Rorschach Psychodiagnostic Test, the

Thematic Apperception Test (TAT), or the Children's Apperception Test (CAT), all of which require fairly extensive verbal expression. Drawing tests, which require little verbal expression, are also often used (e.g,. Draw-A-Person Test, House-Tree-Person test, kinetic family drawings). The usefulness of these projective tests depends primarily on the examiner's experience and familiarity with children who are experiencing emotional problems.

CONCLUSION

The psychologist contributes to the interdisciplinary diagnostic process by obtaining a history of the child's difficulties (from the parents' perspective), an accurate measurement of intelligence, and supplemental information that will assist in understanding the nature of any learning disabilities that might be identified. It is important that the assessment instruments used by the psychologist are reliable, valid, and meet other specific criteria outlined in this chapter. Approach to test administration is also a critical issue, as many children with learning disabilities will exhibit behaviors that typically interfere with testing. Test interpretation should be founded on research-based principles, not on overgeneralized and misconceived views of the "typical" learning-disabled child's cognitive profile.

The interdisciplinary team must, of course, rely on test data in diagnosing learning disabilities. It is important, though, that team members understand that tests are merely instruments to assist in the process of diagnosis. The data should be used cautiously, and only in conjunction with information about the student that has been obtained through other sources.

CHAPTER 4

Educational Evaluation

Elizabeth H. Aylward
Frank R. Brown, III
M.E.B. Lewis
Carol R. Savage

THE EDUCATIONAL HISTORY

The special educator on the interdisciplinary team has access to information that is essential in understanding the child's school difficulties. Although most parents can give a fair chronology of the major events in the child's school career, a complete educational history depends on information that can only be obtained from past and present teachers, other school staff, and, when appropriate, from the student. The ideal school history will include a review of the school record, interviews with past and present teachers, and classroom observations. Supplemental information can be obtained from parents, although their perspective will have been covered fairly thoroughly by the physician and psychologist.

The Record Review

The school record should be reviewed before interviews, observations, or testing are initiated. Parents' permission must, of course, be obtained in writing before school records are examined. Attention should be given to the following areas of information contained in the school record:

Attendance
- ☐ What schools (including preschools) has the child attended, and what were the years of attendance?
- ☐ What were the reasons for changes from one school to another?
- ☐ Have there been any periods of excessive absence? If so, were reasons for these absences recorded?

Remedial Efforts
- ☐ Have any special education services been provided (past or present), including speech-language therapy and resource help?
- ☐ What types of remedial approaches, if any, have been used with the child? How long was each approach employed, and with what effect?
- ☐ Have there been any repetitions of grades? If so, was the child provided any resource help within the repeated grade?
- ☐ Have individualized educational plans been developed (past and present)?

Classroom Environment
- ☐ In what types of classroom settings (open-spaced or self-contained) has the child been placed (past and present)?
- ☐ Has the child moved from class to class during the school day (past and present)?

Grouping
- ☐ Have children been grouped homogeneously for various academic areas? What was the basis for this grouping (e.g., age, cognitive ability, level of academic achievement, optimal learning modality)?
- ☐ If groups are based on academic achievement, in what level has the child been placed for major academic subjects (past and present)?
- ☐ Has the child been moved into more or less demanding groups during the course of the school career? With what effect?

Grades
- ☐ Has the student been graded on the basis of individual effort extended and improvement shown, or on the basis of comparison with classmates?
- ☐ Has the child shown changes in grade patterns?
- ☐ Were these changes associated with any changes in academic expectations (e.g., shifts from rote learning in lower grade levels to more conceptual learning in upper grades)?
- ☐ Has the child shown a consistent pattern in grades (e.g., high in arithmetic, low in reading, or high during the first quarter with regular drops as the year progresses)?

☐ If teacher comments were included in the reports, what criticisms and commendations were made?

Family/Social History

☐ Have any family members had a history of learning disabilities, symptomatology compatible with attention deficit disorder, grade repetitions, or remedial efforts?

☐ Have there been any factors that might limit the family's ability to support the school's efforts (e.g., language proficiency, economic resources, health and emotional status)?

Previous Testing

☐ What is the child's record of performance on group-administered standardized tests? Has performance on these tests been fairly consistent over the years?

☐ Have any individualized tests been administered? What were the reasons for these tests? What were the results?

Behavior

☐ Is there any record of behavior problems? Have behavior problems been consistent throughout the school career?

☐ Have there been any suspensions or expulsions?

Visual/Hearing

☐ Have vision and hearing screens been administered? Were any difficulties identified? Have more extensive tests been administered, if warranted?

☐ Has it been recommended for the child to wear glasses or hearing aids?

Medical Record

☐ Has there been any evidence of medical difficulty that would interfere with learning?

☐ Has the child taken any medication on a regular basis that might affect school performance?

Teacher Interviews

The most complete and spontaneous way of gaining information about a child is through direct contact with teachers (past and present) and others who have knowledge of the child (e.g., school principal, guidance counselors). Such interviews are best conducted after the school record review has been completed in order to avoid redundancy and to follow up on questions generated by the review. Of course, such exchanges of information demand that the interviewer obtain the parents' permission.

The interviewer should use a structured format, which should cover the following areas:

Teacher/Student Ratio
☐ How many students are in the class? How many teachers and aides serve the classroom?
☐ Is any individual student instruction possible?

Attendance
☐ What is the child's current attendance record? What reasons are offered for poor attendance?

Grouping
☐ Is the child able to keep up academically with classmates?
☐ If students are grouped homogeneously within the classroom, what is the basis for the grouping? In what group is the child placed? Is this group placement appropriate?
☐ Has the child been moved into more or less demanding groups during the school year? With what effect?

Classroom Environment
☐ Is the current classroom open-spaced or self-contained?
☐ Does the child move from class to class during the school day?
☐ How is seating arranged, and where does the child sit in relation to the teacher?
☐ What is the level of auditory and visual distraction?

Curriculum
☐ What teaching methods, materials, and strategies are used in various subject areas?
☐ Have any special approaches been employed to remediate academic weaknesses?
☐ Have any special approaches been employed to enhance academic strengths?
☐ Have any special approaches been employed to circumvent the child's particular learning difficulties (e.g., shortened assignments for children with handwriting difficulties, Talking Books for children with reading disabilities)?
☐ How long should the child be spending on homework each evening?

Evaluation
☐ What grades is the child currently earning in each subject area?

☐ On what basis are grades assigned (e.g., individual effort and improvement, or comparison with classmates' achievement)?

☐ Are grades based on class participation, daily assignments, or test performance? In which, if any, of these areas does the child exhibit particular difficulty?

☐ Does the child seem to be satisfied with the grades received?

☐ What evaluation techniques are used most frequently (e.g., true/false, multiple choice, essay, oral response)? Does the child appear to have more difficulty with some types of evaluation techniques than with others?

☐ What special accommodations have been made in evaluation procedures for children with particular weaknesses (e.g., allowing extra time for children with reading or handwriting difficulties, substitution of oral presentations for essay tests)?

Attention Deficit and Impulse Control

☐ Does the child exhibit developmentally appropriate attention in class? Does attention span vary according to task demands, size of instructional group, level of auditory and visual distractions, or other factors?

☐ Does the child currently take any medication for attention deficit disorder? Is the medication administered consistently?

☐ Are attention deficits associated with any excess motor activity (restless, squirmy, fidgety)?

☐ Does the child appear to have particular difficulty in making transitions from class to class or from subject to subject?

☐ Does the child have difficulty inhibiting inappropriate responses or engage in impulsive behavior that disturbs the class (e.g., difficulty staying in his or her seat, talking out of turn, making silly noises)?

☐ Does the child rush through his or her work, resulting in careless errors? Does the child exhibit erratic performance?

Work Habits

☐ Does the child complete independent work? Are there problems in specific work areas (e.g., difficulty completing written work in alloted time)?

☐ Does the child have difficulty organizing materials? (For example, does he or she have difficulty remembering materials needed for homework, does he or she have difficulty finding materials in his or her notebook or folder?)

☐ Is the child's response to frustration appropriate? How does the child respond to correction?

Inappropriate Behaviors
☐ Does the child exhibit any of the following?
—destructiveness
—aggressiveness
—oppositional behavior
—noncompliance
—pouting, sulking
—tantrums
—other forms of attention-seeking behavior
☐ Could these inappropriate behaviors reflect inappropriate placement?
☐ What behavior management strategies have been employed and with what effect? Are school and home strategies coordinated?

Peer Relationships
☐ How satisfactory are peer relationships?
☐ What factors interfere with good peer relationships (e.g., impulsivity, aggressiveness, withdrawal, language difficulties, poor self-concept)?

Self-Concept/Emotional Stability
☐ How does the child appear to feel about himself or herself?
☐ Does the child make derogatory comments about himself or herself or apologies for his or her work?
☐ How does the child feel about going to school?
☐ Does the child show any symptoms of depression (e.g., mood swings, withdrawal, weight change)?
☐ Does the child show signs of excessive anger, tension, or other emotional disturbance?

Family/Social Situation
☐ Are there any family circumstances that interfere with learning (e.g., financial problems, divorce, births or deaths of family members, language proficiency)?
☐ How much contact does the school have with the family?
☐ How receptive are the parents to school suggestions?

Classroom Observation

Just as it is important to review school history and to interview staff familiar with the student, it is important to visit and observe the current classroom. It must be remembered that the observer's presence in the classroom creates an artificial environment. This is unavoidable, and dictates that all observations be judged with this limitation in mind. The areas covered by the classroom observation will be similar to those covered in the Record Review and Interview. The questions addressed by the observation should include:

Teacher/Student Ratio
☐ How many students are present? How many teachers and aides are present?
☐ Is any individualized student instruction occurring?

Grouping
☐ Does the child appear to be able to function in his or her current grouping?
☐ How many students are working on the same task?

Classroom Environment
☐ Is the classroom open-spaced or self-contained?
☐ How is seating arranged, and where does the child sit in relation to the teacher?
☐ What is the level of auditory and visual distraction?

Instruction
☐ What teaching methods, materials, and strategies are used in various subject areas?
☐ Do the methods, materials, and strategies seem clear to the student? Does the lesson appear to be well-organized?
☐ Is the child given opportunity to ask questions and seek clarification? Are these requests appropriately met?
☐ Are any remedial approaches being employed?
☐ Are any enrichment approaches being employed?
☐ Are any special approaches being employed to circumvent the child's particular learning difficulties?

Evaluation
☐ Is the child given appropriate feedback on his or her classroom performance?

Attention Deficit and Impulse Control
☐ Does the child exhibit developmentally appropriate attention in class? Does his or her attention span vary according to task demands, size of instructional group, level of auditory and visual distractions, or other factors?
☐ Are attention deficits associated with any excess motor activity?
☐ Does the child have difficulty inhibiting inappropriate responses or engage in impulsive behavior that disrupts the class?

☐ Does the child rush through his or her work, resulting in careless errors?

Work Habits
☐ Does the child complete independent work?
☐ Does the child have difficulty organizing materials?
☐ Is the child's response to frustration appropriate? How does the child respond to correction?

Inappropriate Behaviors
☐ Does the child exhibit any of the following?
  —destructiveness
  —aggressiveness
  —oppositional behavior
  —noncompliance
  —pouting, sulking
  —tantrums
  —other forms of attention-seeking behavior
☐ What behavior management strategies are employed and with what consistency and effect?

Peer Relationships
☐ How satisfactory are peer interactions?
☐ What factors interfere with good peer relationships?

Self-Concept/Emotional Stability
☐ How does the child appear to feel about himself or herself?
☐ Does the child make derogatory comments about himself or herself or apologies for his or her work?
☐ Does the child show signs of excessive anger, tension, or other emotional disturbance?

When possible, observations should be followed with a brief teacher conference to clarify lingering questions.

Parent Interview

After reviewing material from the physician and psychologist, reviewing the school record, interviewing school staff, and observing the child in the classroom, the special educator is in a unique position to understand both the origins and extent of school difficulties and the parents' perceptions of these difficulties. In order to avoid duplication of material already gathered by the physician and psychologist, the special educator will want to limit his or her interview with the parent to two major areas. First, the parents' explanations should be solicited for such issues as excessive absences, failure to consistently administer medication for attention deficit disorder, or the child's failure to complete homework. Second, the special educator will want to address areas where there appears to be discrepancy between the parents' perceptions and information gathered from the school.

EDUCATIONAL TESTING

One of the most valuable aspects of the interdisciplinary approach is the opportunity it affords professionals in a variety of fields to do what they do best, without the burden of trying to cover less familiar fields. There are discrete areas of assessment for each team member, and although some testing might appear to overlap, the areas in an educational assessment are specific and particularly apt for the special educator to cover. Educational evaluation should serve to qualify as well as quantify the student's capabilities, and to provide suggestions for promoting strengths and remediating weaknesses.

Test Selection

Because accurate assessment of academic achievement, like assessment of cognitive ability, is essential to diagnosis of learning disability, the special educator will want to select tests with proven reliability and validity. The test selected should meet the eleven considerations outlined in Table 3-1. Hundreds of tests are available for the assessment of academic achievement. Because most of these are of poor technical quality (e.g., inadequately normed, of poor or unproven reliability or validity), the educational evaluator must be very conscientious in selecting tests and interpreting the results obtained from them. Several of the most common (but sometimes inappropriate) tests of academic achievement will be discussed. For further information regarding these or other tests, the educational evaluator is encouraged to consult the *Ninth Mental Measurements Yearbook* (Mitchell, 1985), *Test Critiques* (Keyser and Sweetland, 1985), or reviews included in educational journals.

As with the tests of cognitive ability, the tests of academic achievement must be individually administered. In conducting individual evaluations for diagnosing learning disabilities, educators occasionally use tests that were designed for group administration, such as the Metropolitan Readiness Tests or the Stanford Diagnostic Reading Test. Individual administration of these tests, because it does not follow standard procedure, invalidates the norms and makes scores uninterpretable. Thus, tests must not only be individually administered, but must be normed for individual administration.

There are obviously many subskills within each area of academic achievement and, in assessing an individual student, it is important to cover as many of these facets as possible. For example, an assessment of reading achievement should minimally include measures of word attack skills, passage comprehension, and sight vocabulary. When possible, it is desirable to employ a single test instrument, as this will allow valid comparisons among the subskills. (As described in Chapter 3, comparisons between individual tests are more valid if the tests have been normed on the same or similar populations.) For this reason, primary focus is placed on those instruments that permit the most comprehensive evaluation. There are other instruments that reliably measure more discrete skills, and these may be used to supplement the comprehensive batteries. If limitations are properly appreciated, other informal, nonstandardized instruments can be used to get a subjective feel for strengths and weaknesses in isolated areas.

Comprehensive Educational Batteries

There are several comprehensive test batteries on the market that have been used widely by school systems in the past. Many of these do not, however, meet the criteria for tests used in making the diagnosis of learning disabilities (as outlined in Table 3-1). The most widely used comprehensive educational test battery that does meet these criteria is the Woodcock-Johnson Psycho-Educational Battery. This battery and other comprehensive educational test batteries are described in the following paragraphs.

WOODCOCK-JOHNSON PSYCHO-EDUCATIONAL BATTERY (WJPEB). As described in Chapter 3, the WJPEB contains three sections: Tests of Cognitive Ability, Tests of Academic Achievement, and Tests of Interest Level. Although we have reservations regarding the use of Part I (Tests of Cognitive Ability) as a measure of intellectual functioning in the learning-disabled population, Part II (Tests of Academic Achievement) is viewed as an appropriate, well-standardized, and comprehensive instrument to assess academic achievement in this population.

Part II, like the other sections of the WJPEB, is designed for children and adults, ages 3 through 80. Most children will have difficulty reaching basal level on the academic achievement subtests before the age of 4 or 5. Beyond twelfth grade, the norms are less adequate than those for the school-age population, and scores should be interpreted cautiously. A Spanish edition is available, with appropriate norms.

Part II consists of ten subtests that can be combined to measure five different areas of academic achievement (termed *Clusters*): Reading, Mathematics, Written Language, Knowledge, and Skills. The Reading, Mathematics, and Written Language Clusters are the most widely used in diagnosing learning disabilities. The Knowledge Cluster assesses general information in science, social studies, and humanities. It is often omitted because learning disabilities in these areas are rarely addressed. Furthermore, the score from the WISC-R Information subtest, if administered, can provide a good measure of general knowledge. The Skills Cluster may be useful in assessment of preacademic skills for children who cannot base on all of the subtests required for calculation of scores in the Reading, Mathematics, and Written Language Clusters.

The WJPEB Reading Cluster is composed of three subtests:

1. The Letter-Word Identification subtest assesses ability to identify individual letters and words out of context.
2. The Word Attack subtest assesses ability to decode nonsense words (e.g., "quog," "shomble," "tiff").
3. The Passage Comprehension subtest uses a cloze procedure, whereby the student is required to read a short passage in which a single word is omitted, and to supply the word that makes the sentence make sense.

A major drawback of the Reading Cluster is the limited manner in which passage comprehension is assessed. Children who are good at using context clues may do very well on this subtest, without having good inferential or critical reading comprehension skills or good memory for the details of material they have read. Another major drawback is the lack of opportunity for the examiner to hear the child read passages, as the material on the Passage Comprehension subtest is read silently. This prevents the examiner from drawing any conclusions regarding reading speed, accuracy, fluency, and so forth.

The Mathematics Cluster is composed of two subtests:

1. The Calculations subtest requires the child to complete a page of written computation problems, ranging from simple addition and subtraction facts to calculus and trigonometry.
2. The Applied Problems subtest requires the child to respond to orally presented math problems that involve the application of math concepts. Visual aids are provided, and the child is allowed to use paper and pencil.

The Written Language Cluster is composed of two subtests:

1. The Dictation subtest requires the child to spell dictated words, demonstrate knowledge of plurals, punctuation marks, contractions, and abbreviations.
2. The Proofing subtest requires the child to read short passages and identify errors in punctuation, spelling, and word usage, and tell how errors should be corrected.

Like most tests of written language skills, the WJPEB Written Language Cluster assesses only the mechanics of writing, not the child's ability to organize his or her thoughts in writing. No measure of handwriting speed or legibility is included.

Most reviewers agree that the WJPEB is technically excellent, with especially good reliability and concurrent validity. Norming samples are adequate, at least for the school-age population. The WJPEB is easy to administer. Scoring is objective, but cumbersome, and it is easy to make errors in calculating scores. (Computer scoring is available, however.) Despite certain limitations, The WJPEB Tests of Achievement should be considered a valuable instrument in the educator's test battery.

KAUFMAN ASSESSMENT BATTERY FOR CHILDREN (K-ABC). As discussed in Chapter 3, the K-ABC is composed of the Mental Processing Scales (represented by two separate intelligence scales: Simultaneous and Sequential Processing) and the Achievement Scale. The Mental Processing Scales, unlike the WJPEB Tests of Cognitive Ability, are viewed as an appropriate measure of intelligence for use in diagnosing learning disabilities.

The Achievement Scale is made up of six subtests, with different age ranges:

1. Expressive Vocabulary, which requires the child to name objects pictured in photographs (ages 2.5 through 5 years).
2. Faces and Places, which requires the child to name well-known people, fictional characters, or places pictured in photographs or drawings (ages 2.5 through 12.5 years).
3. Arithmetic, which requires demonstration of knowledge of numbers and mathematical concepts, counting and computational skills, and other school-related arithmetic abilities (ages 3 through 12.5 years).
4. Riddles, which requires the child to infer the name of a concrete or abstract concept when given a list of characteristics (ages 3 through 12.5 years).
5. Reading/Decoding, which involves letter and word identification (ages 5 through 12.5 years).
6. Reading/Understanding, which requires the child to follow commands given in written sentences (7 through 12.5 years).

As Kaufman (1983) explains, the Achievement Scale is interpreted as a measure of the child's "applied intelligence." Review of the individual tests reveals that several assess abilities in areas not traditionally included in academic achievement batteries (e.g., vocabulary, general knowledge, verbal concept formation). On the other hand, several areas generally considered to be in the arena of academic achievement are not covered (e.g., word attack skills, written calculation, spelling).

It should be noted that the K-ABC Achievement Scale may obscure learning disabilities in some bright children. If a child has good verbal skills (as measured by the Expressive Vocabulary and Riddles subtests) or a good fund of general knowledge (as measured by the Faces and Places subtest), the Achievement Scale score may be commensurate with overall intelligence (as measured by the Mental Processing Composite), despite poor reading or math abilities. For these children, a diagnosis of learning disability might be missed. However, this problem can be minimized if subtest scores are considered separately.

The Achievement Scale is a technically sound test with many of the same positive characteristics as the Mental Processing Scales (see Chapter 3). Despite these favorable qualities, the nontraditional content of the Achievement Scale prevents many educators from considering it to be the instrument of choice when assessing academic achievement.

KAUFMAN TEST OF EDUCATIONAL ACHIEVEMENT (K-TEA). The K-TEA offers two forms, the Brief Form and the Comprehensive Form, for assessment of academic skills in grades 1 through 12. The Brief Form provides individual scores in the areas of reading, math, and spelling, and takes approximately 30 minutes to administer. The Brief Form is recommended for screening and would not, therefore, be as appropriate as the Comprehensive Form for use in establishing a diagnosis of learning disabilities.

The Comprehensive Form is composed of five subtests:

1. Mathematics/Application—Measures understanding of a wide variety of arithmetic concepts and their application. Items are presented orally with visual aids.
2. Reading/Decoding—Measures recognition of letters and words, both phonetic and nonphonetic.
3. Spelling—Measures the ability to spell dictated spelling words in writing.
4. Reading Comprehension—Measures literal and inferential reading comprehension, using two types of items. One type requires the child to follow commands presented in written sentences. The other type requires the child to read a paragraph and respond orally to questions regarding the passage.
5. Mathematics Computation—Measures ability to do written computation.

In terms of content, the K-TEA has certain advantages over the WJPEB. The most significant of these is the measurement of literal and inferential comprehension on the Reading/Comprehension subtest. The format of items on this subtest is more in line with what is generally termed *reading comprehension* than is the cloze format used by the WJPEB. Unlike the WJPEB, the K-TEA does not contain separate measures of word attack and word recognition. The single Reading/Decoding subtest does, however, allow an item analysis which can identify specific weaknesses in word-attack skills. Finally, the K-TEA, unlike the WJPEB, provides no measure of written language skills other than spelling.

K-TEA norms are based on a large, representative sample. Reliability appears to be fairly good. Validity, to the extent it has been measured, is also promising. Because of its relative recency (published in 1985), the K-TEA is not as widely used or as well-known as the WJPEB. It appears, however, to be a viable option in the educational evaluation.

THE PEABODY INDIVIDUAL ACHIEVEMENT TEST (PIAT) AND THE WIDE RANGE ACHIEVEMENT TEST—REVISED (WRAT-R). Two tests that were used extensively before the introduction of the WJPEB are the WRAT and the PIAT. (The WRAT was restandardized and minimally revised in 1984, and is now entitled the WRAT-R.) Although both of these tests are of adequate reliability, their item content is too limited for the purpose of diagnosing learning disabilities. The WRAT-R Reading subtest, for example, involves word recognition only. The math test measures only rote mathematical computation, and does not assess ability to apply mathematical concepts. Although the PIAT includes a test of reading comprehension, its only measure of written language is a multiple-choice spelling test. The PIAT is also hindered by the fact that norms are out of date (they were developed in 1969), resulting in inflated scores for today's population.

Because the PIAT and WRAT-R are relatively quick to administer, educators often view them as screening devices for obtaining rough estimates of achievement levels. Because the purpose of the education evaluation is to determine as precisely as possible the child's level of achievement in a variety of areas, the use of the PIAT or WRAT-R is not appropriate. Furthermore, there is no reason to invest time administering these instruments if a more comprehensive battery is being used. It is also important to note that educators sometimes use a brief measure, such as the WRAT-R or PIAT, to check the validity of a score obtained from a more comprehensive test. This use is also clearly inappropriate.

Tests of Specific Academic Skills

As discussed previously, it is preferable to select a comprehensive battery that measures abilities in all the basic academic areas (usually considered to be reading, mathematics, and written language). Because each of the subtests within a comprehensive battery is normed on the same group of students, comparison among an individual student's subtest scores can be made with confidence. This is not possible if a variety of tests is used, with each measuring a specific skill area. It is sometimes useful, however, to supplement the comprehensive battery with tests that measure specific skill areas. This is especially true if the results of certain subtests within the comprehensive battery are questionable, or if the evaluator wants to pinpoint difficulties more precisely. In selecting tests that measure specific academic skills, evaluators must be cautioned that the technical qualities of these tests (e.g., norms, reliability, validity) are often less sound than those of the well-researched comprehensive test batteries.

Some of the most common tests of specific academic abilities will be described.

WOODCOCK READING MASTERY TEST. This test, published in 1973, is very similar in structure to the Reading Cluster of the WJPEB. The only additional skill measured by the Woodcock Reading Mastery Test is represented by the Word Comprehension subtest, which requires the student to solve verbal analogies. It can be argued that this skill is more related to verbal reasoning than to reading ability and, thus, its addition to the test battery may not be particularly beneficial in assessing reading ability. The test includes many more items than the WJPEB Reading Cluster, which may allow for easier diagnosis of specific weaknesses. The Woodcock Reading Mastery Test suffers from the same weaknesses as the WJPEB Reading Cluster (e.g., limited assessment of reading comprehension, lack of opportunity for the evaluator to hear oral reading). Because of the similarity between the WJPEB Reading Cluster and the Woodcock Reading Mastery Test, administration of both would be redundant.

GRAY ORAL READING TEST AND DURRELL ANALYSIS OF READING DIFFI-CULTY. As discussed previously, a major drawback of the WJPEB Reading Cluster is its lack of a test that allows the examiner to observe oral reading of passages. Although the relationship between oral and silent reading has not been established, it is certainly true that some of the characteristics that impede a child's silent reading (e.g., word substitutions, inversions, slow rate) can only be assessed through an oral approach. Furthermore, oral reading skill is clearly important for performance in the early elementary grades.

Two tests commonly used to measure oral reading are the Gray Oral Reading Test (GORT) and the Durrell Analysis of Reading Difficulty. The GORT provides 13 passages of increasing difficulty, ranging from a preprimer level to college or adult levels. As the child reads the passages orally, the examiner records errors in eight areas: assistance needed on words, gross and partial mispronunciations, omissions, insertions, substitutions, repetitions, and inversions. Time taken to read each passage is also recorded. The manual describes procedures for arriving at a grade equivalent score of oral reading. However, because the norms are so inadequate, evaluators would be wise to limit use of the GORT to an informal method of gathering information regarding oral reading.

Another individually administered reading test that is often used is the Durrell Analysis of Reading Difficulty, most recently revised in 1980. Because of the subjectivity in scoring, lack of data regarding validity, and questionable norming procedures, scores cannot be used with confidence. Portions of the Durrell Analysis can be used informally to obtain a sample of the student's oral reading ability. Behavioral checklists are provided that will assist the examiner in careful observation of reading characteristics. Comprehension questions are available for both Oral and Silent Reading paragraphs, but examiners are reminded that these questions only require the student to recall explicit information rather than to make inferences or draw conclusions.

KEYMATH DIAGNOSTIC ARITHMETIC TEST. This test, originally published in 1971, is often used to supplement the more comprehensive achievement batteries. It is designed for use with children in preschool through grade six, and measures skills in three areas of mathematics: content, operations, and application. Reliability and validity are adequate. Norms are available only for the total test score. Thus, the KeyMath norm-referenced scores provide little additional information for the student who has already been given an arithmetic test from one of the comprehensive test batteries. Furthermore, the norm-referenced scores are expressed only in grade-equivalents, preventing meaningful comparison with the IQ and making them of little value in diagnosing learning disabilities.

The KeyMath is designed to be used as a criterion-referenced test as well as a normed-referenced test, and information obtained from it can be used to identify specific weaknesses within the child's mathematical abilities. Use of the KeyMath as a criterion-referenced test is discussed later in this chapter.

TEST OF WRITTEN LANGUAGE (TOWL). As mentioned previously, most tests of written language tap only the mechanics of writing (e.g., spelling, grammar, punctuation, capitalization), not ability to express thoughts in writing. The TOWL, originally published in 1978 and revised in 1983, attempts to address this problem by including a subtest requiring spontaneous writing. Designed for children in grades 2 through 12, the TOWL consists of four subtests, from which the examiner derives six subscores. Word Usage assesses syntactic skills through a cloze procedure. Spelling ability is assessed through written spelling of dictated words. The Style subtest requires the student to correctly rewrite sentences that are presented without any punctuation or capitalization. The Story subtest requires the student to examine three pictures and create a written story. This subtest generates scores in thematic maturity, vocabulary, and handwriting. Administration is fairly easy and takes about 40 minutes.

Scoring for the three subtests that use a more traditional test format (Spelling, Style, and Word Usage) is fairly straightforward, whereas scoring for the Story subtest requires considerable practice and is somewhat subjective. Reliability, validity, and standardization for the Spelling, Style, and Word Usage subtests are adequate, at least for the elementary school population. Reliability and validity of the Story subtest, which distinguishes the TOWL from its competitors, are not as well established. For example, the test developers report questionable test-retest reliabilities for the Thematic Maturity and Vocabulary scores. Information regarding interscorer reliability (probably the most important type of reliability for a test whose scoring necessarily involves so much subjectivity) is based on an inadequately small sample.

Because the Story subtest presents only one topic on which the student is directed to write, evaluators must be cautioned that the student's writing may vary considerably depending on his or her interest in the given topic. Furthermore, it is often difficult to get students (especially learning-disabled students) to write stories that are of sufficient length for adequate scoring. For these reasons, the evaluator should use the TOWL results cautiously, and only in conjunction with further information regarding the student's written language abilities, obtained through interviews with teachers and review of writing samples.

TEST OF WRITTEN SPELLING (TWS). This test assesses spelling ability through a dictated test that includes Predictable Words (those that follow orthographic spelling rules, i.e., have good correspondence between phonemes and graphemes) and Unpredictable Words (those that do not follow orthographic spelling rules). Norms appear adequate, although information regarding reliability and validity is sparse. The major drawback to the TWS is its lack of standard scores. Grade equivalents and "spelling ages" are provided, as well as a "spelling quotient" that is based on a comparison of spelling age with chronological age. None of these scores can validly be compared with the IQ and are, therefore, of little value in diagnosing learning disabilities. The test can be used informally to determine whether spelling errors are related to difficulty with application of orthographic spelling rules or to memorization of configurations of words not following these rules.

Tests of Preacademic Skills

As discussed in previous chapters, it is usually not possible to diagnose learning disabilities until the child has had some formal academic instruction (usually not until the middle of first grade, at the earliest). Parents and teachers are often interested, however, in determining whether younger children might be at risk for developing learning disabilities. As discussed in Chapter 2, the physician is in an opportune position to observe delays in early development that may serve to identify children who are at risk for learning disabilities. Unfortunately, there are no tests designed specifically for assessment of preacademic skills that we view as appropriate for the individual educational assessment of potential learning disabilities.

Two group-administered tests of preacademic skills that are sometimes used in individual educational assessment are the Metropolitan Readiness Tests and the Boehm Test of Basic Concepts. As mentioned previously, group administration of tests cannot be supported because nonstandard administration of any test invalidates its norms. Both tests could be used informally by the evaluator to identify concepts with which the child has difficulty.

Criterion-Referenced Tests

Test developers often distinguish between norm-referenced and criterion-referenced tests. All of the tests discussed so far have been norm-referenced, meaning that the child's score is based on the comparison of his or her performance with that of a sample of children of the same age or grade level. The use of criterion-referenced tests should be reserved for determining whether a child has mastered specifically defined skills, not for diagnosis or placement decisions. They are often used in developing a diagnostic prescriptive program that will attempt to remediate the specific weaknesses identified. Criterion-referenced tests cannot be used as a substitute for norm-referenced tests in diagnosing learning disabilities because they do not provide scores that can be compared with the scores from tests of intelligence.

Although criterion-referenced tests can be of great value in diagnosing specific areas of weakness and developing remediation strategies, we believe that they are most efficiently used after diagnoses of learning disabilities have been established through the use of norm-referenced tests. Because of their comprehensive nature, criterion-referenced tests are often quite time-consuming to administer. It is often recommended that they be readministered regularly to determine where progress has been made. Furthermore, these tests will probably be most meaningful and valuable for the teachers who will actually be working with the student on a day-to-day basis. For these reasons, criterion-referenced tests are more appropriately administered, when possible, by classroom teachers rather than by a special education evaluator. Because criterion-referenced tests are not particularly useful in establishing a diagnosis of learning disabilities, they will not be discussed in detail here.

Educators interested in exploring criterion-referenced tests further may want to examine two tests mentioned in the previous sections that are designed to be used as either norm-referenced or criterion-referenced tests

(Stanford Diagnostic Reading Test and KeyMath). One commonly used instrument designed specifically as a criterion-referenced test is the Brigance Diagnostic Comprehensive Inventory of Basic Skills.

Test Administration

Educational testing should be conducted according to the same considerations outlined for psychological testing in Chapter 3. The testing environment should be conducive to the child's best performance, and special accommodations may need to be made to ensure good rapport between the child and the examiner. The examiner should make special effort to critically observe the child's behavior during the testing session, as the information derived from this observation can be as vital in understanding the child's school difficulties as the test results themselves. Specific behaviors to be observed will be similar to those identified for the psychological evaluation, as described in Chapter 3.

CONCLUSION

This chapter has outlined the role of the educator in the interdisciplinary diagnostic process. The educator gathers information that is vital for a complete understanding of the learning-disabled child's school difficulties. The information obtained from the educator through the school record review, teacher interviews, and classroom observation, considered together with the information obtained through the parent interviews conducted by the psychologist and physician, allows a complete history. The educational assessment usually relies on information obtained through one of the well-researched comprehensive batteries of academic achievement. Using such batteries, the educator should be able to provide the interdisciplinary team with scores for reading, math, and written language that can be confidently compared with measures of intelligence obtained through the psychological evaluation. Supplemental tests measuring limited aspects of specific academic skills may be used with caution. As with psychological testing, team members must recognize that assessment instruments are merely tools to be used in conjunction with information obtained from other sources.

CHAPTER 5

Speech-Language, Occupational Therapy, and Physical Therapy Evaluation

Barbara L. Armstrong
Jean A. Lewis
Beverly D. Cusick

In Chapter 1, we introduced the idea of primary (neurologically based) handicapping conditions occurring in association with learning disabilities. In this chapter, primary deficits in three areas, speech-language, fine and oral motor, and gross motor function, will be discussed. Mixtures of any or all of these conditions can occur in association with learning disability, and therefore, we encourage parents and professionals to look closely for these associated conditions which may compound the already complicated learning disability.

LANGUAGE EVALUATION

The primary responsibility of the speech-language pathologist, as a member of the interdisciplinary team diagnosing learning disabilities, is to identify the presence of associated primary (neurologically based) deficits in understanding or in expressing language. In broadest terms, a communication disorder can be anticipated if a learning-disabled child displays verbal skills in one or more areas that are significantly lower than nonverbal cognitive skills. In the majority of learning-disabled children with intercurrent language disabilities, the language disabilities are relatively mild. For a smaller, but still significant percentage of learning-disabled children, the language disability may be substantial enough to warrant a diagnosis of communication disorder as the primary handicapping condition.

Communication disorders can occur as single or combined problems in language processing, language production, or in speech production. The educational impact of a language dysfunction can be seen in the learning-disabled child's oral, writing, reading, or mathematical skills. When superimposed on a learning disability, a language dysfunction may have an additional negative effect upon the child's social-emotional interaction in the learning environment, the peer group, and within the family setting. The speech-language pathologist can assist the interdisciplinary team by identifying the particular type of communication dysfunction, determining its severity, and estimating its impact.

Language Processing Disorders

Wiig and Semel (1976) present a comprehensive breakdown of the types of language processing disorders encountered in learning-disabled children. The learning-disabled child may exhibit deficits in auditory perception, linguistic processing, cognitive processing, memory, or evaluation skills. This section describes how these language processing deficits manifest in learning-disabled children.

Auditory Perceptual Problems

The learning-disabled child with auditory perceptual problems may appear inattentive, distractible, or confused. He or she may have difficulties attending to a chosen auditory stimulus in the presence of competing stimuli, focusing and maintaining attention to auditory stimuli, or discriminating sounds. He or she may demonstrate problems associating sounds with their sources, blending sounds (synthesizing elements), or segmenting units (dividing words into smallest units).

Linguistic Processing Deficits

Linguistic processing deficits can occur at the speech sound (phonological), word formation (morphological), sentence structure (syntactic), or word meaning (semantic) levels. These hierarchial tasks require information processing at several levels concurrently. The learning-disabled child with linguistic processing deficits may experience problems learning the rules of morphology and syntax, may misinterpret figurative language such as metaphors, similes, proverbs, and idiomatic expressions, and be unable to relate surface (spoken message) and deep structure (underlying message), thus missing the implied meaning of a message.

Cognitive Processing Deficits

The learning-disabled child with cognitive processing deficits may have difficulty interpreting word meanings as well as nonlinguistic signals. He or she may misinterpret environmental cues, facial expressions, gestures, intonational patterns, body language, stress, and pause. There may be difficulties establishing cause-effect relationships, symbolic play schemes, and anticipatory imagery. There may be an inability to analyze the meaning of sentences and make logical deductions based on previous knowledge. There may be weakness with temporal and spatial relationships as well as insufficient generalization of information. Finally, the learning-disabled child with cognitive processing deficits may display an inability to process abstract elements, resulting in a tendency toward literal, concrete interpretations (misinterpreting spoken or written material).

Memory Deficits

Memory involves short and long term elements and interacts with perceptual, linguistic (short-term memory), and cognitive-semantic (long-term memory) processing (Wiig and Semel, 1976). The learning-disabled child with memory deficits may exhibit difficulty recalling phonemes or word sequences and may omit or substitute words in sentence recall tasks. There may be particular difficulty with structurally complex and abstract sentences that rely on semantic and syntactic transformations.

Evaluation Deficits

Evaluation is an important linguistic skill that interfaces language processing and language production. The learning-disabled child with deficits in evaluative abilities may display difficulties with semantic or syntactic aspects of a sentence. He or she may be less efficient in correcting semantic, morphologic, or syntactic errors based on a reduction of logical operation abilities.

Language Production Disorders

The learning-disabled child may display deficient sentence formulation (spoken or written), convergent or divergent language production skills (Wiig and Semel, 1976). Deficits in these areas may be subtle, requiring careful assessment and observation under an array of conditions in order to obtain a representative picture of the learning-disabled child's expressive language problems, including formal and informal testing, spontaneous and elicited conversations with peers, parents, and authority figures.

Sentence Formulation Deficits

Wiig and Semel (1976) propose that sentence formulation skills, either spoken or written, represent the ability to create novel sentences using an established set of linguistic rules (morphologic, syntactic). The learning-disabled child with deficient sentence formulation abilities produces a significant number of grammatically incorrect or incomplete sentences. There may be a tendency to simplify syntactic constructions, with kernel sentences (short active declarative sentences) predominating. Restricted use of prepositional phrases and adjectives involving temporal, spatial, and comparative relations may be noted. Confusion of referents, avoidance or incorrect use of passive, embedded, or interrogative sentences can also be observed in spontaneous language samples. Learning-disabled children may have delayed acquisition of morphological rules and persistence of this problem may relate to chronic reading problems.

Convergent Language Production Deficits

Guilford (1967) postulates that convergent language production depends on adequate long-term memory storage and retrieval capacities. The learning-disabled child with deficient convergent language production skills may be unable to generate sentences that fit within previously established linguistic, semantic, and interpersonal confines. There may be problems asking and answering questions, relaying or responding to messages, or mending conversational breakdowns. He or she may exhibit impaired verbal fluency as a result of dysnomia (word finding problems). Finally, there may be a tendency for the learning-disabled child to perform poorly on tasks requiring verbal analogies, verbal opposites, or definitions of lexical items (words) as a result of imposed semantic restrictions (less freedom to compensate).

Divergent Language Production Deficits

Divergent language production skills signify a person's ability to formulate language while incorporating fluency, versatility, originality, and ornamentation. Wiig and Semel (1976) have suggested that divergent language production skills represent a relative strength (although deficient patterns have been observed) for learning-disabled children. The learning-disabled child may utilize stereotypic responses, circumlocutions (talking around a subject rather than expressing it concisely), perseverations (repetitions of words or phrases), and paraphasias (substitution of a word or phrase), resulting in reduced fluency. Decreased flexibility in formulating syntactic structures is observable as the learning-disabled child relies primarily on simple active declarative sentences. Problems with discourse may include inability to adapt speech styles, conversational patterns, and participation roles when alternating between peers and authority figures. Finally, the learning-disabled child may display a tendency to use immature patterns of formulating, organizing, and elaborating when creating stories or titles. The educational impact is significant as the learning-disabled child moves up the academic ladder.

Speech Disorders

Some learning-disabled children exhibit a phonological deficit characterized by phoneme substitutions, omissions, or distortions, resulting in speech that is mildly to severely impaired. The learning-disabled child, whose speech intelligibility is poor, probably uses a deficient phonological system, rather than simply mispronouncing certain sounds. Phonological disorders will not be covered in this chapter.

Evaluation Process

Assessing Auditory Sensation and Perception

A comprehensive speech-language evaluation includes a hearing screening. This can be performed by the school nurse or speech-language pathologist. It is imperative to determine early in the evaluation process if the peripheral auditory system is adequate for speech reception purposes. Individuals are cautioned when administering pure tone screening tests in a noisy environment (nurse's office, school hallway, clinician's office), that they may fail to identify children with a mild, but academically disadvantageous hearing loss (Keith, 1981). In the case of a child who has failed the hearing screening, further testing by a certified audiologist is warranted.

The audiological assessment begins with the administration of the following tests (performed by a certified audiologist) under ideal conditions (sound proof booth) in order to assess the status of the peripheral auditory system, thus obtaining a differential diagnosis. Based on these test results, the audiologist may choose to perform additional tests of central auditory processing.

1. The pure tone audiometric evaluation yields pure tone thresholds (measuring auditory acuity/sensitivity).
2. Impedance audiometry measures middle ear function (eardrum mobility).

3. Speech audiometry yields speech reception thresholds (the level
   at which a person can repeat words or understand conversational
   speech) and speech discrimination scores (the percentage of words
   heard correctly).

History Taking

The importance of incorporating background information, as well as
developmental data, into the evaluation process has been established in
Chapters 2, 3, and 4. The speech-language pathologist may reduplicate
the information gathering process; however, the emphasis is on the child's
communicative competence and performance in a variety of contexts and
with an array of communication partners (peers, parents, and authority
figures). This information will aid in the selection of primary and supplemental evaluative instruments. In the case of the school-aged child, an
interview should be scheduled with the child in order to assess his or her
views about the communication disorder, and willingness to put forth the
necessary effort toward remediation.

Parent Interview

A parent interview is recommended in order to ascertain the family's
concerns regarding the child's speech or language disorder. It is helpful
to note the parents' perceptions of their child's communication problem
(strengths and weaknesses), as well as their estimate of level of development. Familial, birth, and developmental history is gathered in addition
to investigation of specific speech, language, and hearing difficulties. A
prepared case history form (see Figure 5-1) provides the speech-language
pathologist with a useful framework from which to refer.

Teacher Questionnaire

The teacher is in a unique position to provide quantitative and qualitative data regarding the learning-disabled child's speech, language processing, and language production skills over a range of conditions (e.g.,
structured and nonstructured environments, spontaneous versus confrontation tasks, and interactions with peers and authority figures). Possess-
ing first-hand knowledge of the classroom and ancillary service programs,
the teacher has an opportunity to make inferences about the child's performance in academic areas and its relationship to the associated or primary
communication disorder. Two methods of obtaining information on a
teacher questionnaire (see Figure 5-2) are available to the speech-language
pathologist: mailing the form or setting up a personal interview. The latter
method is preferred, barring time limitations, in order to avoid possible
misunderstanding of questions and to afford the teacher an opportunity
to elaborate.

FIGURE 5-1

Parental Case History Form

Name: _____   Date of Interview: _____

Birthdate: _____   Examiner: _____

Age: _____

1. Describe your child's speech, language, hearing problem (give examples):
   _____
   _____

2. What is your child's primary means of communication? _____
   _____

3. Is English the primary or secondary language spoken in the home? _____
   _____

4. Have there been speech, language, hearing problems in the family? _____
   _____

5. Developmental History
   Difficulty in chewing _____ , sucking _____ ,
   swallowing _____ , management of saliva _____
   When did child begin babbling? _____
   Age first word was spoken: _____ Did vocabulary continue to
   expand? _____ When did sentences begin? _____ Was
   your child quiet or talkative? _____
   When did you first notice a problem? _____
   Do you suspect a hearing loss? _____
   Has there been a history of otitis media? _____
   What treatment has been used: medication, ventilation tubes? _____
   _____
   Has your child had formal testing performed: audiometric, impedance, brain
   stem evoked response audiometry? _____
   Where? _____
   When? _____
   Test Results? _____

6. Background Information
   Is your child on any medication? _____
   Has your child expressed frustration about speech, language, or hearing
   problem? _____
   Has your child ever talked better than he or she does now? _____
   Is the child teased by others about speech, language, hearing problems?.
   _____
   Has your child ever been enrolled in therapy to improve speech, language,
   hearing problems? _____

7. Communication Skills:
   Auditory Perceptual Processing
   Does your child respond to and localize sounds and their sound source?
   _____
   Does your child need verbal information repeated? _____
   Is your child inattentive, distractible, confused? _____
   Can your child follow 2 to 3 part directives in sequential order? _____
   Does your child confuse similar sounding words/speech sounds? _____

   (continued next page)

FIGURE 5-1 *(continued)*

Linguistic Processing

Does your child appear naive (misunderstanding idioms, puns, ambiguous sentences)? _____

Can your child repeat complex messages? _____

Is your child slow to process complex messages? _____

Cognitive Processing

Does your child understand verbal analogies? _____

Does he or she comprehend word relationships (spatial, temporal, comparative, familial)? _____

Does your child classify words by attributes? _____

Memory

Does your child have problems following complete directions? _____

Does your child have difficulty with word recall? _____

Does your child forget information when told a story or when complex sentences are used? _____

Evaluation

Does your child correct his or her spoken mistakes (grammar, words)? _____

Does your child confuse the idea and the result (premise and conclusion)?

_____

Sentence Formulation

Are your child's sentences incomplete or incorrect? _____

Does your child use complex sentences? _____

Do you notice if your child uses prepositions, adjectives, verbs (temporal, spatial, comparative)? _____

How long are your child's typical sentences? _____

Convergent Language Production

Does your child have word finding problems? _____

Can your child define words? _____

Can your child answer questions using the correct words? _____

Divergent Language Production

Does your child use a restricted repertoire of words and sentence structures?

_____

Does your child have problems telling a story and elaborating when questioned? _____

Does your child have word finding problems? _____

8. Speech

Does your child have a speech problem? _____

Does your child consistently make the same errors? _____

How easy is it for you to understand your child's speech: easy, adequate with careful listening, difficult, impossible? _____

FIGURE 5-2

Teacher Questionnaire

Name: _____   Date of Report: _____

Birthdate: _____   Teacher: _____

Age: _____   Grade/Class: _____

1. Primary Concern (explain, give examples): _____

   _____

   _____

2. Vision/Hearing Screenings: passed/failed/referred for further testing

   Wears corrective lenses/hearing aids (circle one)
   Diagnosis: _____

3. Medical Information
   Is child on medication: yes/no
   Type of medication: _____

   _____

4. School Attendance Record: _____

   _____

5. Ancillary Services Received
   Occupational therapy: yes/no   When: _____
   Physical therapy: yes/no   When: _____
   Speech-language therapy: yes/no   When: _____
   Progress noted (explain): _____

   _____

   _____

6. Remedial Programs Received
   Special education services: resource/self-contained
   Length of service per day: _____
   Emphasis of Program: _____
   Length of time enrolled in Program: _____
   Progress noted (explain): _____

   _____

7. Individualized Educational Plans
   Specify programs: _____
   Progress noted (explain): _____

   _____

8. Classroom Setting/Behavior
   Student/teacher ratio: _____
   Level of auditory or visual distraction: _____

   _____

   Child's seating in class: _____

   _____

   Child's behavior during structured activities: _____

   _____

   Optimal size of group instruction: _____
   Peer interaction skills: _____

   _____

(continued)

FIGURE 5-2 *(continued)*

ļɪ ˙ Interactive skills with authority figures: _____

_____

Child's activity preferences: _____

_____

Activity strengths: _____
Activity weaknesses: _____

9. Communication Skills:
Auditory perceptual processing
Is child inattentive, distractible, confused? _____
Can child follow three-part directives sequentially? _____
Does child need verbal information repeated? _____
Can child focus attention to auditory stimuli (tune out irrelevant information)?

_____

Does child confuse similar sounding words/speech sounds? _____

Linguistic Processing
Does child comprehend implied messages? _____
Does child have difficulty repeating complex sentences? _____
Does child need more time to process sentences? _____
Does child appear naive (misunderstands idioms, puns, ambiguous
    sentences)? _____

Cognitive Processing
Does child have problems sequencing and segmenting auditory-symbolic
    units (form or separate words by units)? _____
Does child have difficulty comprehending word relationships (spatial,
    temporal, comparative, familial)? _____
Does child comprehend verbal analogies? _____
Can child classify and organize information? _____
Does child have difficulty comprehending abstract words? _____

Memory
Does child have difficulty remembering sound sequences? _____
Does child have poor word recall? _____
Does child confuse semantic implications? _____

Evaluation
Can child correct incorrect sentences? _____
Does child use critical judgment of verbal information and make an
    inference? _____

Sentence Formulation
Are child's sentences incomplete or agrammatical? _____
Does child use complex sentences: passive, embedded, negative? _____
Does child use prepositions, adjectives (temporal, spatial, comparative)?

_____

Does child seem delayed in use of verb tenses, plurals, adjectives, inflections?

_____

Convergent Language Production
Does child have word finding problems? _____

Does child retrieve words fitting within tight constraints (analogies, opposites)?

Can child define words? _____

Divergent Language Production

Does child use stereotyped remarks? _____
Can child formulate ideas using an array of words and sentence structures?

Does child use circumlocutions, paraphasias, and association errors in word recall tasks? _____

10. Does child have a speech problem? (describe) _____

Does child consistently make the same errors? _____
How intelligible is child's speech: good, fair, poor? _____
Is child aware of the speech errors? _____
Is child frustrated when misunderstood? _____

Clinical Observations

An important component of the diagnostic process includes observation of the learning-disabled child's behaviors (verbal and nonverbal) prior to and during the language assessment. The speech-language pathologist is encouraged to compile an accurate log describing the child's behaviors (including antecedent or ongoing events), and to analyze and organize the data as it relates to language processing and production. The child with a language-learning disability frequently displays a pattern of strengths and weaknesses that relates to the social and academic problems identified by the family or teachers. As test items increase in difficulty (linguistic loading, cognitive content) the clinician typically observes a change in the child's behavior.

Observation and evaluation of the child's conversational skills during spontaneous speech and confrontation tasks provide qualitative data useful in answering questions (posed by the family and teacher) and in determining the need for supplemental testing. Does the child display word finding problems (circumlocutions, perseverations, paraphasias) or produce immature or agrammatical sentences? Does he or she omit or confuse pronouns, adjectives, verb tenses, and plurals? During the interactive process, does the child perceive a social give and take, wait his or her turn, respond to message content, answer and ask questions relevant to the topic? Does the child reauditorize or echo (verbally or nonverbally) to aid in processing information? Are similar sounding words confused (child misses actual message), and is there a problem tuning out irrelevant auditory stimuli?

Testing

Monitoring external environment factors (cf. Chapters 3 and 4) and test selection are crucial steps in the evaluation process. Consideration of the following factors when choosing a test has already been established in Chapters 3 and 4: content, validity, reliability, efficiency and economy of administration and scoring, normative data reflecting a cross-cultural representation of the population, age level, and task analysis (modalities and processes tested). No test is perfect; therefore, the speech-language pathologist is cautioned about choosing a single instrument or subtest in making a differential diagnosis. Supplementary tests are recommended in order to corroborate test results and diagnose the presence of a language processing or language production disorder. Knowledge regarding the learning-disabled child's responses over a range of conditions provides useful diagnostic and remedial information: single word utterances, pointing responses, manipulation of objects, imitation tasks, spontaneous speech sample. An ideal assessment yields quantitative and qualitative data outlining the child's relative strengths and weaknesses through a combination of formal and informal test procedures.

This section will review two primary evaluative instruments considered useful in assessing disorders of language processing and language production. Supplementary tests can be found in Table 5-1 (pp. 92-93).

Goldman-Fristoe-Woodcock Auditory Skills Battery (GFW)

The GFW (1976) is recommended for assessment of auditory perceptual processing skills. Normative data cover the age range of 3 years to 80+ years. Scores include percentile ranks, age equivalents, and standard and stanine scores. The child's responses include: pointing, oral, oral imitation, or written response. Test administration is designed for use with a high quality stereo tape player and ear phones (not included in the test kit). The test is divided into four auditory clusters:

1. GFW Auditory Selective Attention Test—measures the child's ability to attend to auditory stimuli in the presence of competing stimuli.
2. GFW Diagnostic Auditory Discrimination Tests—measure the child's ability to discriminate between specific speech sounds. Three tests are included and Part I (most frequently confused sounds) is recommended for administration to all individuals. Parts II and III are administered if the child scores below the 25th percentile.
3. GFW Auditory Memory Tests—include Recognition Memory (measures the child's ability to recognize words that have been heard in the recent past), Memory for Content (measures the child's ability to recognize a set of words recently presented, while disregarding presentation sequence), and Memory for Sequence

(measures the child's skills in remembering the order of a set of words presented in a recent auditory event).

4. GFW Sound-Symbol Tests—measure the skills that are fundamental to the development of an array of oral and written language skills. Tests include: Sound Mimicry (ability to imitate syllables), Sound Recognition (ability to isolate and identify elements of syllables), Sound Analysis (ability to isolate and identify elements of syllables), Sound Blending (ability to integrate isolated sounds into words), Sound-Symbol Association (ability to learn new auditory-visual associations), Reading of Symbols (ability to translate graphemes to phonemes), and Spelling of Sounds (ability to translate phonemes to graphemes).

The GFW represents the most comprehensive assessment of auditory perceptual skills on the market to date. It very clearly differentiates between adequate and deficient auditory perceptual skills in the learning-disabled population. From a format standpoint, the GFW provides the examiner with clear administration and scoring procedures. Tests are not timed, allowing maximum time for the child to respond. The use of picture stimuli in the training sections is followed by the test section, thus reducing the effects of vocabulary variance among individuals being tested. Finally, background noise conditions used in the Selective Attention Test approximate the auditory-figure ground distractions typically encountered in the academic setting, and students wear headphones, thus reducing the level of ambient noise and distractibility.

Some of the weaknesses of the GFW include the fact that test-retest reliability across the 12 tests has not been adequately established, and clinicians need to be cognizant when using the percentile rank norms that the standardization sample for each age range is somewhat restricted (Butler, Oakland, and Bannatyne, 1978). Older children tend to obtain almost perfect scores on some of the tests, thus restricting the effectiveness of the battery (the useful age range of the test is 3 years to 12 years). Finally, although the GFW provides useful diagnostic information, it is insufficient to develop intervention strategies.

Clinical Evaluation of
Language Functions-Diagnostic Battery (CELF)

The CELF (Wiig and Semel, 1980) is one of the most comprehensive tests available for evaluating a child's language processing and production abilities. Normative data are available for the grade-age range of kindergarten through grade twelve (6 years through 18 years). Scores obtained include language age scores and percentile ranks by grade for total processing and total production, and subtest pass-fail criterion scores for each

TABLE 5-1

Supplementary Tests for Language Evaluation

Test	Normative Data	Scores Available
Test of Language Development - Primary (TOLD-P)	4 years, 0 months to 8 years, 11 months	Raw scores, scaled scores, percentile ranks, language age equivalents, language quotients for composites.
Test of Language Development - Intermediate (TOLD-I)	8 years, 6 months to 12 years, 11 months	Raw scores, percentile ranks, standard scores, composite quotients.
Test of Adolescent Language (TOAL)	11 years, 0 months to 18 years, 5 months	Scaled scores, adolescent language scores.
Test of Auditory Comprehension of Language - Revised (TACL-R)	3 years, 0 months to 10 years, 0 months	Percentile ranks, standard scores, age equivalents, grade level norms.
Carrow Elicited Language Inventory (CELI)	3 years, 0 months to 7 years, 11 months	Percentile ranks, standard scores.
Illinois Test of Psycholinguistic Abilities (ITPA)	2 years, 0 months to 10 years, 11 months	Composite psycholinguistic age, estimated mental age, scaled scores for each subtest.
Peabody Picture Vocabulary Test - Revised, Form L and M (PPVT-R)	2 years, 6 months to 40 years, 11 months	Raw scores, standard scores, percentile ranks, stanine scores, single word receptive vocabulary age equivalents.
Developmental Sentence Scores (DSS)	3 years, 0 months to 6 years, 11 months	Mean value of sentence scores divided by the sum of sentences.

Response Mode	Test Domains	Subtests
Pointing, oral, imitation	Linguistic Processing Cognitive Processing Memory Evaluation Sentence Formulation Convergent Language Production Divergent Language Production Phonology	Picture Vocabulary, Oral Vocabulary, Grammatic Understanding, Sentence Imitation, Grammatic Completion, Word Discrimination, Word Articulation.
Oral	Linguistic Processing Cognitive Processing Memory Evaluation Sentence Formulation Convergent Language Production Divergent Language Production	Sentence combing, Characteristics, Word Ordering, Generals, Grammatic Understanding.
Oral, writing, imitation, reading	Linguistic Processing Cognitive Processing Memory Evaluation Sentence Formulation Convergent Language Production Divergent Language Production	Listening: Vocabulary, Listening: Grammar, Speaking: Vocabulary, Speaking: Grammar, Reading: Vocabulary, Reading: Grammar, Writing: Vocabulary, Writing: Grammar.
Pointing	Cognitive Processing Linguistic Processing	I - Word classes and relations, II - Grammatical morphemes, III - Elaborated sentences.
Imitation	Linguistic Processing Memory	No subtests
Oral, pointing, manipulation of objects and illustrations	Auditory Perceptual Processing Linguistic Processing Cognitive Processing Memory Evaluation Sentence Formulation Convergent Language Processing Divergent Language Processing	Auditory Perception, Auditory Association, Auditory Sequential Memory, Auditory Closure, Visual Perception, Visual Association, Visual Closure, Visual Sequential Memory, Verbal Expression, Manual Expression.
Pointing	Cognitive Processing	No subtests
Oral	Sentence Formulation Convergent Language Processing Divergent Language Processing	No subtests

grade level. The test is designed to assess the complete range of language processing and production skills: linguistic and cognitive processing, memory and evaluative skills, sentence formulation, convergent and divergent language production abilities. Two supplementary subtests, processing and production of speech sounds, are included. CELF subtests include:

1. Processing Word and Sentence Structure measures the child's ability to process and interpret words and syntactic structures.
2. Processing Word Classes assesses the child's ability to appreciate word relationships and classifications.
3. Processing Linguistic Concepts measures the child's ability to process and interpret directions containing linguistic concepts necessitating logical operations.
4. Processing Relationships and Ambiguities evaluates the child's ability to interpret ambiguous and logico-grammatical statements.
5. Processing Oral Directions measures the child's ability to interpret, recall, and carry out verbal directives increasing in length and complexity.
6. Processing Spoken Paragraphs assesses the child's ability to process and interpret spoken paragraphs. Retention and recall of prominent information is emphasized.
7. Producing Word Series evaluates the child's ability to recall and produce automatic-sequential word series. Fluency and speed are emphasized.
8. Producing Names on Confrontation investigates the child's ability to name colors, forms, and color-form combinations. Fluency, accuracy, and speed are emphasized.
9. Producing Word Associations measures the child's ability to retrieve semantically related words from long-term memory. Fluency, flexibility, quantity, quality, speed, and use of associative grouping strategies are emphasized.
10. Producing Model Sentences evaluates the child's sentence imitation skills using sentences varying in length and complexity.
11. Producing Formulated Sentences investigates the child's ability to generate sentences when provided with a target word. Sentences are evaluated by the syntactic structures employed.
12. Processing Speech Sounds (supplementary subtests) assesses the child's ability to perceive differences in minimally contrasting word pairs.
13. Producing Speech Sounds (supplementary subtests) evaluates the child's articulation skills.

Strengths of the CELF include the fact that test-retest reliability coefficients for combined subtests over a 6 week period are stable, and raw scores can be compared to criterion scores at the child's grade level (Sanger, 1985). From a format standpoint, the CELF test manual provides the examiner with clear and concise administration procedures and allows scoring of subtests individually rather than in totality. This allows the examiner to prevent fatiguing the child and to deal more effectively with the distractibility commonly encountered in the learning-disabled population.

The speech-language pathologist employing the CELF is cautioned that, although data accumulation documenting reliability and validity of the diagnostic battery is underway, this process in not complete at present (Wiig and Semel, 1980). Additionally, standardization norms are considered experimental, based on the number of children evaluated and the non-finalized criteria (Wiig and Semel, 1980).

Summary

The speech-language pathologist employs the quantitative (standardized test results) and qualitative data (parent case history, teacher questionnaire, clinical observations, informal test results) discussed in this section to determine the presence of language processing and production deficits in learning-disabled children and to estimate their impact on academics and social interactions. The incorporation of these individual findings in the interdisciplinary diagnostic process will be discussed in Chapter 6 and appropriate service delivery models will be presented in Chapter 7.

OCCUPATIONAL THERAPY EVALUATION

The occupational therapist can assist the interdisciplinary team evaluating the learning-disabled child by identifying deficits in fine motor, postural, perceptual motor, play, and self-care skills, and by suggesting home- and classroom-based accommodations to promote emotional adjustment to the learning disability. Many occupational therapists use sensory integrative procedures (Ayres, 1972a, 1979) to evaluate and treat learning-disabled children. This frame of reference addresses disorders in sensory processing and will serve as the central evaluation and conceptual model for this section. Learning-disabled children may have difficulties in some or all of these areas, and Public Law 94-142 mandates provision of occupational therapy as an educationally related service when these services are anticipated to improve the child's ability to benefit from the overall educational experience. The procedure used in determining the need for occupational therapy services includes history taking, standardized testing, and clinical observations.

History

The occupational therapist typically initiates the evaluative process by obtaining a history from the parents prior to standardized testing and clinical observations. This can be achieved through a parent questionnaire (Figure 5-3). This questionnaire might also be employed by the classroom

FIGURE 5-3
Sensorimotor History*

Place a check in the appropriate column. Items marked ''yes'' may indicate sensorimotor problems.

QUESTIONS	NO	YES	COMMENTS
Tactile sensation			
Does the child:			
1) Object to being touched?			
2) Dislike being cuddled?			
3) Seem irritable when held?			
4) Prefer to touch rather than be touched?			
5) React negatively to the feel of new clothes?			
6) Dislike having hair and/or face washed?			
7) Prefer certain textures of clothing?			
8) Avoid certain textures of food?			
9) Isolate self from other children?			
10) Frequently bump and push other children?			
School activities			
Does the child:			
1) Lose place when reading?			
2) Reverse letters or words?			
3) Confuse left from right?			
4) Have poor handwriting?			
5) Have poor school grades in reading, spelling, math?			
Behavior			
Does the child:			
1) Seem distractible?			
2) Have difficulty paying attention?			
3) Have a poor self-concept?			
4) Get mad easily (aggressive)?			
Visual sensation			
Does the child:			
1) Have a diagnosed visual defect?			
2) Have difficulty eye-tracking?			
3) Make reversals when copying?			
4) Have difficulty discriminating colors, shapes?			
5) Appear sensitive to light?			
6) Resist having vision occluded?			
7) Become excited when confronted with variety of visual stimuli?			

QUESTIONS	NO	YES	COMMENTS
Vestibular sensation			
Does the child:			
1) Dislike being tossed in the air?			
2) Seem fearful in space (e.g., going up and down stairs, riding teeter-totter)?			
3) Appear clumsy, often bumping into things and/or falling down?			
4) Prefer fast-moving, spinning carnival rides?			
5) Avoid balance activities?			
Muscle tone			
Does the child:			
1) Have any diagnosed muscle pathology (e.g., spasticity, flaccidity, rigidity, etc.)?			
2) Seem weaker or stronger than normal?			
3) Frequently grasp objects too tightly?			
4) Have a weak grasp?			
5) Tire easily?			
Coordination			
Does the child:			
1) Manipulate small objects easily?			
2) Seem accident prone? (e.g., have frequent scrapes and bruises)?			
3) Eat in a sloppy manner?			
4) Have difficulty with pencil activities?			
5) Have difficulty dressing and/or fastening clothes?			
6) Have a consistent hand dominance?			
7) Neglect one side of the body, or seem unaware of it?			
Reflex integration and development			
1) Was the child slow to reach the usual developmental milestones (e.g., sitting, walking, talking)?			
2) Was the child irritable in infancy, particularly when held?			
3) Does the child have difficulty isolating head movements?			
4) Does the child lack adequate protective reactions when falling?			

*Adapted from Pat Wilbarger, OTR. Special Education Workshop, St. Paul Public Schools, St. Paul, Minnesota, August, 1973.

teacher to identify learning-disabled children for whom referral to an occupational therapist would be warranted. Areas to be covered by the history include sensory processing, balance, muscle tone, gross and fine motor coordination, behavior, and school performance.

Standardized Testing

The sensory integrative procedures approach is one of the most commonly used assessment and treatment approaches in occupational therapy with learning-disabled children. Sensory integration (Ayres, 1972a, 1979) provides a developmental framework for understanding how inadequate organization and integration of sensory input (primarily vestibular, tactile, and proprioceptive) can influence higher level cognitive and social skills. Ayres's premise is that acquisition of higher function is dependent on adequate subcortical neural organization. For example, if a child is distracted by abnormal sensitivity to touch or is unable to easily maintain posture against gravity, attention may focus upon these basic automatic functions versus school work. Ayres classified types of sensory integrative dysfunction occurring in learning-disabled children following completion of several factor analytic studies. Further research was conducted to determine which of these dysfunctions would be amenable to therapy (Ayres 1972c, 1976, 1978). Evaluation of these types of sensory integrative functions consists primarily of a standardized norm-referenced test, the Sensory Integration and Praxis Test (Ayres, 1986), and nonstandardized clinical observations (Ayres, 1972a). In addition to these tools, the therapist may wish to observe the child's performance on certain fine and gross motor tasks (e.g., handwriting, cutting with scissors, typing, buttoning, zippering, or balancing). The reader is referred to Clark, Mailloux, and Parham (1985) for a more thorough overview of sensory integrative procedures and other occupational therapy approaches pertinent to learning-disabled children.

Sensory Integration and Praxis Test (SIPT)

The SIPT is a revised and restandardized version of the Southern California Sensory Integration Tests (SCSIT) (Ayres, 1972b). The battery is developed for children between the ages of 4 and 9 years, with some subtests standardized up to 12 years. In order to administer and interpret this test, it is recommended that therapists be certified by Sensory Integration International. The SIPT consists of 18 subtests that evaluate skills in visual perception, praxis, motor performance, somatosensory (tactile) perception, and vestibular functioning.

VISUAL PERCEPTION. The space visualization test measures mental manipulation of objects in various orientations. Blocks are presented which match a model that has been placed in different spatial orientations; accuracy, speed and hand use are recorded. The figure ground perception test requires selection of a foreground figure from a rival background. Design copying is a visual motor test which measures visual perception of a geometric design and graphic praxis.

PRAXIS AND MOTOR PERFORMANCE. The motor performance section addresses five types of praxis (ability to plan unfamiliar motor tasks). Postural praxis evaluates the child's ability to imitate unusual positions or postures demonstrated by the examiner; speed and accuracy are recorded. Praxis on verbal command measures the child's ability to motor plan various body postures following verbal directions without visual cues. Constructional praxis requires the child to replicate simple and complex block structures, measuring motor planning and visual spatial relations. Sequential praxis measures the child's ability to replicate a series of hand and finger movements demonstrated by the examiner. Oral praxis requires the child to motor plan oral positions and sequences of movements, such as putting the tongue in the right cheek, followed by the left cheek. Standing and walking balance is tested with and without vision. The bilateral motor coordination test measures motor planning and integration of the two sides of the body. The child imitates both arm and feet patterns noting timing and sequencing. The motor accuracy test measures speed and accuracy of both left and right hand when drawing with a pen along a line in a particular direction.

SOMATOSENSORY PERCEPTION. Perception of touch is measured by testing proprioceptive awareness of the upper extremities (perception of joint position and movement), stereognosis (ability to name objects by touch with the eyes closed), and tactile discrimination of the fingers, hands, and forearms. All items are done with vision occluded and are administered at one sitting, as there may be a cumulative effect of the child's ability to tolerate tactile stimulation. This information is useful in determining presence of tactile defensiveness.

VESTIBULAR FUNCTIONING. Vestibular processing is assessed by measuring duration and extent of nystagmus (involuntary rapid back and forth eye movements) in response to rotation, using the procedure developed for the Southern California Post Rotary Nystagmus Test (Ayres, 1975).

Because the SIPT is still under development, it is not possible to provide conclusive data regarding reliability, validity, or adequacy of the norms. Early reports from the test developers indicate good inter-rater and test-retest reliability. Therapists who wish to use the SIPT are urged to review the test with particular attention to these technical qualities, once it has been published.

Clinical Observations

Clinical observations, a nonstandardized instrument, allows the therapist to systematically observe a series of neuromotor and behavioral functions related to learning (Ayres, 1972a). In the clinical observations, the following areas are tapped:

Muscle tone refers to the amount of tension and readiness in a muscle group at rest. Some learning-disabled children may exhibit hypotonia (low muscle tone) that can result in difficulties in posture, balance, muscle strength, or fine motor skills. To assess muscle tone, the occupational therapist looks for excessive joint range of motion in the shoulder, elbow, thumb, and fingers, and observes the child's overall posture in standing.

Extraocular muscle control refers to the child's ability to efficiently control eye movements, such as visual tracking, convergence, and quick localization. These skills are essential for reading as well as visual motor activities. The examiner assesses control over eye movement by asking the child to visually track a pencil as it moves through different planes.

Bilateral coordination refers to the child's ability to coordinate the two sides of the body, and is essential in many fine and gross motor activities. It is assessed by observing the child's symmetry, coordination, timing, and rhythm during imitation of specific arm and hand movements.

Laterality refers to efficient performance of motor tasks requiring the child to consistently use one hand in preference to another. Hand preference is determined by recording which hand the child prefers to use to receive objects offered at the midline. Eye preference is assessed by asking the child to look through a kaleidoscope, tube, and pinhole.

Motor planning (praxis) is the child's ability to organize and execute unfamiliar motor tasks. The examiner assesses praxis of the arms (diadokokinesia), hands (thumb to finger touching), tongue (tongue to lip movement), and whole body by asking the child to imitate various movements.

Postural control is the child's ability to maneuver his or her body in relation to gravity. Postural security is assessed by observing the child's level of tolerance for being off the ground and inverted. The child's postural background movements are evaluated by observing the child's automatic and appropriate adjustments of posture during activities. Quality of equilibrium reactions are determined by observing the child's ability to maintain balance when his or her center of gravity is displaced in a variety of positions. Coordination in hopping, skipping, and jumping is also assessed.

Cocontraction refers to simultaneous contraction of opposing muscle groups (e.g., flexors and extensors) to stabilize a joint. Poor cocontraction will make it difficult for the child to maintain the postural stability needed to efficiently produce coordinated movements. To assess cocontraction, the child's ability to resist the examiner's opposing force (e.g., attempts to push the child off balance) is observed.

Primitive Postural Reflexes (e.g., asymmetrical tonic neck reflex, tonic labyrinthine reflex) represent immature postures that are generally inhibited during infancy. Persistence of these reflexes can interfere with progression of more mature automatic movement reactions (righting and equilibrium). To assess existence of these reflexive postures, the occupational therapist asks the child to assume various positions and assesses the degree of flexion or extension of various muscle groups in response to head position and gravity.

Clinical observations may also include assessment of the level of activity, presence of tactile defensiveness, hypersensitivity to movement, gravitational insecurity, and choreoathetosis.

Interpretation of Evaluation Results

Data from the screening, history, standardized testing (SIPT) and the clinical observations are combined to formulate hypotheses regarding the type(s) of sensory integration dysfunction the child is demonstrating. Ayres (1979) identifies five major types of sensory integrative dysfunctions: developmental dyspraxia, vestibular bilateral integration dysfunction, left or right hemisphere dysfunction, and generalized dysfunction. Three problems in modulation of sensory input (hyperresponsivity to motion and touch) were also identified: gravitational insecurity, intolerance to movement, and tactile defensiveness. Analysis of data will reveal one or more of these problems. Only those problems most commonly seen in learning-disabled children will be discussed here.

Developmental dyspraxia indicates difficulty in planning nonhabitual motor tasks (Ayres, 1972a, 1979). Children with developmental dyspraxia generally develop basic level motor milestones such as crawling or walking on time, but have difficulty with the more complex motor skills such as riding a bicycle, cutting with scissors, using a pencil, or maneuvering a fork and knife together. The basis for motor planning difficulties may be due to poor tactile perception (referred to as somatosensory dyspraxia) that results in a poor body scheme, or from poor organization of spatial information and difficulty with ideation (constructional dyspraxia).

The learning-disabled child with developmental dyspraxia appears clumsy, demonstrating poor sequencing and timing of movements. The child may be more dependent in self-care skills than would be expected for his or her age (e.g., he or she may have difficulty with buttoning, zippering, tying shoes, or understanding directionality of clothing), and everyday tasks become monumental. Because of such difficulties, these children sometimes develop a poor self-concept, are easily frustrated, and have a tendency to avoid new situations.

Children who exhibit developmental dyspraxia respond well to sensory integrative procedures, according to Ayres (1981). Treatment focuses on remediation of the basis of dyspraxia, postulated to be a poor body scheme due to inadequate tactile, proprioceptive, and vestibular integration. Therapy attempts to enhance ideation and body scheme and motor planning abilities.

Vestibular bilateral integration dysfunction is postulated to reflect an "underreactive" vestibular system. The major areas affected for the child with this type of dysfunction include poor postural control and inadequate bilateral integration. The basis for the poor postural control includes: poorly integrated primitive reflexes, immature righting and equilibrium reactions, poor muscle tone (hypotonia), and poor cocontraction. These children will also look clumsy because they do not have the postural base to perform coordinated movements.

Children with bilateral integration dysfunction sometimes demonstrate poor ocular control due to inadequate vestibular functioning affecting the ocular systems. They tend to have difficulty sustaining a stable visual field necessary for skilled eye movements in reading.

Poor bilateral integration is evident by poor performance of both hands working together. The child may not develop a hand preference by the expected developmental age. These children tend to use each hand independently, which is inefficient for manipulative skills. Difficulty crossing the midline or determining directionality may also be present.

The focus in therapy is to remediate the vestibular dysfunction by addressing postular and ocular control and to facilitate bilateral integration. Ayres (1976) indicates that these children respond well to sensory integrative procedures.

Generalized dysfunction describes children with severe sensory integrative problems. Children with diffuse dysfunction and prolonged nystagmus may not be prime candidates for sensory integrative procedures as they impact on learning. However, therapy may improve general adaptive behavior.

Gravitational insecurity and *intolerance to movement* refer to problems in modulation of sensory input and represent hypersensitivity to vestibular input. Children with gravitational insecurity tend to be anxious and fearful of movement due to inaccurate feedback they receive from gravity receptors (located in the inner ear). They may be fearful of heights, uneven surfaces, playground equipment, or climbing. Intolerance to movement is a result of poor modulation of input from receptors that monitor rotation. Children with intolerance to movement have difficulty with rapid circular movements or spinning, and may experience dizziness or car sickness. Given the nature of these problems, the major areas affected are motor performance and emotional security. The child's school performance may be affected indirectly, as fear and anxiety related to movement can create overdependence. Treatment activities providing vestibular stimulation are graded to allow the child to accommodate to movement off the ground.

Tactile defensiveness is an aversive reaction to touch. It is hypothesized that this condition occurs due to an imbalance between the protective and discriminative tactile systems, whereby the protective system predominates (Ayres, 1964). These children perceive touch as uncomfortable and threatening, and may be uncomfortable wearing certain fabrics, washing their hair, face, or hands. These children may appear to be hyperactive or distractible in response to the tactile defensiveness. Treatment focuses on decreasing the tactile defensiveness by providing tactile experiences in order to facilitate a better balance between the protective and discriminative system. Vestibular stimulation is also recommended for its modulating effects on the tactile system.

Summary

This section has delineated the role of the occupational therapist in the identification and evaluation of children demonstrating problems in basic foundational skills categorized as sensory integrative dysfunctions. Information gathered from the history, standardized testing, and clinical observations is used to determine the presence of difficulties which may impact on the child's physical, social, emotional, and academic performance. This information is combined with data from other team members evaluating the child. A decision is then made regarding the need for occupational therapy services. A treatment plan is formulated to address the child's individual needs. Treatment will be further discussed in Chapter 7.

PHYSICAL THERAPY EVALUATION

As discussed in Chapter 2, the learning-disabled child may demonstrate subtle deficits in gross motor (large muscle) coordination, organization, and execution of movement skills. When discussing gross motor function in the learning-disabled child, it is important to remember that young children relate and interact with each other through two primary avenues, their verbal (communicative) skills and their physical play (gross and fine motor skills). Deficits in gross motor function can contribute to a child's sense of failure and inability to participate positively with peers in organized play activities.

Since the inception of Public Law 94-142, the physical therapist has joined the educational team in assessing areas of difficulty, developing treatment plans, and implementing comprehensive programming for children with learning disabilities. In the assessment process, the physical therapist works closely with parents and teachers to obtain a history of problem areas in the motor system and in sensory/perceptual functioning. Following a thorough history, the physical therapist will use both standardized and nonstandardized assessment tools to diagnose and describe specific weaknesses.

History

The physical therapist will first want to question parents and teachers regarding obvious gross motor difficulties observed at home and in the classroom. Parents may report that the child has had longstanding difficulty with clumsiness, excessive falling and bruising, and repeated collisions with furniture or other objects. Parents may also report that the achievement of play skills such as tricycle and bicycle riding, skipping rope, and playing ball occurred late (if at all) and with extra effort on the child's part. Inability to perform at the level of unaffected peers often results in either a disinterest in or an avoidance of organized sports or group games. Parents and teachers may report that the learning-disabled child actually fears playground equipment or play activity that involves scaling, climbing on gymnastic apparatus, or experiencing rapid acceleration and deceleration on devices such as slides or swings. On the other hand, many younger affected children (under 5 years of age) may appear to crave the experience of spinning, as long as it is self-imposed. They may, for example, use a swing as a spinner by lying prone over the seat, twisting the ropes, releasing their feet, and allowing the ropes to unwind.

Clinical Observations

Nonstandardized assessments incorporate the therapist's clinical observation skills pertaining to joint alignment, muscle tone, posture, and quality of movement. These clinical observations are essential to the process of interpreting the findings of standardized motor achievement tests. The therapist should focus particular attention on the following:

Skeletal Alignment. This factor concerns spinal curvature and alignment of the legs and feet in standing. A common observation is a swaying of the low back (lordosis) or a forward tip of the pelvis.

A position of protraction (forward displacement) of the head and shoulders is also commonly encountered. The shoulder blades rest loosely and widely apart on the upper back and are inclined to protrude at the inner borders (scapular winging). In the legs, the knee joints might be hyperextended (too straight), so that the ligaments and tendons at the back of the knee are relied upon for support.

The feet and ankles might also show a mild to moderate degree of collapse inward, which brings on an associated inward twist of the leg and thigh above. These postural features are generally associated with low muscle tone (hypotonia) of a mild to moderate degree, and laxity of the supportive ligaments.

Muscle Tone. Muscle tone may be described as the amount of tension apparent in a resting muscle. The most commonly observed abnormality of tone in children with learning disabilities is hypotonia or low muscle tone, particularly through the trunk, where back and abdominal muscles are required to anchor the pelvis and the shoulder girdle in order to permit efficient use of the arms and legs.

The Postural Reflex Mechanism. This area of observation entails assessment to determine the extent of integration of total body reflexes, along with the child's ability to balance and to automatically adjust to changes in weightbearing.

Considering reflex motor behaviors, the asymmetric (ATNR) and the symmetric (STNR) tonic neck reflexes are no longer observed in most normal children beyond infancy. However, full integration of these reflex reactions, such that they are no longer apparent, is not normally achieved until 9 years of age or even later (Silver, 1952). The lack of full integration of these reflexes in older children has been revealed by altering the procedures used to determine their presence in the infant. For instance, the child assumes the quadriped (all fours) position, his or her head is turned actively or passively to either side, and the degree of flexion on the skull-side elbow is measured. Rating scales and age expectations relative to this test have been established (Dunn, 1981; Parmenter, 1975; Parr et al., 1974). Other methods for identifying subtle signs of the persistence of the ATNR have been developed and are described by DeQuiros and Schrager (1979), and Ayres (1972a).

Methods for determining the persistence of the STNR are described by Bender (1976) and Ayres (1972a), using static and dynamic (moving) evaluation procedures. The purposes of ascertaining the persistence of these reflexes are primarily to acknowledge the existence of neurological deficit and to establish a baseline against which to evaluate the effectiveness of intervention measures.

In assessing the postural reflex mechanism, the therapist selects assessment tasks that challenge the child's balancing skills (equilibrium), and watches for exaggerated motions of the limbs, head, or trunk as the child attempts to maintain or to regain balance. Also, a rigid quality of adjustment at the trunk, or a reliance on immature protective mechanisms might be observed, such as propping on hands to prevent a fall rather than relying on the muscles at the trunk exclusively.

Symmetry. This term refers to the capacity to use both sides of the body in an integrated fashion. The child with problems in this area may exhibit differences in distribution of muscle tone between left and right sides of the body.

Variety of Movements. Among learning-disabled children with gross motor problems, there is often a poverty of approaches to movement tasks, such that the initiation of movement and the selection of movement transitions and postures is very often limited and somewhat predictable. Movements may frequently be initiated with peculiar patterns of extension, particularly at the head and neck.

Sensory Awareness Relative to Body Awareness. The child with problems in this area may have difficulty identifying body parts (body image) and realizing the relative position of trunk and limbs in space (proprioception). They may also demonstrate distorted or underdeveloped sensitivity to touch.

Coordination. The therapist will assess coordination through such activities as finger movements (touching each finger tip to the thumb, for instance), foot tapping and heel-toe walking (touching the heel on the advancing foot to the toe of the standing foot as the child walks on a straight line). Although body balance is considered a part of the assessment of coordination, ineptness may be most apparent when complex motor activities are attempted, as in gym class.

Movement Quality. The physical therapist will observe specific motor tasks, with particular attention focused on the following features of "quality":

1. The ability to use both sides of the trunk and neck simultaneously and with general skill against gravity.
2. The ability to shift weight dynamically (as assessed in such tasks as wheelbarrow walking on hands, one foot stance, and hopping on a line), whereby efficiency, strength, and organization are observed.
3. The ability to incorporate both sides of the body in relatively equal fashion (as demonstrated in bilateral rhythmic tasks, such as jumping forward and backward on both feet and performing jumping jacks).
4. Precision in task executions, without extraneous or purposeless movements at the trunk, head, or arms.
5. Facility, timing, and functional similarity in the switch from one side of the body to the other during execution of alternating rhythmic tasks, such as skipping.
6. Availability of true stability for function, as demonstrated by postural set prior to or during execution of a task. Evidence of poor postural set includes shoulder elevation, neck hyperextension

(tipping the head back), wide base of support, unnecessary locking of elbows when extending arms, or holding arms close to the chest, palms turned upward and elbows near each other in preparation for catching a ball.

7. Reliance on immature or limited posture and movement systems, as demonstrated by W-sitting (kneel-sitting with feet positioned beside rather than under the pelvis) or "bunny hopping" (as opposed to crawling reciprocally).

Standardized Assessment Tools

There are several standardized instruments for screening gross motor function (Cermak and Henderson, 1985; Connolly, 1984), but there are few technically sound tools that thoroughly assess gross motor functional levels in children with mild motor deficits. Screening tools will not be discussed here, as it can be presumed that a referral to physical therapy for problems related to clumsiness warrants administration of a thorough evaluation. However, the therapist, out of concern for time limitation, may select subtests from comprehensive assessments in order to focus attention primarily on gross motor function. The selection of subtests should reflect the therapist's goals in assessment, which include establishing the existence of gross motor deficits that may interfere with academic performance and describing the specific deficit areas. The following assessment tools should be considered.

Bruininks-Oseretsky Test of Motor Proficiency

This is perhaps one of the most appropriate tools for assessing gross motor functioning in learning disabled children. Designed for children between 4.5 and 14.5 years, the complete battery comprises eight subtests from which three scores can be derived: Gross Motor, Fine Motor, and Total. The physical therapist may wish to administer the four Gross Motor subtests, which include running speed and agility, balance, bilateral coordination, and strength. Standardization appears to be adequate. These four tests can be administered in less than 30 minutes. However, because some subtest reliabilities are relatively low, therapists are cautioned against using the subtest score profile to diagnose relative strengths and weaknesses or to plan remediation strategies.

The Basic Motor Abilities Test-Revised (BMAT-Revised)

The BMAT-Revised (Arnheim and Sinclair, 1979), is composed of 11 subtests, 9 of which assess gross motor skills: Target Throwing, Back and Hamstring Stretch, Standing Long Jump, Face Down to Standing, Static

Balance, Basketball Throw for Distance, Ball Striking, Target Kicking, and Agility Run. Percentile scores are provided for each subtest, based on a broad cross-cultural sample. Test-retest reliability for the overall battery is good, but reliability information on individual subtests is not provided. Because of the paucity of information regarding standardization, reliability, and validity, this test should be used only as an informal tool for observing the child's abilities. Results should be used only to supplement data from other sources.

Summary

It is essential that the physical therapist consider any clinical observation or test result as a component of an interdisciplinary diagnostic process. Information drawn from parents and other professionals is essential in arriving at an accurate diagnosis and in understanding the true nature of the child's difficulties. Information derived from the physical therapy assessment will be used in combination with data from other sources in developing a comprehensive treatment plan, as discussed in Chapter 7.

CHAPTER 6

Interdisciplinary Diagnosis

Elizabeth H. Aylward
Frank R. Brown, III

IDENTIFYING SIGNIFICANT DISCREPANCY BETWEEN ACADEMIC ACHIEVEMENT AND INTELLECTUAL ABILITIES

The diagnosis of learning disabilities is based on a significant discrepancy between a child's intellectual abilities and academic achievement. The previous chapters have described the methods for obtaining accurate assessments of intelligence and academic achievement, as well as other information relevant to understanding the child's learning difficulties. Using discrepancy between intellectual ability and academic achievement as the basis for definition, it would appear that the task of diagnosing a learning disability would be fairly straightforward after these assessments have been completed. There is, however, much controversy regarding what constitutes a "significant discrepancy" between intellectual abilities and academic achievement.

Neither Public Law 94-142 nor other federal guidelines provide precise diagnostic criteria for establishing a significant discrepancy between academic achievement and cognitive expectation. Although many states and local school districts have convened committees to study this issue and have outlined procedures for identifying a significant discrepancy, there is, as yet, no universally accepted method for doing this. General agreement has been reached, however, on inappropriate methods for identifying significant discrepancy, and these will be discussed before considering more appropriate methods.

Inappropriate Methods for
Identifying Significant Discrepancy

Many school districts are still basing a diagnosis of learning disability on a discrepancy between a child's academic performance and the performance of his or her grade-level peers. According to this system, a child must be one or two grade levels below his or her actual grade placement to be considered learning disabled. This method is clearly not consistent with the definition of learning disability as outlined in Public Law 94-142. It will bar from services the bright child who is at or near grade level in academic skills, but performing significantly below cognitive expectation. Similarly, children who are slow both cognitively and academically may be mislabeled as learning disabled. This method is also inappropriate because it generally delays the identification of learning disabilities until at least second grade. If a child does not qualify for special education services until he or she is two years below grade level, the child must experience at least two years in an inappropriate learning environment before receiving any special services, which results in undue frustration and wastes valuable time. Finally, the method is inappropriate because a child who is two years below grade level in the early elementary grades is clearly more seriously impaired than the child who is two years below grade level in secondary school. Many school systems fail to make this distinction when using this method to identify learning disabilities.

A second method that is commonly used, but is now being criticized, involves comparing standard scores from intelligence tests and achievement tests, and looking for a certain discrepancy measured in standard deviations. The WISC-R and K-ABC, described in Chapter 3 as appropriate tests for use in making the diagnosis of learning disabilities, each has a mean score of 100 and a standard deviation of 15. (The Stanford-Binet Intelligence Scale has a mean of 100 and a standard deviation of 16.) Using tests of intelligence and tests of achievement that have standard deviations of 15 points, significant discrepancy between cognitive expectations and academic achievement might be defined as a discrepancy of 1, 1.5, or 2 standard deviations (15, 22.5, and 30 points, respectively). A child with an IQ of 100 would have to obtain a standard score of 85 or below on the achievement test to be considered learning disabled, assuming that a cut-off of one standard deviation were being used. Similarly, a child with an IQ of 115 would have to obtain a standard score of 100 or below on the achievement test to be considered learning disabled. This method is certainly superior to the one described in the previous paragraph, which did not take into account the child's intelligence. The major problem with this second method involves a statistical phenomenon called *regression toward the mean*.

The Concept of Regression Toward the Mean

Regardless of the trait being measured or the measurement instrument being used, there is always going to be some amount of error. A test with good reliability will have less "error of measurement" than a test that is less reliable. The WISC-R, which is considered to be one of the most reliable of all psychological instruments, has a standard error of measurement of 3 points. That is, a child's "true IQ" (the average IQ that would be obtained if the test could be given an infinite number of times without any retest effects) will be no more than 3 points higher or lower than the measured IQ approximately 68 percent of the time (the percent of cases falling between +1 and −1 standard deviations on a normal curve). One can assume that the more deviant a score is, the larger the error of measurement it probably contains (Campbell and Stanley, 1963). Thus, the child with an extremely high score can be considered to have had unusually good "luck" (large positive error) and the extremely low scorer bad "luck" (large negative error). Because luck is capricious, one would expect students with extremely high scores on one test to score somewhat less well on a subsequent test. Similarly, the child who was unfortunate enough to receive a very low score on an initial test can be expected to score somewhat higher on a subsequent test. This phenomenon is known as *regression toward the mean*. That is, when a particular child has a score on one test that is above or below the mean, one can expect the score on a subsequent test to be nearer to, or to regress toward, the test mean. This is especially true when scores are farther from the mean or when the test is less reliable.

When one is comparing scores on two tests (e.g., an intelligence test and an academic achievement test), the problem of regression becomes even more serious than when one is comparing scores on the same test given on two occasions. The lower the correlation between the two tests, the greater the amount of regression that can be expected. Although regression toward the mean cannot be eliminated, it can be minimized by selecting tests that have good reliability.

Predicting Educational Quotients

School systems have begun to take the phenomenon of regression toward the mean into account by charting predicted Educational Quotients (EQs) for children with various IQ scores. By looking at Table 6-1, it becomes clear that a child whose IQ is above average can be expected to have a lower EQ than IQ. Similarly, the child whose IQ is below average can be expected to have a higher EQ than IQ. For example, a girl with an IQ of 130, which is considerably above average, can be expected to perform very well on an achievement test, but not quite as high as the

TABLE 6-1

Predicted Educational Quotients (EQs) for Given VIQs, PIQs, and Full Scale IQs

VIQ or Full Scale IQ	Predicted EQ	PIQ	Predicted EQ
130	118	130	115
125	115	125	113
120	112	120	110
115	109	115	108
110	106	110	105
105	103	105	103
100	100	100	100
95	97	95	98
90	94	90	95
85	91	85	93
80	88	80	90
75	85	75	88
70	82	70	85

(Predicted EQs are somewhat different for PIQs than for VIQs or Full Scale IQs because the correlation between academic achievement and nonverbal intelligence is lower than that between academic achievement and verbal intelligence. See McLeod, 1979, for a more in-depth discussion of this issue.)

130 score. Table 6-1 indicates that she should be expected to have an achievement test standard score of approximately 118, assuming that academic achievement has progressed at a level commensurate with her IQ. If the achievement test score is significantly below 118 (not 130), one can make a diagnosis of a learning disability (assuming that other causative factors, such as emotional disturbance or lack of educational opportunity, have been ruled out).

As discussed previously, school systems differ in what they consider to be a significant discrepancy between scores. McLeod (1979) suggests a cut-off of 1.5 standard deviations. Thus, if a student's score on a test of academic achievement is 22.5* points lower than the predicted EQ, a significant discrepancy has been identified, and the diagnosis of learning disability can be made. In the case described in the previous paragraph, the student's standard score on the test of academic achievement would have to be 95.5 (118 minus 22.5) in order for her to be diagnosed as learning disabled. Some school systems may choose a cut-off of one or two standard deviations in defining significant discrepancy. The cut-off level chosen

---

*This number is derived by multiplying 1.5 times 15 (which is the standard deviation of most intelligence tests and academic achievement tests).

will depend upon the system's philosophy regarding learning disabilities, as well as on its ability to provide services for children identified as learning disabled.

Further Considerations in Identifying Discrepancy

Choosing the Measure of Intelligence for the Cognitive-Achievement Comparison

Even after determining which tests of intelligence and academic achievement will be administered, and the degree of discrepancy needed to constitute significance, the interdisciplinary team must decide which individual scores will be compared in making the diagnosis of learning disabilities. For children whose Verbal IQ-Performance IQ (VIQ-PIQ), or Simultaneous-Sequential discrepancy is small, it is not unreasonable to compare the WISC-R Full Scale IQ or K-ABC Mental Processing Composite standard score with the standard scores from the test(s) of academic achievement. However, when there is a large VIQ-PIQ discrepancy, several different approaches to the discrepancy issue can be justified. Take, for example, a child with a WISC-R VIQ of 85, PIQ of 115, and Full Scale IQ of 99, and a WJPEB Reading Cluster standard score of 85. Because of the child's significant VIQ-PIQ discrepancy, it would not be appropriate to consider the child's Full Scale IQ of 99 as an accurate representation of intellectual functioning. Therefore, it would not be feasible to use the Full Scale IQ in determining the presence of significant discrepancy between intellectual and academic abilities.

Because reading ability is more highly correlated with verbal abilities than with visual-spatial abilities, it could be argued that the child should not be expected to be reading at a level higher than the level of the child's verbal abilities. Thus, using the VIQ of 85 alone as the measure of cognitive functioning, Table 6-1 indicates that the predicted EQ would be 91. The difference between the predicted EQ of 91 and the actual reading achievement score would be 6 points. Because this does not meet the cutoff of 1.5 standard deviation discrepancy (22.5 points), no learning disability would be identified.

It could, however, be argued just as reasonably that the mechanism that is preventing verbal skills from developing at the same rate as nonverbal (visual-spatial) skills is the same mechanism that is preventing better development of reading skills. Using this reasoning, the Reading Cluster score could be justifiably compared with the PIQ of 115. Table 6-1 indicates that an EQ of 108 would be predicted for an IQ of 115.* The

---

*Column 2 of Table 6-1 is used in predicting the EQ from the PIQ because the correlation between PIQ and academic achievement is approximately .5, whereas the correlation between academic achievement and either the VIQ or the Full Scale IQ is .6.

discrepancy between the EQ and the actual reading achievement score in this case is 23 points, which would be significant, if a cut-off of 1.5 standard deviations (22.5 points) is used. Thus, a learning disability would be identified. We believe that this approach is more attuned to the definition of learning disabilities outlined in Public Law 94-142, which includes disorders in "the understanding of language" as learning disabilities. Similarly, it would be justifiable to compare the score of academic achievement with the VIQ alone, if it were significantly higher than the PIQ, as the Public Law 94-142 definition includes such conditions as "perceptual handicaps."

The procedure for determining predicted EQs is not necessary if one uses the K-ABC for both measures of intellectual functioning and academic achievement, as the cut-offs for significant discrepancy between tests are provided in the manual. The K-ABC routinely requires the examiner to compare the standard scores for each of the Mental Processing Scales (Sequential, Simultaneous, and Composite) with the standard score for the Achievement Scale. Thus, a significant difference between achievement and any of the scores of Mental Processing could be an indication of a learning disability.

The K-ABC does not, however, encourage routine comparison of each of the Mental Processing scores (Sequential, Simultaneous, and Composite) with individual Achievement subtest scores, but rather with the overall Achievement composite score. Thus, the routine comparison of Mental Processing scores with the overall Achievement scale may not detect the child who is seriously delayed in only one area of academic achievement. Kaufman and Kaufman (1983) caution that the Mental Processing scores can be compared with individual Achievement subtest scores, if the number of comparisons is limited by selecting wisely the most appropriate comparisons to make, based on background information about the child. Of course, the interdisciplinary team will often want to compare the child's K-ABC Mental Processing scores with scores from achievement tests other than the K-ABC. In this case, the procedure for predicting EQs outlined earlier should be followed.

Considering Individual Subtest Scores in the Cognitive-Achievement Comparison

It is important to point out that the interdisciplinary team, in making the diagnosis of learning disability, may sometimes need to consider the individual subtest scores that go into making up the overall scores of intellectual functioning (WISC-R VIQ, PIQ; K-ABC Sequential Processing standard score, Simultaneous Processing standard score) and overall scores of academic functioning (e.g., WJPEB Reading Cluster, Mathematics

Cluster, and Written Language Cluster scores). For example, on the WISC-R, several of the subtests (Similarities, Comprehension, Vocabulary) are often considered to measure more "important intelligences" than other subtests (Information, Arithmetic, Digit Span). As described in Chapter 3, the Arithmetic and Digit Span scores can often be depressed in a child who has attention deficit disorder, and the Information subtest is greatly influenced by environmental stimulation (including reading). Thus, when a child's scaled scores on Similarities, Comprehension, and Vocabulary are significantly higher than his or her scaled scores on Information, Arithmetic, and Digit Span, his or her VIQ may not be an accurate reflection of the "more important" verbal skills—abstract thinking, verbal concept formation, and verbal expression—but may be depressed by verbal skills often considered less important—auditory attention, fund of general knowledge, short-term memory. The team may want to take this pattern of scores into account when making the diagnosis. If, for example, the child with the pattern just described did not have quite enough discrepancy between the VIQ and scores of academic achievement to meet the cut-off for the diagnosis of learning disabilities, the team may want to take into consideration other data to determine if the VIQ was not artificially depressed by factors not generally considered indicators of intelligence (e.g., distractibility) and adjust the criteria for diagnosis.

Similarly, the team should take into account variability within the subtest scores that comprise the measures of overall academic achievement. For example, a child may be reading on grade level, according to the overall Reading Cluster score from the WJPEB. However, the child might perform three years above grade level in Letter-Word Identification (word recognition) and Word Attack (application of phonics skills), but be functioning five years below grade level in Passage Comprehension. In this case the child's overall Reading Cluster score does not adequately summarize his or her reading abilities. The interdisciplinary team should again not abide by the strict criteria established for making the diagnosis of learning disability, but should consider other data that might explain the discrepancy within reading skills.

Need for Flexibility in Diagnosis

It is imperative that professionals use the formula for identifying learning disabilities as a guideline, and not as an absolute authority. For many children, it will be just as important to take into account reports from teachers and parents, observations during testing, and other data sources before arriving at a diagnosis. In some cases, it will not be possible to find a reliable and valid test to measure the child's skill in a

particular area. For example, many children perform quite well on measures of written language ability, although teachers and parents insist that
the child has a great deal of difficulty when required to express himself
or herself in writing. Because most of the tests available for obtaining a
score in written language focus on the mechanics of writing (e.g., spelling,
punctuation, usage, capitalization), it may not be possible to diagnose a
learning disability in written language by using test scores alone. It would
be necessary in such a case for the team to take into consideration teacher
and parent reports, to observe the child in a situation that requires him
or her to write a paragraph, and to subjectively evaluate the child's written
work in terms of content, organization, neatness, and time taken to complete it, as well as correct use of spelling, punctuation, grammar, capitalization, and so forth. Only then can an accurate diagnosis be made,
regardless of the presence or absence of significant discrepancy between
test scores.

It is especially important that the interdisciplinary team consider
factors other than the EQ-IQ discrepancy when making the diagnosis of
learning disabilities in younger children. Because academic testing in the
early grades (kindergarten and first grade) is based primarily on material
that can be learned rotely (e.g., letter and number identification, sight
words, addition facts), it may be difficult to identify the child who will
have problems with more complex processes (e.g., application of phonics
rules, reading for comprehension, understanding math concepts). For these
young children, it is very important that the interdisciplinary team rely
heavily on teacher and parent reports in identifying the child at risk for
learning disabilities.

IDENTIFYING STRENGTHS AND WEAKNESSES IN THE LEARNING STYLE

Many investigators have attempted to classify children with learning
disabilities (particularly reading disabilities) according to their specific
difficulties. Children with reading disabilities are often thought to fall into
one of two categories. Children in the first group (sometimes called *dysphonetic* dyslexics) have difficulty with auditory processing and are unable
to make accurate phoneme-grapheme correspondences, are unable to break
words into their phonetic components and blend the sounds together to
form the correct word, and have difficulty sequencing phonemes correctly.
These children make bizarre spelling errors, unrelated to the sound of the
word. Children in the second group (sometimes called *dyseidetic* dyslexics)
have difficulty with visual-spatial perception and may be unable to recognize individual letters, are slow to recognize simple sight words (visual
gestalts), have poor visual discrimination of words closely similar in
configuration, and have trouble recognizing nonphonetically spelled words.

These children read very slowly, as they must decode each word as they go along. They spell words the way they sound, ignoring irregular patterns usually learned through a sight approach (e.g., "tough" may be spelled "tuff").

Some investigators have divided children with reading disabilities into these or similar groupings based on the direction of the VIQ-PIQ or Sequential-Simultaneous discrepancy, subtest profiles from the intelligence tests, or by an analysis of reading and spelling errors. In some schools, attempts have been made to tailor the curriculum to address the strengths and weaknesses presumed to be exhibited by the different groups. Sadly, there is not much evidence for success in this type of approach. Learning disabilities must certainly be considered a heterogeneous disorder. The differences among learning-disabled students are, however, probably too complex to allow us to base treatment on the child's membership in one of a limited number of broadly defined subgroups.

This is not to imply, however, that the team cannot learn much about the nature of the child's learning disabilities by examining test results and other data for specific patterns. After one has identified whether or not a learning disability exists, it may be helpful for those who are going to be working with the child to identify strengths and weaknesses in the child's learning style. In identifying strengths and weaknesses, the team should consider subtest patterns on the intelligence test as well as scores from some of the tests that were suggested as possible additions to the psychologist's battery. For example, it may be helpful for the child's teacher to know that he or she has excellent ability to perceive visual-spatial stimuli (as indicated by a high Performance IQ and good performance on the Motor-Free Test of Visual Perception), but poor fine motor skills (as evidenced by slowness on the Coding subtest, sloppiness on the Mazes subtest, and poor performance on the Developmental Test of Visual-Motor Integration). The teacher would then know that he or she should not waste time on activities to strengthen visual-perceptual skills, but should instead work on strategies to remedy or circumvent the poor fine-motor skills. Kaufman and Kaufman (1983) provide many suggestions for approaching children with various profiles on the K-ABC (difficulties with Simultaneous Processing, Sequential Processing, or both). Although strategies based on the test pattern profiles have reasonable face validity, there is little evidence that they are the most effective approaches to remediating the learning disabilities.

IDENTIFYING ASSOCIATED PROBLEMS

In addition to diagnosing learning disabilities and identifying areas of strength and weakness in the cognitive and achievement profiles, the team should attempt to identify associated problems that may be interfering with learning. Many of the problems that teachers consider most disruptive to the learning process are sometimes thought of as "behavior problems." By better understanding the basis of these problems, the teacher can better help the child overcome them. The interdisciplinary team has available several sources of data for identifying these problems that interfere with learning: teacher reports, parent reports, child interview, classroom observation, neurodevelopmental evaluation, test results, observation during testing, and subtest profiles. Various combinations of these data will be needed to identify the problems that exacerbate, or are exacerbated by, the learning disabilities.

Attention Deficit Disorder

A disorder commonly seen in conjunction with learning disabilities is attention deficit disorder (ADD), with or without hyperactivity. In the Diagnostic and Statistical Manual of Mental Disorders ([DSM-III], American Psychiatric Association, 1980) ADD is defined in terms of a developmentally inappropriate lack of attention (inattention) with associated poor impulse control. A child with this disorder typically exhibits an inconsistent application of cognitive abilities to academic tasks, producing variable and inconsistent performance that confounds teachers, parents, and the child. It is important to appreciate, both diagnostically and therapeutically, that disorders of attention and a physically high motor activity level may exist separately or together. Although it is rare, there are children who exhibit hyperactivity with no apparent attention deficits. More common are children with attention deficits with no apparent excesses of physical activity.

According to the DSM III, a child must meet criteria for inattention (e.g., failure to finish things he or she starts, failure to listen, easy distractibility, difficulty in concentrating and/or sticking to a play activity) and criteria for impulsivity (e.g., acting before thinking, shifting from one activity to another, difficulty in organization, need for supervision, frequent calling out in class, and difficulty awaiting turns) to be diagnosed as having ADD. For a diagnosis of ADD with hyperactivity, the child must demonstrate, in addition to distractibility and poor impulse control, a level of excessive motor activity. This excessive motor activity may be apparent as difficulty sitting still or staying seated, excessive running or climbing, moving excessively during sleep, and/or acting as if "driven by a motor" (American Psychiatric Association, 1980, p. 44). As noted in the DSM III, these behaviors will generally be reported by the parents or the school. Because "signs of the disorder may be absent when the child is in a new or one-to-one situation" (p. 43) the clinician often observes no evidence for ADD.

Although the diagnostic elements of ADD are the finding of developmentally inappropriate attention deficits coupled with poor impulse control, there is no single measure that can positively identify ADD. Although identification of attention deficits seems simple enough, it is sometimes a quite complicated process. It may be very difficult to determine whether a child's failure to perform stems from an attention span that is inappropriate for his or her cognitive level or whether there is an overall cognitive delay that would entitle a child to a degree of inattentiveness appropriate to the more immature level of functioning. Ascertaining correspondence between cognitive level and attention span is a bit simpler process for the child with substantial cognitive delays (e.g., mental retardation), but can be an extremely difficult process with children in a more normal range of function.

The interdisciplinary team needs to combine data from several sources to determine if ADD is a problem associated with the learning disability. More emphasis should be placed on data gathered from the environment in which the child typically functions (i.e., the classroom and the home) than on data from the clinicians' evaluations, as the child may not display distractibility and impulsivity in the novel one-on-one situation.

The team will want to consider information gathered through the teacher(s) interview (see Chapter 4), focusing especially on items regarding the child's activity level, ability to pay attention, follow directions, complete assignments, and control impulsivity. Similar information gathered through a classroom observation should also be considered. Data gathered from the parent interview will be of great importance in determining the existence of ADD. The team should focus especially on the parents' responses to questions regarding the child's ability to listen to and follow directions, complete regular chores, and complete homework. Observations by the physician, psychologist, and educator who conducted testing with the child may provide important information in making the ADD diagnosis. (See specifically Chapter 3 for discussion of some of the test behaviors that might indicate distractibility.)

Some of the most important diagnostic clues from the individual assessments (medicine, psychology, and special education) are discussed as follows:

Inattentiveness may be evident from the neurodevelopmental assessment in terms of variability in performance with tests of rote auditory memory, including, on occasion, an improved performance with digits reversed as opposed to digits forward, and in impulsive execution of the Gesell drawings (see Chapter 2).

In the medical, psychological, and special education assessments, a child with ADD may evidence difficulty paying attention and staying on task, frequent requests for repetition of oral questions and directions, easy distractibility to visual and auditory stimuli, irrelevant comments or attempts to relate personal experiences that are brought to mind by various test stimuli, and tendencies to "lose track" of the tasks presented.

The impulsive components of ADD may manifest as tendencies to give the first answer that comes to mind, to begin tasks before instructions are completed, and to grab for materials before the examiner is ready to present them.

From the psychological assessment, a pattern of excessive distractibility can be hypothesized when relatively low scores are obtained on the WISC-R Arithmetic, Digit Span, and Coding subtests or on the K-ABC Magic Window, Face Recognition, Hand Movements, Number Recall, Word Order, and Spatial Memory. (See Chapter 3 for a discussion of subtest patterns.) These subtests, which are affected by the child's ability to focus attention, are naturally also affected by many other unrelated factors. For this reason, a pattern of poor performance on these subtests should not be used as the primary determinant for making a diagnosis of ADD. The team should use the subtest patterns in conjunction with some of the general observations listed previously to help identify ADD.

To repeat, in the diagnosis of ADD it is important to assess attention span within the setting in which the child is asked to function, that is, in the classroom. This requires discussion with school personnel to determine the appropriateness of that situation and the child's attentional profile in the school setting with its attendant demands and distractions. It is inappropriate to attempt to diagnose ADD without input from the school.

As stated previously, there is no single measure that can confirm or deny the existence of ADD. Only by considering data from many sources can the diagnosis be made, and even then it is often difficult to be certain. Because the pertinent issue is the child's attention span and impulse control in the home and school settings, professionals on the interdisciplinary team should place greater value on parents' and teacher's reports than on their own observations during evaluations of the child.

It is important to note here that ADD (with or without hyperactivity) is sometimes seen in children who are doing poorly in school but who do not exhibit learning disabilities. Many of these children have managed to master skills in basic academic areas (reading, mathematics, written language), but do poorly in school because they are unable to stay on task, complete assignments, and organize themselves. The strategies discussed in Chapter 8 for dealing with attention problems are equally appropriate for the child who exhibits ADD with or without learning disabilities.

Problems with Organizational Skills or Study Skills

Children with ADD often demonstrate difficulties with organizational and study skills. However, these problems can be observed in other children with learning problems as well, and will, therefore, be discussed separately. As with the diagnosis of ADD, the primary sources of data for identifying problems in organizational and study skills are the teachers, parents, and, if appropriate, the student. Their responses to questions regarding completion of homework (amount of homework assigned, actual time taken to complete it, need for supervision), reasons for poor grades (lack of preparation for tests, failure to complete homework or classwork, lack of class participation), and the child's need for structure at home and school will be important for determining if there are problems with organizational and study skills. Relevant information may also be gathered from observation of the child during testing and from the results of certain intelligence subtests that require good planning ability. (See Chapter 3 for a discussion of these subtests.) It is important to note that problems with organizational and study skills are observed more frequently as the child gets older and is expected to take more responsibility. Especially as children reach middle school, they are often expected for the first time to move from class to class on their own, and no longer have one primary teacher who will "look out" for them. Also, as children get older, long-term assignments are made that require more planning, more independent studying of texts is required, and parents often provide less supervision of homework.

Handwriting Slowness and Inefficiency

Although difficulties in written language are usually considered when making the diagnosis of learning disability, many of the tests that measure abilities in this area focus primarily on spelling and the mechanics of writing (e.g., punctuation, grammar, capitalization, word usage). Handwriting speed and efficiency, which is largely based on fine-motor skill or visual-motor integration, is less often measured, but can play an important role in determining whether or not a child is able to perform in school at a level commensurate with his or her intellectual functioning. In order to determine if handwriting speed and efficiency are adequate, the interdisciplinary team should review data from the teacher and parent interviews, focusing particularly on responses to questions regarding completion of assignments, time needed to complete assignments, and neatness of work. If possible, teachers should be questioned regarding the reasons for slow or inaccurate completion of assignments (e.g., daydreaming, slow but diligent work pace, failure to follow instructions, difficulty copying from the board).

Children with slow or inefficient handwriting often show difficulties with other fine-motor skills, such as those presented during the occupational therapy evaluation or the neurodevelopmental evaluation. Scores on certain tests (e.g., tests of visual-motor integration, the WISC-R Coding subtest) may be low. Observation during testing may also indicate reasons for the child's slow completion of assignments (e.g., perfectionistic approach, tendency to repeatedly lose his or her place during copying, off-task behaviors, awkward pencil grasp). Specific suggestions for circumventing handwriting difficulties can be made if the team can pinpoint the areas of weakness. (See Chapter 7 for a discussion of these strategies.)

Gross Motor Clumsiness

Some children with learning disabilities also demonstrate poor gross motor skills. These gross motor (play) skills represent one of the two major ways children relate to each other (the other being language). Although poor gross motor skills may not interfere with learning per se, they can certainly affect the learning-disabled child's already vulnerable self-concept. Difficulties with gross motor skills are assessed through the physical therapy evaluation and the neurodevelopmental examination. Teachers and parents will often comment regarding a child's clumsiness. Responses to questions about extracurricular activities (especially athletics) will provide data regarding the extent to which gross motor difficulties influence the child's selection of pastimes.

Language or Speech Problems

Children with learning disabilities often have a history of slow language development. Language problems may continue into school age. Language problems may be first mentioned by parents or teachers, who might say that the child appears to have difficulty processing information, gives inappropriate responses to questions, has weak vocabulary skills, is unable to relate common experiences or tell stories. Language difficulties might also be evidenced by a WISC-R profile where the PIQ is significantly and unusually higher than the VIQ. Observation during medical, psychological, and educational testing might also suggest language difficulties. (See Chapter 3 for a discussion of some of the signs examiners might observe in children with language difficulties.) A complete language evaluation should be obtained for children with suspected language difficulties. (See Chapter 5 for a discussion of the language evaluation.)

Speech problems will be more easily observed. The interdisciplinary team should attempt to determine whether speech difficulties are severe enough to interfere with learning. Consideration should also be given to the effects of speech difficulties on social/emotional adjustment. Evaluation by a speech pathologist will provide important information in determining the need for speech therapy.

Significant delays in speech or language warrant special education services, regardless of the existence of learning disabilities.

Emotional Problems

The child whose learning difficulties are assumed to be primarily the result of emotional handicaps is not diagnosed as learning disabled. However, the child with learning disabilities can and often does have concomitant secondary emotional difficulties. If learning disabilities are thought to be the primary handicapping condition, special education services that lead to improved academic achievement may be sufficient to correct emotional problems. Conversely, if an emotional disorder is the primary handicapping condition, psychotherapy may be sufficient to correct the learning problems. However, it is sometimes very difficult to determine the primary handicapping condition—that is, to determine whether emotional problems are causing learning difficulties or vice versa. Regardless of the cause-effect relationship, the child with serious emotional and learning difficulties will benefit from help with both.

Data for determining the existence of emotional problems may come initially from the interview with the parents, teachers, and child. The team should focus especially on responses to questions regarding the child's self-concept, peer relations, eating or sleeping disorders, separation difficulties, level of motivation, unusual fears, mood swings, tendency to withdraw, and so forth. Observation during testing will also play an important role in identifying emotional disturbance. The child who shows excessive anxiety, anger, destructiveness, lack of confidence in his or her responses, avoidance behaviors, lack of eye-contact, inappropriate demonstrations of affection, low tolerance for frustration, or inappropriate affect should receive further evaluation. Results from projective psychological tests will be of value in making a determination regarding the presence of emotional disorders.

Family Problems

The presence of a learning disabled child, especially one who has associated ADD (with or without hyperactivity), can be very disruptive to family life. Parents (and teachers) may feel the child is lazy, not working up to his or her potential, deliberately failing to follow instructions, stubborn and willful, or simply "dumb." Some parents may blame their child for poor school performance, rather than being supportive and attempting to help the child overcome his or her difficulties. Other parents may blame themselves for the child's difficulties and try to overcompensate by making excuses, providing excessive help with assignments, or allowing the child to avoid school. Especially as children get older, parents expect them to take more responsibility for their schoolwork, but become frustrated as they observe their child fail to do so. Children become more resentful of parental interference with school work, although they need the additional structure.

Identification of family problems is based primarily on information gathered from interviews with the parent and the child. School personnel may also be aware of information pertinent to this topic. Projective tests can also provide valuable insights into family dynamics.

Specific Behavior Problems

Most behavior problems that will be mentioned by parents and teachers are, broadly speaking, manifestations of the child's reaction to his or her learning disability, ADD, or emotional problems. Therefore, the strategies used to deal with these disabilities and disorders (e.g., special education services, medication, psychotherapy) will generally be effective in improving the child's overall behavior and in reducing specific behavior problems. Many specific behavior problems will, however, respond well to behavior management techniques (described in Chapter 9). It is therefore advisable to identify the most salient problems at home (e.g., lying, failure to follow instructions, difficulty getting ready for school, temper tantrums, excessive fighting with siblings) and at school (e.g., failure to complete assignments, talking out of turn, wandering about the classroom, tardiness). Interviews conducted with the parents and teachers are generally the best sources for identifying these problems. When possible, attempts should be made to identify the nature of the problem, when and where the problem is most likely to occur, any specific occurrences that are likely to trigger the problem, strategies that have been used in an attempt to control the problem, and the success of these strategies. Specific behavior management strategies can be suggested by the interdisciplinary team if this information is carefully gathered and clearly presented.

CONCLUSION

As outlined in this chapter, the first task of the interdisciplinary team, when it meets to review the individual team members' data, is to determine whether a significant discrepancy exists between the child's level of cognitive functioning and level of academic achievement in one or more areas. Appropriate and inappropriate methods for determining whether this discrepancy is significant were discussed. Because learning disabilities cannot be defined strictly according to statistical formulae, the team is urged to consider factors in addition to test performance. The next task is to examine data from a variety of sources to determine factors that underlie the disability or help to clarify its nature. Finally, the team must determine the existence of problems often associated with learning disabilities. After completing this procedure, the team will have the information necessary to develop a comprehensive plan for treatment.

PART II

PLANNING FOR TREATMENT

CHAPTER 7

Planning for Treatment of Learning Disabilities and Associated Primary Handicapping Conditions

Elizabeth H. Aylward
Frank R. Brown, III
M. E. B. Lewis
Carol R. Savage

C hapter 6 included discussion of the diagnosis of learning disabilities, attention deficit disorder (ADD), and associated problems. It is important for the team, once it begins to develop therapeutic recommendations, to appreciate that some of these conditions are neurologically based. The primary handicapping conditions include (but are not limited to) learning disabilities, speech-language disabilities, gross and fine motor dyscoordinations, and ADD. Because of these primary neurological handicapping conditions, the learning-disabled child (if provided with no special programming) falls progressively behind in achievement, and may develop a variety of secondary handicapping conditions, including behavioral and emotional problems. Treatment of learning disabilities and any associated deficits in language and gross or fine motor dyscoordinations is the subject of this chapter. Treatment of ADD will be discussed in Chapter 8. Treatment of secondary handicapping conditions will be discussed in Chapter 9.

In planning for treatment of the learning disabilities, team members must keep in mind that special education services are mandated in Public Law 94–142, the Education for All Handicapped Children Act. This legislation requires the provision of a free, appropriate public education for all students identified as handicapped. Furthermore, it defines learning disability as a handicap, and requires that services for learning-disabled students be provided in the least restrictive environment. That is, education must be provided in a setting that permits the learning-disabled student to remain among nonhandicapped peers as much as possible.

As outlined in Chapter 1, the interdisciplinary team will diagnose primary and secondary handicapping conditions and develop general therapeutic recommendations. For example, the team may recommend that a child with reading disability be provided with reading resource help and special accommodations to help him or her circumvent reading difficulties in other subjects. The interdisciplinary team will not usually outline the specific goals and objectives to be accomplished as part of the child's curriculum for the school year or specify particular instructional methods. Individual team members will be given responsibility for ensuring that more specific guidelines are developed and implemented. The following sections discuss the development and implementation of a plan for providing the special education services that are legally mandated for the learning-disabled student.

THE INDIVIDUALIZED EDUCATIONAL PLAN (IEP)

The IEP is a comprehensive plan of instructional activities designed to address specific areas of weakness. The IEP should be a "map" of the year's or semester's program for the student, including goals and objectives, as well as strategies for reaching them. A new teacher or therapist should, without assistance, be able to read the document and determine where the student is headed during the period covered by the IEP.

The IEP Development Team

The development of the IEP is done by a committee, usually based in the child's school. This committee might be composed of the same members as the interdisciplinary team. In most cases, however, the IEP development committee will be composed primarily of school-based personnel and include few outside professionals, although input from outside professionals should, of course, be welcomed. The committee usually includes the child's current teacher, a special educator, a school psychologist, and an administrator. The committee will sometimes solicit the participation of other professionals (e.g., physicians, speech-language therapists, behavioral psychologists, occupational and physical therapists).

It is helpful if at least one member of the interdisciplinary team assists in developing the IEP or is at least readily available to the IEP development committee.

In addition to professional staff, parents should be asked to contribute their understanding of their child's needs, as well as their desires for outcome. Parents are too often ignored until the IEP is actually written, and then they are asked to "rubber stamp" the document with their signature as consent and agreement for implementation. Parents should be encouraged to understand their child's learning strengths and weaknesses and assist in the development of reasonable and realistic goals for instruction. Parents are much more likely to share in the educational process and support educational programming at home if they have a vested interest and have been heard by those who design the instructional program.

Components of the IEP

Although, by definition, each IEP is individualized to meet the particular student's needs, all IEPs have certain components in common, including:

Current Levels of Achievement

Present levels of achievement must be stated from the most recent assessments. A diagnostic term such as *developmentally delayed* or *dyslexic* is not acceptable to describe the current achievement of the student. Test scores, expressed as grade equivalents, standard scores, percentiles, or descriptive statements (when quantifying is not feasible) are acceptable. Scores or levels should be stated in understandable terms, so that members of the IEP development committee (including parents) can comprehend them without the assistance of test manuals or other supplemental materials.

Goals and Objectives

Planning for the learning-disabled student should reflect long-range or global goals. Goals reflect the committees' expectations for the student's accomplishments in a particular area during the period specified (e.g., "The student will demonstrate one year's growth in reading comprehension").

In addition, the committee must specify short term objectives for attainment of the goal (e.g., "Given a ten sentence paragraph written at the fifth grade level, the student will identify the main idea and two supporting details"). Objectives are measurable or observable steps toward the achievement of the goal. Objectives should be reasonably detailed, but IEPs are not meant to resemble daily lesson plans.

Criteria for Mastery of Objectives

Appropriate objective criteria must be included to determine if and when an objective is achieved. Such criteria may be stated as a percentage: "The student will transcribe a vocabulary list from dictation with 85 percent accuracy" or as a ratio: "Given five chances to name the Thirteen Colonies, the student will do so correctly at least four times." In some cases, the criteria for achievement is an implied 100 percent, as the task is either achieved or not: "The student will correctly state his or her name."

Criteria can change throughout the course of programming. For example, a student whose IEP calls for 60 percent accuracy for an objective during the first quarter of the school year may progress through the year to a more challenging 80 or 90 percent by the last month of the IEP's duration.

Specific Service

The IEP should indicate the extent of special education and related services that will be needed to help the student meet the outlined goals and objectives. The amount of time the child will spend receiving special services is often defined according to levels. (These levels will be addressed later in the chapter.) Related services represent intervention provided by professionals other than educators and may include, for example, speech-language therapy, occupational therapy, physical therapy, or counseling. These services should be outlined, as well as the amount of time the child will need to spend with each specialist.

In addition to specifying extent of special education and related services, the IEP may specify particular methods to be used with the student, such as the Orton-Gillingham method or the VAKT approach. (Specific remedial approaches will be elaborated later in this chapter.) The IEP may outline modifications to be made in the instructional program, such as special seating, special management techniques, supplemental equipment or materials, computer assistance, or cassette recorders to supplement note-taking. Special remedial or treatment methods, such as sensory integration therapy, pragmatic language therapy, articulation therapy, supplementary vocational or prevocational training may also be specified.

Duration

An IEP should state when the program will take effect and when attainment of goals and objectives is expected. Usually, duration is for either a school year (9 months) or a calendar year. An IEP can be reviewed, revised, or rewritten at any time during implementation (with the parents' knowledge and consent), but all IEPs must be reviewed and updated at least annually.

□   □   □   □   □

IEPs, although incorporating the components discussed, should be designed to allow flexibility in their implementation. This can be accomplished in several ways. For example, several methods can be suggested for instruction of specific skills, criteria for attainment of objectives can be adjusted, and provisions can be made for allowing the child to demonstrate attainment of skills in a variety of ways (e.g., orally, in writing, with manipulation of objects).

Implementation of the IEP

The IEP must be developed before a student is placed in special education programming, and must be implemented no later than 30 days after its development. Although not always legally required, the parents' acceptance of the IEP should be indicated by their signature.

Teachers and other personnel providing related services must review the IEP 60 days after initial placement. In addition, they should periodically update the IEP to note objectives met, success of methods, and whether or not the IEP is still an accurate reflection of realistic programming for the student. If the IEP is inappropriate in any area, it should be revised. Change in the nature or level of service provided cannot be made without the parents' consent. An addendum to the IEP or an entirely new document can be drafted by the committee. The student remains in the current program until the modifications are approved. The IEP must again be reviewed 60 days after any major revisions.

Considerations for Developing and Implementing the IEP

In developing and implementing the educational plan, consideration should be given to the following assumptions regarding the learning-disabled student and the learning process:

□ *Learning-disabled students are "normal" people with special needs.* Learning-disabled students have the same desire to learn and the same desire for acceptance in the process as their peers. They are entitled to enjoy the learning process, to have a good self-concept, and to be able to relate as normally as possible to other children, despite their learning handicap. Without some accommodations in the learning process, they probably will not have these experiences.

□ *Learning-disabled students require more structure.* Because learning-disabled children often exhibit distractibility, poor impulse control, and poor organizational skills, they will usually benefit from increased structure and organization imposed from outside sources. Increased structure

involves the clear presentation of expectations, clear delineation of consequences for meeting or failing to meet expectations, and consistency in
feedback. Specific strategies for increasing structure and consistency are
outlined in Chapter 8. Structure will also enhance the effectiveness of other
treatment modalities (e.g., medication for ADD, behavior management
strategies).

□ *Many learning-disabled students require more control of distractions.*
Distractions in the classroom should be minimized in order to maximize
the learning-disabled child's ability to attend. Suggestions for decreasing
distractions are discussed in Chapter 8.

□ *Students learn best through direct experience.* Abstract concepts
and prolonged debate of esoteric issues do not work well as a foundation
for teaching the learning-disabled student. Instruction should be practical, and teachers should ask themselves "What can the student do with
what he or she is learning?" Topics of interest are generated from daily
experiences, and, when possible, can be presented in conjunction with
activities such as field trips, films, and special projects.

□ *Skills taught in isolation have a transient effect.* The curriculum for
the learning-disabled child should emphasize relationships among skills
and repetition over time. Skills taught in one subject area should be reinforced in other subject areas. For example, application of language skills
is not taught in the English or reading class alone, but must be reinforced
by teachers in other content areas. Goals of today should relate to the goals
of yesterday and tomorrow. The development of any curriculum for
learning-disabled students requires provision for repetition of concepts and
procedures. Reinforcement and repetition will enhance internalization of
concepts.

□ *Learning is a multisensory experience.* Internalization of concepts
is believed to be enhanced though presentation in a variety of sensory
modalities (e.g., visual, auditory, kinesthetic, and tactile). Multisensory
strategies include audio-visual instruction, laboratory experiences, manipulation of materials, and so forth.

□ *There is a point of diminishing return in remedial programming.* In
programming for the learning-disabled student, there is sometimes an automatic assumption that more remediation is necessarily better. The goals
of special education should include instruction in content as well as remediation of skills. For example, the fifth grader, who for remediation of word
attack skills, is required to read first grade material, will not be provided
with ideas, concepts, and information appropriate for his or her cognitive
level. The child's vocabulary and fund of information will suffer as a result
of "overremediation." There must, therefore, be an appropriate balance
between remediation of skills and instruction in content. Of course, instruction in content will have to be modified to circumvent areas of weakness.
Suggestions for such modifications (e.g., Talking Books) will be discussed
later in this chapter.

☐ *The most important issue for the learning-disabled child is how he or she feels about himself or herself.* Well-balanced programming affords the learning-disabled student an opportunity to shine in his or her areas of strength. Successful experiences will serve as a reminder that he or she is normal and capable, despite his or her handicapping condition. This reassurance will, in turn, encourage the child to use and develop his or her inherent strengths, thus enhancing self-concept.

If these opportunities for developing strengths are not provided, the reverse may occur. The learning-disabled child with a poor self-concept may realize less than his or her inherent potential, and the prospect of disability becomes self-fulfilling.

LEVELS OF SERVICE

Once a child has been identified as meeting the eligibility criteria for special education, the IEP should detail the extent and types of special education intervention required to enable the student to meet the goals and objectives. In determining the extent of special education required, the IEP development committee should keep in mind that Public Law 94-142 mandates education in the least restrictive environment. Depending on the nature and severity of the disability, placement in special education settings will vary along a continuum, extending from mildly intrusive modifications in instructional programming to complete exclusion from the mainstream of education. This continuum of special education services might be portrayed as in Figure 7-1. As suggested by Figure 7-1, most children are placed in programs that offer the most normalized settings, such as regular classrooms and resource rooms. There will be fewer children requiring the more restrictive settings, such as self-contained classrooms and out-of-school placements.

Although the descriptive terms applied to each level of service and the number of levels may vary from state to state or from district to district, the concept of a continuum of available services is generally applied. The levels of service portrayed in Figure 7-1 will be described as follows:

☐ *Regular Classroom with Consultative Special Education Assistance to the Teacher.* The regular classroom teacher may receive consultative assistance from professionals in a variety of areas (e.g., special education, psychology, speech-language therapy, occupational and physical therapy). At this level, there is no direct contact between these professionals and the student.

☐ *Regular Classroom with Limited Services Outside of Class.* At this level of resource placement, the student typically receives up to an hour per day of instruction outside of the regular classroom. Resource help is usually restricted to one subject area. A resource teacher usually

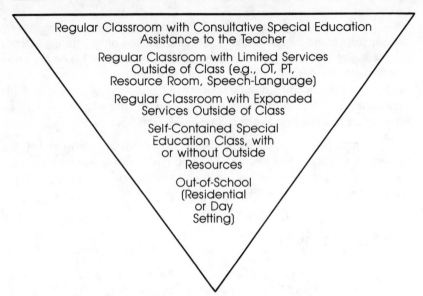

FIGURE 7-1. *Levels of Special Education Service*

schedules three to four children at a time to work on similar specific skill deficits.

One difficulty with a resource room placement is that a child who may already have problems with distractibility, impulsivity, and organizational skills must now relate to two teachers and complete two separate sets of assignments. For this reason, it is essential for resource teachers and regular classroom teachers to have good communication and to coordinate assignments. Because the child must typically leave the regular class to receive resource help, it is important that the child not be held accountable for the regular class instruction he or she misses.

At this level, the child is receiving his or her first direct exposure to any type of special education service. Careful monitoring at this level is important in order to determine whether the special education services should be continued at the same level, expanded, or deleted. If the child's performance and behavior in the resource room is markedly better than his or her performance and behavior in the regular class, this may be a good indication that more resource help would be beneficial. In addition, the resource teacher is in a particularly good position to monitor the child's distractibility, impulsivity, and organizational skills, as the materials presented in the resource room are specifically designed to match the child's ability level and are presented in a less distracting environment.

☐ *Regular Classroom with Expanded Services Outside of Class.* At this level of resource placement, the student typically spends up to one-half of each day (three hours) outside of the regular classroom. Resource help may be provided in more than one subject area. Considerations discussed in the previous paragraphs continue to apply at this level.

☐ *Self-Contained Special Education Class.* If resource placement is still too distracting for the child, or if disabilities are too severe or too numerous, a self-contained classroom may be the best alternative. These classes usually contain 10 to 15 students with one special education teacher and perhaps an aide. Of course, a smaller pupil-teacher ratio is preferred. It is important that the learning-disabled student be placed in a special education class designed specifically for students with similar learning disabilities.

In some schools, all children with learning difficulties are placed in noncategorical special education placements. Thus, slow learners, students with language deficits, and perhaps retarded students might be placed together with the learning-disabled students. This is inappropriate and prevents the most efficient use of instructional time. Most school systems provide self-contained classrooms for a variety of disabling handicapping conditions, including mental retardation, orthopedic handicaps, communication disorders, emotional disturbances, and learning disabilities.

☐ *Out-of-School Placement.* Out-of-school placements for learning-disabled children are generally needed only for those students who have concomitant severe emotional or behavioral difficulties that prohibit their functioning in typical academic settings. Out-of-school placement also may be acquired in rural areas where there are too few learning-disabled students to warrant special education classes within the school.

EDUCATIONAL APPROACHES TO REMEDIATING LEARNING DISABILITIES

So far in this chapter, the amount of time spent in special programming (i.e., levels of service) has been discussed. The other important variable is, of course, the approach to special programming. In discussing remedial approaches, it will be assumed that attempts have already been made to teach the child through traditional approaches. For this reason, only special education techniques typically used with the learning-disabled student will be discussed.

Multisensory Approach

Multisensory approaches are designed to employ as many of the child's sensory modalities as possible. They are presumed to be particularly useful when a child has a specific deficit in either auditory or visual processing (e.g., language processing difficulties, poor visual-spatial perception, poor visual or auditory memory). The two major multisensory approaches are the VAKT (Visual-Auditory-Kinesthetic-Tactile) or Fernald approach and the Orton-Gillingham approach. Teachers may use components of both methods in the classroom, and many alter parts of each to suit their purposes.

The VAKT or Fernald Approach

This approach attempts to use a comprehensive balance of visual, auditory, kinesthetic, and tactile methods for introducing new words to the reading and spelling vocabulary. The student selects a word he or she wishes to learn. The teacher then writes the word in cursive on paper. Cursive is used for its fluid effect, both for the purposes of training and verbalization. The student then traces the word with his or her finger, saying the word (sounding out each letter or letter combination) as he or she traces. This is repeated until the child can write the word without looking at the printed model. After the student has mastered a collection of words (i.e., the "bank"), he or she practices recollection and reproduction, seeing the word (visual), saying the word (auditory/oral), and writing the word (kinesthetic/tactile).

Once a sufficient number of words is "banked," the student uses the vocabulary to make up stories that he or she and the teacher write together. The teacher assists the student by providing any additional words necessary for completion of the story. Once written, the story is typed and given to the student. As additional words are introduced and learned, the student is taught synonyms for words already in the bank. Oral and written reinforcement of the printed vocabulary and regular practice and review of words are vital to this approach.

The VAKT approach is very useful with children who have severe reading disabilities. It is highly individualized and reinforcing to the student because he or she writes and collects stories in areas of personal interest. On the negative side, the VAKT approach is time consuming and must be adhered to rigidly. Because the student can introduce nonstandard words, words that do not follow spelling rules, or that follow spelling rules not yet introduced, the benefits of the VAKT approach to spelling are debatable.

The Orton-Gillingham Approach

The Orton-Gillingham approach was originally designed to incorporate penmanship with reading and spelling instruction. This approach requires the student to make constant associations between the spoken and written characteristics of words (e.g., their visual construction, their pronunciation, the movements of the mouth when speaking the word, the movements of the hand when writing the word). The method is an extension of phonetic analysis, or the "sounding out" approach. Students analyze and recognize the letters of the alphabet first, associating a word with the letter ("b is for boy"). The students learn via different colored stimulus cards to isolate vowels from consonants and to remember from practice the physical production movements for each letter. Sound and letter production are associated by the SOS (spontaneous oral spelling) method, which links sound to symbol for phonetic and nonphonetic words. Unlike the VAKT approach, the Orton-Gillingham method rigidly controls the introduction of letters and words.

The Language Experience Approach

This approach is predicated on the idea that students can be motivated to read from materials they create themselves when they might not be interested in reading other materials. This method is useful for all students, but is particularly useful for adolescents who may be "turned off" by the more infantile subject matter of stories written at their low level of reading ability.

Using this approach, students dictate stories and the teacher writes the story, exactly as dictated, on a blackboard or chart. The teacher then reads the story aloud, including any grammatical errors. Students may spontaneously correct their material when it is read aloud. The teacher may also introduce corrections, depending on the language goals and the student's tolerance for correction. Students can type from the corrected draft, refining and ultimately "authoring" their work.

The Thematic Approach

In this approach, a common theme is used as the basis for instruction in all subject areas over a given period of time. Instruction may be implemented through a variety of approaches, including multisensory, language experience, structural and phonetic analysis, and may be presented in a variety of formats (e.g., large group, small group, one-on-one, peer tutoring, or computer-assisted instruction).

Instruction in all subject areas revolves around a central theme. This allows students to integrate instruction in subject areas that might otherwise be viewed as isolated from one another. Although not limited to the special education population, this approach has been used successfully with learning-disabled students. Examples of topics that might be used with the thematic approach are outlined in Table 7-1.

Of course, the teaching approach selected is not nearly as important as the capabilities, level of understanding, and personality of the individual teacher implementing the approaches. It is important that teachers choose

TABLE 7-1
Examples of Topics That Might Be Used with a Thematic Approach

September:	"Who am I?"	An introduction to individuals and their limitations
October:	Mystery	Observation and inferential thinking skills
November:	Sports	Discussion of athletic abilities, power, and socialization skills
December:	Money	Planning a budget, reading advertisements, making decisions
January:	Travel	World cultures, traditions, religions, cooking, map-reading
February:	Politics	Issues, debate, expression of opinions, reading and listening to the news
March:	Entertainment	Media, live performance, writing
April:	Animals	Sex education, wild life, survival, evolution, responsibilites of keeping a pet
May:	Local geography	Ethnic groups, historical sights, cooking, local attractions, community problems

approaches and materials with which they have expertise and feel comfortable, and in which they have confidence. Teachers should feel free to use an eclectic approach that incorporates the best facets of the approaches discussed in the preceding paragraphs with the best facets of the more traditional approaches used with non-learning-disabled students. Although information obtained through testing will be useful in determining the most effective methods to use with individual students, some "trial and error" will be necessary. Most importantly, the approach must fit the student. It is futile and potentially damaging to attempt to force the student to adapt to an inappropriate, arbitrarily selected curriculum.

APPROACHES TO REMEDIATING PRIMARY HANDICAPPING CONDITIONS ASSOCIATED WITH LEARNING DISABILITIES

Speech-Language Therapy for Learning-Disabled Children

As previously mentioned in Chapter 5, the majority of learning-disabled children with intercurrent language disabilities display relatively mild language disorders. Their school placement and intervention needs will differ from the smaller percentage of learning-disabled children diagnosed as having more severe "communication disorders."

For those children diagnosed as having a mild language disorder in conjunction with a learning disability, assignment to a regular classroom with resource services provided by a certified speech-language pathologist will be appropriate. The speech-language pathology services will be designed to meet the individual child's need (based on information obtained through the language assessment) and they may include diagnostic therapy (extension testing), comprehensive direct clinical intervention, or a specific program designed in association with and delivered in part by other members of the interdisciplinary team (e.g., occupational therapy). Children assigned to such resource speech-language programs are not excluded from obtaining the benefits of consultation and support services provided to classroom teachers and families, rather, these benefits are recommended as additional services provided on an as-needed basis.

For the learning-disabled child with more severe language disability, it is the responsibility of the speech-language pathologist and the rest of the interdisciplinary team to determine whether the child's needs would best be met in a learning-disabled or a communication-disordered classroom. This decision will hinge in large part upon the team's perception of whether the child's major handicapping condition is the learning disability with an associated language deficit or vice versa. Additional factors might include whether it is anticipated that the child will require specially designed curriculum of the speech-language pathologist, and whether language disabilities are of severe enough degree to cause a child to significantly lag behind other children socially. If, on balance, the language disability is felt to be the predominant cause of disability, a decision may be made to place the child in a self-contained program for children with primary communication disorder (and the associated learning disabilities will be addressed within this classroom setting). Specific speech-language intervention methods and strategies will not be addressed here, rather the interested reader may refer to texts by Wiig and Semel (1976, 1980, 1984).

Occupational and Physical Therapy for Learning Disabled Children

The place of the physical and occupational therapist in the educational environment is one of support service to the overall effort to provide each child with an optimum education. Flexibility, attention to the teacher's concerns for scheduling classroom versus out-of-classroom activities, and making an effort to understand the teacher's philosophy and approach to education are essential features of functioning effectively as a therapist in the educational setting. The therapist must also acquire a sound knowledge of the legal responsibilities and limits of his or her role.

Kalish and Presseller (1980) have identified five functions of the physical or occupational therapist in the public school:

1. Screening and evaluating children with a wide variety of functional
    deficits.
2. Program planning based on evaluation results and related to a
    child's ability to receive maximum benefit from his or her educa-
    tional experiences.
3. Designing treatment activities to meet program goals.
4. Consulting with teachers, other school personnel, and parents
    regarding the provision of carry-over of services into the class-
    room and the home.
5. In-service training for individuals and/or groups, relative to the
    needs of disabled children.

Readers are referred to Cermak and Henderson (1985) and Connolly
(1984) for their descriptions of several well-known treatment approaches
and for their critiques relative to current research findings regarding the
impact of the various approaches on academic performance.

Occupational Therapy Program Implementation

Occupational therapists may address development of specific skills
(e.g., handwriting) or, through sensory integrative procedures, address basic,
foundational skills (e.g., postural control). Existence of a sensory integrative dysfunction warrants a specific treatment program directed to the
child's type of disability. Occupational therapy services are provided either
directly to the child or on a consultative basis to the classroom.

As discussed in Chapter 5, some learning-disabled children have
difficulties in a number of areas, including maintaining adequate posture
in a chair, crossing the midline, and writing legibly and at a speed necessary to keep up with peers. The learning-disabled child may lack a clear
body scheme, which will affect fine and gross motor skills. The child may
not accommodate to particular textures due to tactile defensiveness. He
or she may be unable to command control of both sides of his or her body
against gravity. All of these dysfunctions can disrupt the child's ability to
attend and to perform adequately in the classroom.

The occupational therapist consults with the teacher to identify those
aspects of classroom performance that may be addressed in treatment. The
goals of therapeutic intervention involve the remediation of basic skills
and automatic movements required for postural control and movement.
Goals of treatment are summarized by Clark, Mailloux, and Parham (1985)
and include the following:

1. Increasing the frequency and duration of successful, adaptive
    responses and sensory input.
2. Producing more complex adaptive behavior.
3. Increasing self-confidence.

4. Enhancing language and cognitive abilities and increase performance in some academic skills (Ayres, 1972c, 1976, 1978).
5. Enhancing daily living and personal-social skills.

Issues addressed in treatment include: hypotonia, poor postural control, inadequate balance, poor ocular control, tactile defensiveness, poor motor planning, inadequate bilateral coordination, lack of hemispheric specialization (development of laterality), lack of self-confidence, poor fine motor control, poor organizational skills, and behavioral problems.

Therapy is done ideally on a bi-weekly basis, one-to one, and activities are chosen to address the type of dysfunction present. The child is encouraged to be self-directed in activities, but at the same time is given guidance by the therapist to enhance progress. Activities incorporate play with equipment that is carefully chosen and arranged to enhance the child's sensory integrative development, that is, to foster vestibular, tactile, and proprioceptive organization. Change is documented by use of other standardized tests such as the Bruininks-Oseretsky Test of Motor Proficiency (Bruininks-Oseretsky, 1978).

Information is shared with the parents as well as the teacher to create a supportive environment. The parents may be given a better understanding of the types of activities needed to enhance their child's development by observing therapy sessions and discussing the activities with the therapist. The occupational therapist can similarly give suggestions to the individual(s) involved in organizing the child's physical education during the school day.

Sensory integrative procedures, when considered together with other team members' approaches, may be a valuable adjunctive treatment modality for the learning-disabled child. Sensory integration provides a different perspective on why a child may be having difficulty with academics, independence in activities of daily living, and in emotional adjustment. By developing good foundational skills versus splinter skills, sensory integration addresses a holistic approach for the child.

For additional information regarding sensory integrative procedures, refer to Ayres (1979). Knickerbocker (1980) presents another occupational therapy approach for learning-disabled children which combines sensory integrative procedures and perceptual motor techniques.

Physical Therapy Program Implementation

The availability of trained therapists within the school system must be considered relative to the question of providing individual versus group treatment. For instance, Denver public schools service approximately 60,000 children. Taking the more conservative estimate of the incidence of learning disability at 10 percent, one could reasonably presume a learning-disabled population of 6,000 within that school system. Taking again the more conservative estimate that 50 percent of children with learning disability will show motor deficit (Klasen, 1972), the potential caseload of screenings of motor-impaired children could conceivably total 3,000. Currently, Denver's public school system supports 10 full-time and 3 part-time physical and occupational therapists. Excluding children with obvious motor and orthopedic handicaps, each therapist would be expected to assume responsibility for evaluation and programming for over 230 children. This situation is not at all unusual.

Presuming, therefore, that the therapist can offer only limited individual attention to the children with milder motor deficits, alternatives to individual treatment must be sought, including the following:

1. Arrangement of treatment sessions for small groups of up to eight children.
2. Arrangement of training of classroom and/or therapy assistants and aides to carry out various components of the program.
3. Reliance on the physical education staff to support the effort to promote specific sensory motor skills and to assure each child of successful movement experiences.
4. If available, incorporation of adaptive physical education programs as a remedial resource for the gradual application of those activities undertaken in therapy to the higher, more demanding skills needed for group games.

Taking time to build rapport with gym teachers is time well spent, as close collaboration between the therapist and physical educators can gradually bring about a successful process of mainstreaming the child with motor deficits into the regular gym class. Together, the physical therapist and the physical educator can develop a checklist of motor skills which can be administered by the physical educator at the start of the school year and again at midyear, as a means of assessing progress and of determining the need for program revision.

Ideally, daily gross motor time will be provided in the child's school curriculum, with the purpose of promoting both alertness and general physical fitness. Arnheim and Sinclair (1979) describe a vicious cycle in which the child with poor motor ability avoids physical activity, which results in poor physical fitness secondary to the lack of exercise, with a consequent reduction in motor ability. Cratty and Martin (1969) advocate training to develop motor proficiency primarily for the impact of such training on the child's health, self-concept, and acceptance by peers. Cratty and Martin make no claims for the effect of such training on academic achievement, but suggest that classroom performance can be enhanced if the child feels both more healthy and more positive about himself or herself.

There will be times when the therapist will confront a conflict between his or her concern regarding a child's need for individual treatment and the legal or time restrictions imposed within the school system. It is reasonable, then, to refer such a child for individual treatment outside of the school setting, and for the school therapist to monitor the child's functional performance informally or in a group setting, such as sensory/motor group, consulting at regular intervals with the attending therapist.

The therapist should also attend any community-based sensory/motor programs available, in order to determine the appropriateness of the instruction, supervision, activities, and expectations of such programs. For the therapist who is faced with impossible numbers of appropriate candidates for services, such programs outside the school system can be a valuable alternative resource.

The Clumsy Child (Arnheim and Sinclair, 1979) lists equipment needed for sensory motor programs and suggests specific activities programs. For additional resources for treatment activities, please refer to Embrey, Endicott, Glenn, and Jaeger (1983). The problem of alignment deviations, particularly through the ankle and foot (as noted in Chapter 5), should be addressed through appropriate referral for the provision of orthotics or molded shoe inserts. Either a pediatric physical therapist, a podiatrist, or a pediatric orthopedist can be expected to address this concern.

The reader is referred to Appendix D for suggestions regarding overall planning for remedial services within the public school curriculum, with additional considerations for planning for carryover of treatment principles into the home.

ACCOMMODATIONS TO CIRCUMVENT LEARNING DISABILITIES

As discussed previously, there must be a balance between amount of time spent in attempting to remediate weaknesses and amount of time spent in instruction of content. The learning-disabled student, whose intelligence is generally average or above, must continue to be exposed to appropriate cognitive stimulation, despite the fact that academic skills are impaired. In order to provide this stimulation, teachers will have to make certain accommodations in their instructional methods, assignments, and methods of evaluation. The following paragraphs provide some suggestions on specific accommodations that may be necessary to ensure that the learning-disabled student can fully utilize his or her cognitive potential and to ensure that his or her mastery of material is acknowledged.

Accommodations for Reading Disabilities

For the student with reading disabilities, it will be necessary to select (or develop) text material that presents content at the appropriate cognitive level, but that is written at the appropriate reading level. For students with less severe reading disabilities, the teacher may wish instead to read the regular text material together with the student, writing in appropriate substitutions for those words the student cannot decode alone.

Another approach, which allows the student to participate in regular classes and use regular text material, requires that the text material be dictated onto tape. This can be done by the teacher, parent, or another student. The learning-disabled student can then listen to the tapes as he or she follows along in the text. Although time consuming for both teacher and student, this approach reinforces reading skills, while at the same time circumventing reading disabilities.

Parents and teachers should be aware that the United States Library of Congress provides a service known as Talking Books to individuals who are blind, reading disabled, or otherwise unable to read regular materials. Students who have documented reading disabilities can borrow, free of charge, tape-recorded versions of books and magazines, as well as a cassette tape player. Librarians at the school or public library should have information regarding this service. If not, parents or teachers should contact the Chief, Network Division, National Library Service for the Blind and Physically Handicapped, Library of Congress, Washington, D.C., 20542.

Students with reading disability may also need special accommodation in evaluation. For example, students may need to have someone read test items and test instructions to them. Extra time might also be allowed for completion of tests.

Accommodations for Written Language Disability

Students with written language disability often demonstrate extreme frustration because they are unable to express their thoughts in writing. Despite the fact that they can gather information with no difficulty and process the information intelligently, their efforts often fail to be acknowledged because they are unable to demonstrate what they know in writing. Teachers should allow these students to substitute oral presentations for written assignments and to substitute oral tests for written tests. Whenever possible, tests should use an objective format (e.g., true/false, multiple choice) rather than an essay format. When written work is required in content areas, it should be evaluated on the basis of content, not spelling, mechanics, or organization. Alternatively, teachers might give one grade for content and one grade for writing.

Students whose written language difficulties are limited to the area of spelling might be encouraged to keep a list of those words that regularly give them trouble and be allowed to consult the list whenever necessary. These students might also benefit from the use of a word-processor that will automatically check their work for spelling errors.

Accommodations for Handwriting Difficulties

Because handwriting difficulties, like attention deficits, are often neurologically based, attempts at remediation in this area are often futile. For this reason, accommodations for students with poor or inefficient handwriting must be made to prevent excessive frustration. The suggestions made for accommodation of children with written language disability are equally appropriate for children with handwriting difficulties. In addition, the amount of written work required of these students should be decreased. Students with handwriting difficulties should be allowed to dictate assignments onto tape, or to dictate them to a parent or to another student. They should be allowed to use a tape recorder in class to supplement note-taking. If copying assignments from the blackboard presents problems, the student with handwriting difficulties should be allowed to dictate onto tape the material he or she does not have time to copy. Alternatively, another student might be asked to make a carbon copy when he or she is writing the assignment. Unnecessary copying should be avoided. For example, if an assignment requires students to copy sentences and underline the subject of each sentence, students with handwriting difficulties should be allowed to write only the subject of the sentence. These students may find it easier to use a typewriter or word-processor than to write by hand (although poor fine motor skills often interfere with attempts to learn to type). If the student can learn to use a typewriter or word-processor efficiently, he or she should be allowed to use it for both class assignments and homework.

Accommodations for Mathematics Disability

Accommodations for children with learning disabilities in mathematics will depend upon the areas of specific weakness. If, for example, the child has difficulty with computation, but not mathematical concepts, he or she might be allowed to use a calculator when working on applied problems. Alternatively, he or she might be evaluated separately on his or her ability to determine the correct procedure for solving the problem and his or her ability to complete the calculations correctly. Some students may have difficulty remembering the sequence of steps needed for certain mathematical operations (e.g., long division, finding lowest common denominators) or may be easily distracted before completing all the steps. These students should be allowed to refer to a written list of steps for each problem. Children with handwriting difficulties often have trouble copying math problems. Accommodations should be made to avoid unnecessary copying. Of course, children with learning disabilities in math should be given extra time for tests.

CONCLUSION

After the interdisciplinary team has formulated diagnoses and outlined general recommendations for treating the disorders identified, a separate committee is usually convened to outline specific methods for
remediating and circumventing learning disabilities. The Individualized
Educational Plan (IEP) is written to outline the goals and objectives to be
met by the student during a specified period of time. The amount and type
of special education services and related services that will be needed to
help the student meet these goals are also outlined in the IEP. Special
instructional techniques, as well as accommodations needed to help the
student circumvent weakness, must also be delineated. In developing and
implementing the plan for legally mandated special education services, the
IEP development committee must keep in mind that the most important
component in the process is the student. By pinpointing specific weaknesses, identifying potential strengths, and placing primary emphasis on
the student's self-concept, the committee will be able to develop a plan
that allows the student to meet the goals and objectives they have outlined,
as well as to minimize the stigma of being labeled as "learning disabled."

CHAPTER 8

Planning for Treatment of Attention Deficit Disorder

Frank R. Brown, III
Elizabeth H. Aylward

In earlier chapters we introduced a distinction between primary and secondary handicapping conditions for learning-disabled children. As discussed, primary handicapping conditions are neurologically based, and include learning disabilities, speech-language disabilities, gross and fine motor dyscoordination, and attention deficit disorder (ADD). Chapter 7 discussed remediation of learning disabilities and any associated deficits in speech-language and gross or fine motor dyscoordination. This chapter addresses remediation of ADD.

In general, children with learning disabilities exhibit two problems that might be associated with the word *attention*. They may have *too little attention* (span) and *too much attention* (seeking). The lack of a developmentally appropriate attention span (ADD) represents a primary neurological handicapping condition (analogous to learning disability) that is, for the most part, out of the child's control. This neurological deficit interferes with the learning process and compounds the already complicated learning disabilities profile. Attention-seeking, on the other hand, is a secondary handicapping condition that is behaviorally rather than neurologically based and stems in part from the fact that learning-disabled children do not receive the normal positive reinforcements that go along with school achievement. In reaction to this situation, the learning-disabled child may exhibit a variety of a negative attention-seeking behaviors that again interfere with the learning process.

The learning-disabled child will typically exhibit some mixture of "attentional" problems, that is, both a lack of and an inordinate seeking of attention. This fact has created a lot of confusion in choosing appropriate environmental accommodations (both at home and at school), use of stimulant medications (e.g., methylphenidate, Ritalin), and behavior modification techniques. In this section the two major treatment modalities for children with a primary attention deficit, environmental accommodations and stimulant medication, will be discussed. Chapter 9 will address behavior management strategies appropriate for children with secondary attention-seeking behaviors.

MANAGEMENT OF ATTENTION DEFICIT DISORDER—
ENVIRONMENTAL ACCOMMODATIONS

All children need structure and consistency. As children grow older, however, parents and teachers usually expect them to take more responsibility for their actions, to require less structure and supervision, and to be able to deal with less consistency in the daily routine. Children with primary neurologically based ADD (who are often thought of as "immature") need more structure and consistency for a longer time than most children their age.

It is not easy, for many reasons, to deal with children who have ADD. At times, they appear quite able to function at an age-appropriate level, making parents and teachers believe that the child's inappropriate behavior is completely volitional. At times (especially as they reach adolescence), children often resent interference from parents and teachers, and want to be responsible for themselves, but do not have the organizational abilities that will allow them to do so successfully. Their impulsivity causes them to do "stupid" things that they know are inappropriate, causing frustration for both themselves and adults.

Parents and teachers need to understand that ADD is a primary, neurologically based disability that prevents children from paying attention, following instructions, organizing themselves and their materials, completing work on their own, tuning out distractions, and controlling impulsivity. Just as parents and teachers of a physically impaired child would not insist on taking away the child's wheelchair or braces when he or she reaches a certain age, parents and teachers should not insist that the child with ADD function without the extra support, structure, and consistency he or she needs.

Parents and teachers will need to provide extra support, structure, and consistency of the type discussed in the remainder of this chapter to help the attention-deficit-disordered child function. In some instances, these accommodations may be all that is required and they may substitute for employment of stimulant medication. In most circumstances, however, one finds that a combination of these techniques with stimulant medication usage is more effective than either treatment modality by itself in minimizing the negative effects of ADD.

School-Based Accommodations to Increase Structure and Consistency

Teachers of children with ADD will have to make special efforts to provide the extra support and structure these children need, as well as attempting, as much as possible, to cut down on the number of distractions in the classroom. The following suggestions might be shared with the teachers of children who are diagnosed as having ADD.

Children with ADD have difficulty in making transitions from one activity to another. It is important, therefore, to keep the daily routine as consistent as possible. The child should be able to expect that various activities (e.g., reading, recess, lunch, physical education) will occur at approximately the same time each day. Changes from room to room and from teacher to teacher should be minimized, as the child often has difficulty making transitions and organizing himself or herself in new situations. If the child must be taken out of the room for special education services, the services should be provided at the same time every day. The child should not, of course, be expected to make up work he or she misses when taken out of the room for special education services. The special education services should be provided at the same time that the children in the regular class are being presented with material in the same subject area (e.g., special reading help should be provided at the same time as the regular class is having the reading lesson).

A child with ADD will have more difficulty paying attention to classroom instruction. In order to work around this difficulty, teachers should make certain they have the child's attention before beginning instruction. This can, of course, best be accomplished by working with the child one-on-one or in a small group. Because this is usually impossible, teachers can use other strategies, such as standing next to the child, placing a hand on the child's shoulder, maintaining eye contact, and frequently asking direct questions to make certain the student is following along. When giving directions for a particular assignment, it may sometimes be necessary to repeat instructions individually for the child, or to ask him or her to repeat the instructions to make certain that he or she understands what is expected.

Directions for specific tasks or assignments should be stated precisely and simply. Young children should only be given one direction at a time.

Older children may be able to remember two or three directions, but if the directions are at all complex, they should be put in writing. Teachers must specify clearly what they expect. For example, teachers should not ask the child with ADD to "Organize your materials to go home." Instead, the child should be told to "Check to make certain you have your math book, homework assignment, and notebook."

The child with ADD often becomes overwhelmed when faced with a large assignment. Teachers can help overcome this obstacle by breaking down tasks into small, manageable segments. For example, if the child has a page of 50 math problems to complete, the teacher should cover up 40 of them and tell the child only to complete the first ten. After the first ten are completed, verbal praise should be provided, and the next ten problems should be uncovered. This procedure should be continued until all 50 problems are complete. Gradually, the child can be taught to break assignments into segments on his or her own and to provide his or her own verbal reinforcement.

It may also be beneficial to set a reasonable time limit for completion of each task. A kitchen timer will be helpful, as the child may not have a good concept of how much time is passing. Using the previous example, the teacher might tell the child he has ten minutes to complete the first ten problems. The teacher should then set the timer and come back when it rings. The child should be reinforced for completion of the segment, and the process repeated. The time limits can be adjusted as appropriate.

Teachers should attempt, as much as possible, to cut down on the number of distractions for the child with ADD. Whenever possible, instruction should be provided individually or in small group settings. When instruction is provided in large group settings, the child should be seated near the teacher. When independent work is required, the child might benefit from the use of a study carrel. Alternatively, the child might be allowed to go to the library or other quiet place that would be relatively free of distractions. These strategies should only be used if they can be done in such a way that the child does not feel he or she is being punished by the isolation (for the obvious reason of the child's self-concept).

The classroom environment may also need to be modified for the child with ADD. Too many posters, bulletin boards, and equipment will add unnecessary distraction. An "open space" environment is especially inappropriate because it prevents the teacher from controlling external auditory and visual distractions.

Teachers should attempt to provide plenty of reinforcement for successful completion of tasks. Verbal praise should be provided whenever there is improvement in the child's ability to complete tasks, work independently, or pay attention. Teachers should not expect major changes to happen quickly. By reinforcing the small gains, teachers can motivate the child to work toward larger gains.

These suggestions are for increasing structure and consistency for the child with ADD. If there are specific behaviors that need improvement, teachers should be encouraged to establish a behavior management system, which will be described Chapter 9.

Home-Based Accommodations to Increase Structure and Consistency

Some parents will need assistance from the professional team in providing the extra support, structure, and consistency their child needs. Depending upon the parents' level of sophistication, willingness to cooperate, and own level of organization, they may or may not need assistance in implementing the following strategies. The interdisciplinary team should not assume, however, that parents will be able to follow through in establishing effective behavior management strategies on their own. Regular follow-up will be needed to assist parents with this task. (See Chapter 10 for a discussion of follow-up with the families of learning-disabled children).

The interdisciplinary team may want to share with the child's parents the following suggestions for home management of children with ADD.

Parents should attempt to increase the structure of the daily routine. Children with ADD have difficulty making transitions from one activity to another. It is important, therefore, to keep the daily routine as consistent as possible. Parents should try, as much as possible, to have the child do daily tasks—such as getting up in the morning, getting ready for school, eating meals, starting homework, getting ready for bed, bedtime—at the same time every day. As much as possible, the child should be allowed to finish each task before being asked to start another. For example, parents should not set up the daily schedule so that breakfast comes in the middle of getting ready for school.

A child with ADD will have more difficulty in paying attention to directions. In order to work around this difficulty, parents should make certain they have the child's attention before giving instructions. For example, parents should not walk through the den and say "Pick up your shoes" while the child is watching television if they really expect the job to be done. Instead, the parent should first cut down on all distractions as much as possible (turn the television off for a moment or get the child away from his or her friends or toys for a moment). The child should be called by name, and the parent should wait for a verbal response and eye contact. Instructions should be stated clearly and simply. Younger children should be given only one instruction at a time. Older children may be able to remember two or more directions, but if the directions are at all complex, they will need to be put in writing. The child might be asked to repeat the instructions so the parent knows the child understands what is expected.

When giving instructions parents should specify clearly what they expect. For example, the child with ADD should not be told to "clean your room." Instead, parents should indicate specifically what they mean by "clean your room." (The parent's idea of a clean room and the child's idea of a clean room are probably not the same.) Parents might, for example, say instead, "Pick up your clothes. Put the dirty ones in the hamper. Hang up the clean clothes. Put toys in the toy chest. Empty your waste basket. Make your bed." (Instructions, should not, however, be presented all at one time. Parents may need to give each instruction separately and check to see whether the child has carried it out before giving the next instruction, or instructions might be put in writing.)

The child with ADD often becomes overwhelmed when faced with a large assignment. Parents can help the child overcome this obstacle by breaking down tasks into small, manageable segments. For example, if the child has difficulty getting himself ready for school, the parent might divide the task into segments by first asking the child to wash his hands and face. After this is done, the parent should provide verbal praise and tell the child to get dressed. This procedure can be continued until all steps of the larger task have been completed. Gradually, the child can be taught to break tasks into segments without help and to provide his own verbal reinforcement.

It may also be beneficial to set a reasonable time limit for completion of each segment of a task. A kitchen timer will be helpful for the child who does not have a good concept of how much time has passed. The timer can be set, and the parent can come back when the timer rings. The child should be reinforced for completion of the segment, and the process repeated. Time limits should be adjusted as appropriate.

If the task assigned is one that requires any amount of concentration, parents should attempt to cut down on the number of distractions as much as possible. Homework should not be completed in front of the television or in a room full of activity. Telephone calls should not be allowed during homework time. Some children complete homework best if sent to their room to work alone, but it is important to remember that even a quiet room may have lots of distractions, such as toys and books. (It is also important to remember that the child with ADD can create his or her own distractions!) It may be more convenient for parents to provide the supervision needed by having the child sit at the kitchen table or other centralized place, assuming that the area can be kept fairly quiet. Parents will need to experiment to see what works best for them and their child.

Parents should provide lots of reinforcement for successful completion of tasks. It is unreasonable to expect behaviors to change in one day. Parents must keep in mind how long it took the child to develop the bad habits they are attempting to correct, and realize that the resolution of these problems may also entail a great deal of time. Praise should be provided whenever improvement is observed, no matter how slight that improvement is. Parents should be encouraged to be patient and not give up.

Although the previous suggestions are based on psychological principles that have been tested and proven over the years, there are always exceptions to every rule. It is important for parents to remember that the list contains suggestions for helping their child work around attention problems, not steadfast rules. The suggestions should be implemented consistently for a few weeks. If something is not working, parents should experiment on their own to see if they can find a better approach.

These suggestions are for the management of general behaviors. If there are specific behaviors that need improvement, parents should be encouraged to establish a behavior management system, as described in Chapter 9.

USE OF STIMULANT MEDICATION (METHYLPHENIDATE, RITALIN)

Approximately 50 years ago, a chance observation was made that stimulant medications (amphetamines) improved school performance and behavior and had a paradoxical calming effect on hyperactivity. The use of stimulant medications proliferated, until by the late 1960s about 10 percent of children attending public schools were taking them. In the 1980s, however, about 1.5 percent of school children in the Baltimore school system received stimulant medications. This current decreased utilization of these medications reflects their earlier widespread misuse. Specifically, they were frequently used as a first recourse rather than as a component of a comprehensive remediation program (including environmental accommodations and behavioral modifications). They were frequently used as a "cure-all," which delayed implementation of more appropriate and specific interventions, and commonly, no monitoring systems were in place to assess their efficacy and needs for continuance. Secondary to these abuses, usage of stimulant medication has decreased to a point at present where it may, if anything, be underutilized.

Institution of stimulant medication can be considered with any child who exhibits symptomatology compatible with ADD, and after evaluation of cognitive potential, academic achievement level, and assessment of the appropriateness of the existing academic placement. It should be remembered that stimulant medication is only one part of the management program for the child with ADD. All team members participating in management of the learning-disabled and attention-deficit-disordered child will need to ensure that other important treatment modalities are not ignored.

The major stimulant medication employed with children with ADD is methylphenidate (Ritalin). It is our opinion that related central nervous system stimulants (e.g., dextroamphetamine [Dexedrine] and pemoline [Cylert]) have no particular pharmacologic advantage over methylphenidate, and the physician is best off learning to use one of these medications effectively. In this discussion methylphenidate (Ritalin) will be used as a prototype for these medications.

It is important to appreciate that, both diagnostically and therapeutically, disorders of attention (ADD) and a physically high motor activity level (hyperactivity) may exist separately or together. A number of studies point out that acute control of excessive motor activity level (hyperactivity) with methylphenidate does not necessarily ensure academic improvement. In general, as the dosage of methylphenidate is raised, a child will become quieter. However, above a certain dosage (around 1.0 mg/kg/dose), the child's academic performance may start to decrease, even though he or she is physically less motor active. A dosage of methylphenidate of approximately 0.3 mg/kg/dose is generally better for improving attention span and decreasing impulsivity, although it may not always reduce physical motor activity level (hyperactivity). Our recommendation is that a dosage of approximately 0.3 mg/kg/dose be used as a guideline, to be adjusted on an individual basis. Side effects, consisting chiefly of loss of appetite and disturbance of sleep, can be minimized by starting with a low dosage (perhaps one-half of the anticipated optimal dosage) and increasing gradually for the first week or two to the optimal level (the smallest effective dosage).

The short-term benefits of stimulant medication are easily demonstrated and may include improvement in attention span and in relationships with peers, improvement on visual-motor tasks (handwriting), and decreased impulsiveness. Stimulant medication should be initiated on an empirical basis and should be continued based on feedback from the parents and school regarding its effects on attention span and impulse control. In this feedback process it is important to apprise parents and school personnel of what stimulant medication can and cannot do.

The desired effect is an improvement in attention span and impulse control, that is, the components of primary, neurologically based ADD. Stimulant medication will not impact on behavioral problems under the child's willful control, such as oppositionalism, non-compliance, and attention-seeking. Because problems of ADD (not under willful control, but affected by stimulant medication) and attention-seeking behaviors (under willful control, and not affected by stimulant medication) are typically found together in learning-disabled children, it is requisite that parents and school personnel be aware of what specifically to monitor when stimulant medication is employed. If they are not, they may erroneously conclude that medication has not helped (with willful behavior problems) and it may be discontinued prematurely.

The other responsibilities in monitoring stimulant medication usage are to know about its rate of metabolism, dosage adjustment, and when to discontinue it. Methylphenidate has a very short half-life in the blood stream of approximately 3 to 4 hours. This has several important ramifications for its administration:

1. Children will typically require two doses (approximately 8 A.M. and noontime) to cover the typical school day. If they are having attentional interference with homework activities, they may require a third dose in the day, typically around 4 P.M.

2. Because of the rapid rate of metabolism, one is not concerned with the total dose administered in 24 hours, but rather with what is the correct individual dosage at any one time. This means that if the correct dosage at any one time is, for example, 10 mg, then this same dosage should be used at other times of administration in the day. One does not reduce subsequent dosages out of concern for the cumulative amount taken in the day.

3. A dosage of approximately 0.3 mg/kg/dose is only a rough guideline (which implies that the typical school age child will be taking approximately 10 mg/dose) and the dosage will have to adjusted to fit each child. One usually starts with a somewhat lower dosage (e.g., 5 mg) and slowly increases the dosage to obtain the desired improvement in attention span and impulse control.

4. Professionals sometimes wrongly advise families that children will outgrow their ADD symptomatology at some magical age, particularly in adolescence. This may be generally true, but it is not inviolate. The best way to handle this situation is to monitor periodically the needs for continuance of medication. This can be handled by giving a child drug vacations on a once or twice a year basis, monitoring attention span and impulse control before and after these drug interruptions. In order to remove day-to-day variations in performance, except in very obvious situations, these trials should be of approximately one to two weeks duration. If needs for continuance are monitored in this fashion, legitimate objections about open-ended medication usage can be obviated.

CONCLUSION

Learning disability and ADD represent primary, neurologically based handicapping conditions, which are in large part beyond the child's control. Chapters 7 and 8 have addressed remediation of these primary handicapping conditions. It can be argued that separation of the learning-disabled child's problems into primary handicapping conditions (e.g., learning disability and ADD) and secondary handicapping conditions (e.g., attention-seeking behaviors and poor self-concept) is artificial, in the sense that a learning-disabled child will typically have a mixture of these problems. Nevertheless, we feel that it is useful when thinking about remediation to initially separate the child's problems into those that are neurologically based (and beyond the child's control) and those that are more emotionally and behaviorally based.

The first step in addressing the learning-disabled child's needs will be to identify a remediation setting (as discussed in Chapter 7) that can provide an individualized educational course appropriate for the child's cognitive and academic strengths and weaknesses. The second step is to ensure that appropriate home-based and school-based accommodations are in place to help the child focus attention and control impulsivity. If the child continues to show attention deficits and poor impulse control, additional therapies, including stimulant medication (methylphenidate, Ritalin) can be instituted. Even when an individualized educational plan is established and primary ADD is addressed in this fashion, most learning-disabled children will be left with some secondary handicaps (e.g., attention-seeking behaviors and poor self-concept). Suggestions for minimizing these problems will be discussed in the following chapter.

CHAPTER 9

Planning For Treatment of Secondary Handicapping Conditions

Elizabeth H. Aylward
Frank R. Brown, III

T he primary handicapping conditions of the learning-disabled child (learning disabilities, speech-language disabilities, gross and fine motor dyscoordination, and ADD) are, as discussed in Chapters 7 and 8, "part of the child's wiring" and are, as such, somewhat out of his or her control. The strategies discussed for dealing with these primary handicapping conditions (e.g., individualized educational programs, accommodations both at home and school to increase structure and consistency, and stimulant medication), although appropriate given our present understanding of learning disabilities, are often inadequate to resolve the primary handicaps. As a result, the learning-disabled child may not receive the usual "strokes" that go along with school success, and is very apt to resort to inappropriate attention-seeking behaviors to get the recognition that would otherwise not be received. Additionally, learning-disabled children are cognizant of the fact that their performance does not measure up to the standard of the group, resulting in poor self-concept. Inappropriate attention-seeking behaviors and poor self-concept are examples of secondary handicapping conditions that parents and professionals must attempt to prevent or minimize. This chapter presents strategies for managing these secondary behavioral and emotional problems. It is our opinion that implementation of these strategies is most important for ensuring optimal outcome.

MANAGING BEHAVIOR PROBLEMS

Establishing a Behavior Management System

If there are specific behaviors upon which parents and teachers would like to see the child improve, or certain tasks that need to be completed with less supervision, it may be worthwhile to establish a behavior management system. Quite simply, a behavior management system requires that the desired behaviors be specified clearly, that the child's performance on these behaviors be carefully recorded, and that successful performance be systematically rewarded. The key is consistency, both in recording the child's performance and in administering rewards.

Steps are offered for establishing a behavior management system. They are equally appropriate for the home and the classroom. In some cases, parents and teachers may want to work together to create one behavior management system that covers both home and school behaviors. In order to do this, the teacher might be asked to send home a report each day that tells how many objectives the child accomplished at school. Parents can record on the home behavior management system the child's performance on school objectives. Parents can be responsible for providing a reward at the end of the week if both home and school objectives have been met by the child.

The behavior managment system requires a commitment from the parent or teacher who chooses to establish one. A behavior management system should not be attempted by parents or teachers who do not have the motivation or time to carry through with it. This will only result in the child being taught that parents or teachers do not follow through with their own goals. On the other hand, teachers and parents should remind themselves that it may be easier to work hard to control some undesirable behaviors than to ignore them and have them escalate into more serious problems in the future.

The first step in establishing a behavior management system is to specify the behaviors or tasks upon which the child needs to improve. Objectives for improving the child's behavior and completing tasks should be outlined in writing. In order to do this, the parent or teacher should list the daily tasks that the child is expected to complete, being as specific as possible. For home behavior management, the list should include the child's assigned chores (e.g., clearing the dinner dishes, emptying waste baskets, feeding pets), as well as other tasks that the child may have difficulty completing independently (e.g., getting ready for school on time, completing homework assignments, taking baths). At school, various regular tasks should be listed (e.g., copying the homework assignment, completing daily assignments in reading, spelling, and arithmetic, participating in social studies discussion). Parents and teachers should be specific regarding their expectations. For example, instead of listing "Get ready for school on time," parents may need to specify "Get dressed, brush teeth, wash hands and face before 7:30 A.M." The list can also include behaviors parents and teachers would like to see the child improve. As much as possible, these should be stated in a positive way. For example, instead of listing "Don't wander around the classroom," the teacher might want to state "Ask permission before leaving your seat." It may be more difficult to specify the behaviors that need improvement than the tasks to be completed, but again teachers and parents should try to be as specific as possible. For example, "Be polite to parents," should not be included as an item. Instead, parents may want to specify "Say please and thank you when appropriate, wait your turn before speaking, and look at your parents when they are speaking to you."

The list of objectives should be discussed with the child. The child should have some input regarding which household chores he or she would prefer and when he or she might prefer doing them. Parents and teachers should discuss with the child the reasons they would like the child to take more responsibility for personal tasks and to improve certain behaviors. The child should not be allowed to dictate the list, but his or her cooperation should be elicited in setting objectives.

In selecting objectives on which to begin the behavior management system, the parent or teacher should choose four or five critical objectives on which to start, together with two or three easy objectives. All of the child's shortcomings cannot be expected to improve at once. Both adult and child will become frustrated if the behavior management system attempts to address too extensive a list of objectives. By initially targeting a few selected critical and easy behaviors, and demonstrating some immediate success with these, parents and teachers will be more likely to maintain motivation for continuing the system, and will generalize the system to deal with additional behaviors in their listings.

For each of the objectives selected, the parent or teacher should set reasonable time limits (if appropriate), criteria for success (if appropriate), and any other limitations or restrictions for successful completion. For example, if the objective is "Start your homework on your own," it may be desirable to set a time limit (e.g., "Before 7:30 P.M."). If the objective is "Complete 25 math problems," a criteria for success can be added (e.g., "with at least 90 percent accuracy"). If the objective is "empty the wastebaskets in all rooms every day," the restriction "without reminders" might be added. Clearly, it is inappropriate to set time limits and criteria for each objective. This should be done only when it helps to clarify the expectations for completion of the objective.

The next step is to set up a checklist where objectives are listed down the side of a sheet of paper, and days of the week are listed across the top of the page. (See Tables 9-1 and 9-2.) If some objectives are to be accomplished only on certain days, x's should be placed in the boxes corresponding to the days on which objectives are not to be completed. The child's successful completion of each objective will be recorded each day, with either a check or sticker in the corresponding box. It is important that the child's performance be recorded consistently every day. Parents and teachers should not wait until the end of the week and try to remember what objectives were achieved each day.

TABLE 9-1

Sample Behavior Management System to Be Used at Home

OBJECTIVES	Mon	Tues	Wed	Thurs	Fri	Sat	Sun
Make bed every morning before 7 A.M. without reminder (10 A.M. on nonschool days).							
Get ready for school (wash face, get dressed, get books and papers together, eat breakfast, brush teeth) before 7:30 A.M. without reminders.						X	X
Take out trash cans on garbage pick-up days before school, with one reminder.	X		X	X		X	X
Keep your hands to yourself when playing with your sister.							
Start homework on your own before 7 P.M. without reminder.						X	X

Criteria for reward: Successful completion of 18 out of 26 objectives.

Reward: Going bowling on Saturday with Dad and a friend.

TABLE 9-2

Sample Behavior Management System to Be Used at School

OBJECTIVES	Mon	Tues	Wed	Thurs	Fri
Be seated and have materials on your desk by 8:30 A.M.					
Complete daily assignment in arithmetic without supervision, within a 20 minute time limit, with 90 percent accuracy.					
Ask permission before leaving your seat 90 percent of the time.					
Participate in social studies discussion by making at least two appropriate comments, without being asked by the teacher.					
Walk quietly in the halls.					

Criteria for reward: Successful completion of 20 out of the 25 objectives.

Reward: One-half hour of "free time" on Friday, to be spent on playground, in the classroom, or in the library.

The behavior management system is based on reward for successful completion of objectives. First, parents or teachers need to decide how many of the objectives must be successfully accomplished within a week in order for the child to earn a specific reward. The behavior management system outlined in Table 9-1 has 26 spaces for recording successful behavior. It is a good idea to start with a fairly easy criteria (e.g., "18 of 26 objectives must be met in order to receive a reward at the end of the week"). The number of objectives selected for criteria will depend on the difficulty of the objectives and on the likelihood that the child will be able to complete them. The number of objectives necessary for reward can be increased as the system continues and the child achieves more success.

The next step is to work with the child in deciding what would be an appropriate reward for successful completion of the prescribed number of objectives. It will be important to provide verbal praise for the completion of each objective every day. However, more tangible reinforcement will be necessary for rewarding the child for success at the end of the week. Parents should not get carried away with promises of expensive toys or activities. They should keep in mind that they may have to provide the reward every week. Some rewards that might be appropriate for the behavior management system at home include:

☐ Staying up until midnight on Saturday night to watch a special movie (one that has already been approved)
☐ Having a friend spend the night on a weekend
☐ Money for roller skating, movie, or bowling
☐ Purchase of a small toy, perhaps part of a collection the child has started
☐ Going to lunch or on an outing with mom or dad, without siblings

Rewards that might be appropriate for the behavior management system at school include:

☐ A half-hour of "free time" on Friday afternoon
☐ Being selected as the teacher's "special helper" to run errands or help younger students
☐ Being allowed to use special materials for an art project of the child's choice
☐ Being allowed to play with a particular group of educational toys
☐ Participating on a particular class outing

The teacher might also be able to solicit cooperation from parents in providing a reward for appropriate school behavior.

In selecting a reward, parents and teachers should keep the following in mind:

☐ The reward should be obtainable at the end of the week. Parents should not tell the child, for example, that he or she can have a big reward, such as a bicycle, if he or she succeeds on the objectives for ten weeks in a row. Similarly, a teacher who promises the child an "A" at the end of the term may not be able to elicit much motivation for the system. Most children cannot delay gratification much longer than a week and will lose interest in the system.
☐ The reward should not be a continuation of privileges the child already has. That is, the child should not be threatened with the removal of existing privileges if he or she does not meet criteria.
☐ Money can be used as a reinforcer if parents desire. However, it is better to earmark the money for a particular purchase so that the child has something to work toward. It is better not to use this with younger children, and probably should be used only if the parent and child cannot think of less mercenary reinforcers.

☐ If possible, reinforcers should be chosen that incorporate values parents and teachers would like to see developed (e.g., family togetherness, sharing with classmates, socializing with friends, physical fitness).

☐ If the child does not meet the criteria, parents and teachers must be consistent in not administering rewards, so they should not select as a reward something they intend for the child to have regardless of his or her behavior (e.g., summer camp, birthday party, class picnic).

It may be necessary with very young children (under 6 years) to provide reinforcement on a daily basis rather than on a weekly basis. If so, the parent or teacher should use the same procedure outlined, but make the reward smaller (e.g., playing a game of the child's choice with mom or dad for a half-hour before going to bed, choosing the story that will be read to the class). The time between reinforcers can gradually be lengthened as the child gets older and begins to have consistent success with the system.

Parents and teachers should make certain the child understands the rules of the system from the outset and understands what the reward will be. If the child thinks something about the system is unfair, the problem should be worked out before starting the system, if possible.

The child's success on each objective should be recorded every day. The child can be allowed to put stickers or checks in the boxes on the chart, with supervision.

At the end of the week the parent or teacher should review the child's progress with him or her. If the child does not meet criteria, the parent or teacher should not scold, but should stay calm and say, "We'll try it again next week." (If the system is begun with fairly easy criteria for reinforcement, failure can be avoided in the beginning. Parents and teachers should remember that the objective is to have the child succeed!) The parent or teacher may want to spend some time with the child discussing where he or she experienced the greatest difficulty in meeting the objectives and suggest some ways to help him or her do better next week. If the child has succeeded in reaching the criteria for reinforcement, parents or teachers should provide verbal praise, tell the child how proud they are of his or her accomplishments, and make arrangements for administering the reward as soon as possible. If the child has succeeded in reaching the criteria for reward several weeks in a row, the difficulty for reaching criteria can be increased, either by adding new objectives or by requiring that more of the existing objectives be met each week.

If the child does not reach criteria for reward, no matter how close he or she came, the reward must not be administered. If it is administered, the parent or teacher will be teaching the child to see how little he or she can get away with doing and still get the reward.

In summary, parents or teachers should clearly specify what is expected, the criteria for earning the reward, and what the reward will be.

They must be consistent in recording daily performance and in administering the rewards. Plenty of verbal praise should be given along the way. Nagging and criticism should be avoided.

Psychotherapy for Behavior Problems

The two defining characteristics of ADD are inattention and impulsivity. The child with ADD often misbehaves because he or she impulsively acts before thinking about the consequences of his or her behavior. Therapists have attempted to modify impulsive behavior through many techniques, including imposed delay, modeling, identification of failures, establishing response cost contingencies, and self-instructional training (Kendall and Finch, 1979). One type of therapy that appears to have good potential for success is cognitive behavior therapy. Using this approach, therapists teach children strategies for thinking before responding. In some cases, modeling, self-instruction, and response-cost contingencies are used as part of the training. Some programs (e.g., the "think aloud" program developed by Camp, Blom, Herbert, and Van Doornenck, 1977) emphasize social behaviors by teaching children to evaluate how their behavior affects others, to develop alternative strategies for addressing conflicts, and to think before acting. As with most therapies, the success of cognitive behavior therapy depends a great deal on the skill of the therapist. Furthermore, the strategies presented during therapy do not always generalize sufficiently to situations outside the therapy session. Despite these common drawbacks of psychotherapy, cognitive behavior therapy appears to be quite appropriate for many children with ADD, especially those with good verbal skills.

MANAGING SECONDARY EMOTIONAL DISTURBANCE

The most common emotional disturbance observed in children with learning disability or ADD is poor self-concept. After years of academic failure, social failure, and criticism from parents and teachers, this outcome is not at all surprising. Parents and teachers should make efforts to maintain a young child's self-concept before the effects of learning disability and ADD have a chance to damage it. For the older child whose learning disabilities and ADD are not diagnosed until after self-concept is damaged, special accommodations will be needed to help the child feel more positive about himself or herself. The following suggestions are appropriate for either maintaining or remediating poor self-concept:

The child should be encouraged to participate in structured nonacademic group activities that will allow him or her to compete successfully with peers in areas where he or she is not so far behind. Because so much of the learning-disabled child's poor self-concept derives from academic problems at school, it is especially important to identify, if possible, school-related activities in which the child may be expected to succeed (e.g., participation in school athletics, clubs, and offices). All too often the learning-disabled child is excluded from these activities because of poor grades. These extracurricular activities may be important in drawing the child back into what is inherently a difficult learning process.

Parents and teachers should attempt to identify and encourage any special strengths or talents a child might have (e.g., music, art, leadership, creative writing). It is important for the child to be able to achieve success and earn praise for some special skill or talent, especially if academic achievement is not a source of positive reinforcement.

Parents should make efforts to identify, encourage, and praise strengths that distinguish the child from siblings, especially if siblings are perceived by the child as more successful.

Parents and teachers should make efforts to provide the child with special responsibilities that the child can handle with success. For example, the teacher might regularly ask the child to take messages to the school office, to assist in classroom "chores" (e.g., taking inventory of materials, organizing shelves, taking attendance), to assist younger students, or act as a member of the safety patrol. If possible, the child should be given opportunities that will allow him or her to feel important in the eyes of peers. For example, he or she might be allowed to assist the teacher in directing the class play, teach a lesson on a subject in which he or she has particular expertise, or share a special experience with the class.

The child should be praised for good attempts at new activities, regardless of the outcome of these efforts.

Parents and teachers should solicit the child's input when planning activities. Whenever possible, the child's suggestions should be incorporated into the plans in order to make him or her feel that his or her input is valued.

In general, parents and teachers should attempt to make the child feel that he or she is special in a positive sense in order to overcome all of the negative attention he or she receives as a result of learning disabilities and attention problems. Parents and teachers must become attuned to every opportunity that warrants praise and reinforcement. If strategies for maintaining self-concept are integrated into the educational process as soon as academic difficulties are identified, serious behavioral and emotional problems may be obviated. Sadly, the maintenance of self-concept is sometimes ignored until problems have gotten out of hand. When efforts by teachers and parents are insufficient or delayed, psychotherapy is often necessary. Although poor self-concept is the most common emotional disturbance observed in conjunction with learning disabilities and ADD, other concomitant disorders can include depression, school phobia, eating disorders, substance abuse, excessive tension, anger, or hostility. Most parents and school personnel are unequipped to deal with these more serious emotional disturbances. In these cases, professional counseling for the child must be sought. The physician may be able to help convince the parent of this need and to assist in selecting an appropriate therapist. Family therapy is often necessary when the child's learning disabilities or ADD have led to conflict within the family situation.

CONCLUSION

Strategies discussed in Chapters 7 and 8 for dealing with primary handicapping conditions are often inadequate to fully resolve the problems. As a result, the learning disabled child often experiences secondary handicapping conditions, including behavior problems and poor self-concept. Strategies for dealing with behavior problems include the establishment of behavior management systems, both at home and school, and, when necessary, psychotherapy. Poor self-concept is addressed through the consistent application of positive reinforcement. If these strategies for handling behavior problems and maintaining self-concept are consistently employed, many of the secondary handicapping conditions can be minimized or avoided altogether.

CHAPTER 10

The Summary Conference

Frank R. Brown, III
Elizabeth H. Aylward

The goal of the interdisciplinary team process, as described in the preceding chapters, is to develop a consensus opinion regarding diagnoses and to formulate a comprehensive treatment plan. An equally essential element of the diagnostic and prescriptive process is to convey findings and recommendations of the interdisciplinary team to the parents (and, when appropriate, to the child) through a summary conference. The individual assigned this responsibility (usually the case manager) has a very difficult and important responsibility; this is the subject of the final chapter.

In theory, and in the best of circumstances, any professional participating in the interdisciplinary team process should be capable of functioning as case manager and could be assigned the responsibility of explaining the diagnoses and therapeutic recommendations to the parents and child. It is imperative, however, that the case manager understand, at least to a reasonably complete degree, all the factors involved in formulating the interdisciplinary diagnoses and therapeutic recommendations. It is not sufficient for the case manager to understand only his or her own discipline's perspective, as the result would reflect this limited perspective and bias. The person conducting the summary conference should have a good breadth of understanding of the learning-disabled child and his or her family, and should be able to articulate the team's findings and recommendations to the family in a comprehensive, unbiased, and sensitive way. In particularly difficult cases, it may be beneficial to have several team members present at the summary conference in order to support the case manager's presentation.

The case manager may want to begin the conference by asking the parents to reiterate the concerns and goals they had at the time the evaluation was initiated. Concerns of the individual who initiated the referral (if not the parents) should also be discussed. With these concerns and goals in mind, the case manager can conduct a conference that will produce appropriate closure on the parent's agenda and, when necessary, expand this agenda to reflect additional diagnostic concerns and therapeutic recommendations from the team's perspective.

PRESENTATION OF THE DIAGNOSES

Throughout this book we have attempted to clearly distinguish between primary (neurologically based) and secondary (derivative of primary) handicapping conditions. It is important that the case manager share this distinction with the parents. By making this distinction, the case manager provides the parents and child with a logical and effective framework for the discussion of diagnoses and therapeutic recommendations.

Diagnoses of Primary Handicapping Conditions

In presenting the team's diagnostic data, the case manager will need to define some terms for the parents, especially the term *learning disability*. Throughout this book, *learning disability* has been defined as a discrepancy between cognitive ability and academic achievement, assuming that other conditions have been ruled out (see Chapter 1). It is important that parents understand the difference between intelligence and academic achievement, as many will presume that these concepts are one and the same. The difference between intelligence and academic achievement can sometimes be explained by describing the types of tasks presented on tests of intelligence (which are presumed to reflect underlying cognitive ability) and tests of academic achievement (which reflect the level of mastery of academic skills).

Following definition of terms, the case manager should review the data from the individual evaluations and highlight those findings that support or refute the diagnosis of a specific learning disability. The case manager can begin by describing any delays in early development that often correlate with subsequent learning disabilities (see Chapter 2). This will help the parents understand the long-standing developmental basis of their child's primary handicapping conditions.

Next, the case manager will present data regarding potential for academic achievement, as defined by the results of the psychologist's formal cognitive assessment. Overall cognitive assessment should be discussed, as well as any significant strengths and weaknesses within the cognitive profile (see Chapter 3).

When discussing the child's academic achievement, it is important to present both the results of the formal achievement tests and the classroom teachers' present and past perspectives on the child's rate of progress (see Chapter 4). Strengths and weaknesses within the academic achievement profile should also be discussed with the parents.

After the case manager has explained the defining characteristics of learning disabilities and has outlined any significant discrepancies between cognitive ability and academic achievement, the diagnostic conclusion regarding the presence or absence of learning disabilities should be quite clear to the parents. Definition of relevant individual learning disabilities (dyslexia, dyscalculia, dysgraphia) will further clarify the diagnosis (see Chapter 1). The case manager should help the parents understand how the learning disabilities will interfere with school performance and how the disabilities may prevent the child from learning through traditional approaches.

Following discussion of learning disabilities, the case manager should introduce any other primary handicapping conditions diagnosed by the team (e.g., attention deficit disorder [ADD] with or without hyperactivity, language disabilities, fine and gross motor dyscoordination). As with the discussion of learning disabilities, the case manager will need to clearly define the terms associated with each individual diagnosis. Then data to support or refute each diagnosis should be presented. This data will include test results as well as information obtained through the teacher interview, parent interview, classroom observation, and observation of the child during testing. The case manager should explain how these associated primary conditions will interfere with school performance. For example, parents should be able to easily understand that ADD may result in inconsistent application to task, fluctuating academic performance, and failure to follow directions.

Diagnoses of Secondary Handicapping Conditions

The case manager should next focus discussion on any secondary handicapping conditions that have been diagnosed or are suspected (e.g., poor self-esteem, behavioral problems). Their definitions, diagnostic features, and implications should be discussed. Data relevant to these conditions may include test results, but will more typically involve information obtained through interviews and observation.

At this point, it will be helpful for the case manager to review the relevant diagnoses and their definitions, and to discuss the relationships among the diagnosed conditions. Parents should understand that the primary handicapping conditions are neurologically based, whereas secondary handicapping conditions have probably occurred as a result of the primary disabilities.

It is especially important that the case manager clarify the distinction between primary and secondary handicapping conditions when discussing ADD and attention-seeking behavior (see Chapter 8). It should be emphasized that ADD represents a primary disability frequently associated with learning disabilities, which is to a large extent out of the child's control. This is contrasted with attention-seeking behaviors, which are frequently a secondary condition representing the child's underlying frustration in dealing with the primary handicapping conditions. These attention-seeking behaviors can, with assistance, be brought under the child's willful control. Although these conditions often overlap and may be very difficult to disentangle, it is important that the parents understand the distinction between them before therapeutic recommendations are presented.

PRESENTATION OF THERAPEUTIC RECOMMENDATIONS

Following explanation of the diagnoses, the parents' first question will probably be "What do we do about these problems?" The case manager should attempt to respond to this question by systematically reviewing the types of treatment and accommodations appropriate for each specific diagnosis. In discussing these recommendations, the case manager will find it helpful to again use a format based on the distinction between primary and secondary handicapping conditions.

Therapeutic Recommendations for Primary Handicapping Conditions

The case manager should present the team's therapeutic recommendations by first discussing the relatively straight forward procedures used to address the learning disabilities. The issue of special education services should be presented by explaining to parents that their child's learning disabilities prevent him or her from being taught effectively using traditional approaches. Parents should be provided with information regarding the types of special education services that might be available through the school and introduced to the procedures for obtaining these services.

Following this general introduction, the case manager should discuss with the parents some of the specialized terminology they will encounter when they meet with the Individualized Educational Plan (IEP) development team at their child's school. Some of this terminology will be used in discussing the amount of time the child spends in special programming (e.g., resource classroom, levels of special education service). Other terms will be used in discussing special education methods to which the child will be exposed (e.g., VAKT approach, language-experience approach). It is important that parents be familiar with these terms, as this type of "jargon" is often used by school personnel during the IEP development conference without adequate explanation. If the interdisciplinary team wishes to recommend any other educational treatment (e.g., tutoring, vocational education) or alternative school placements, these options should also be presented.

Next, the case manager should discuss any special accommodations that the child's teachers (regular or special education) will need to make to circumvent additional primary handicapping conditions often associated with learning disabilities. For example, if the child's handwriting is slow and inefficient, the parents need to understand what types of accommodations the child's teachers should be making (see Chapter 7). Similarly, if the child has ADD the parents should expect special classroom accommodations to be implemented (see Chapter 8).

The case manager should also discuss the parents' role in the management of primary handicapping conditions, especially ADD. Specific suggestions for home management of the child (see Chapter 8) should be reviewed with the parents. Strategies for helping the child with homework, organizational difficulties, or other problems associated with the primary handicapping conditions should also be presented.

If the interdisciplinary team (with input from the child's physician) has determined that a trial of medication for ADD is warranted, the case manager will want to convey this recommendation to the parents. The case manager, depending on his or her familiarity with the medication, may want to provide a full discussion of this topic or may instead want to recommend that the parents speak with the child's physician. In any case, it should always be made clear that the final decision regarding use of medication is to be made by the parents and the child's physician.

Therapeutic Recommendations for Secondary Handicapping Conditions

Therapeutic recommendations for the prevention or treatment of secondary handicapping conditions should be presented following discussion of the primary handicapping conditions. This area of discussion is most important because these secondary handicapping conditions, unlike the primary conditions, can almost always be prevented or eliminated, if parents and teachers deal with the child appropriately.

During the evaluation, the interdisciplinary team will have identified inappropriate attention-seeking behaviors that are a cause for concern among parents or teachers. The case manager should explain to the parents how they can help the child control these behaviors through a behavior management system (see Chapter 9). It may be necessary in some cases for the parents and school to coordinate their efforts in establishing a single behavior management system that covers inappropriate behaviors both at home and school. Strategies for establishing such a system should be discussed with the parents.

Finally, and perhaps most importantly, the case manager should discuss strategies for maintaining or improving the child's self-concept. This area is of vital importance because, when all is said and done, the child's image of himself or herself and his or her ability to relate to others are probably the greatest determinants of overall success.

Parents need to understand their role in building the child's self-concept. They should be encouraged to implement some of the specific strategies discussed in Chapter 9 (e.g., identifying and encouraging special strengths or talents, encouraging participation in structured nonacademic group activities). More importantly, they can accept the fact that the basis of many of the child's difficulties is neurological and, therefore, out of the child's control. When parents stop holding the child accountable for learning difficulties, attention problems, and poor impulse control, and focus on providing the extra structure and support needed, the child's self-concept will improve.

Parents also need to understand the school's responsibility for building the child's self-concept. They may need to work as the child's advocate to make certain that teachers each year are making the special accommodations necessary to allow the child maximum success.

ANSWERING PARENTS' QUESTIONS

Through a systematic approach of defining terms, presenting data to support or refute diagnoses, explaining how each handicapping condition will interfere with performance, and presenting therapeutic recommendations to treat or accommodate each condition, the case manager should be able to convey to the parents a fairly comprehensive understanding of their child's situation. Regardless of the case manager's skills at conveying this information, parents will no doubt have many unanswered questions. The most common of these involve the etiology and prognosis of the disorders.

Discussion of Etiology of Disorders

As discussed in Chapter 1, we view learning disabilities and associated primary handicapping conditions as neurologically based. With an understanding of the neurological basis of learning disabilities, parents are sometimes better able to recognize that the child is not at fault and cannot be held responsible for his or her difficulties. Because neurological damage in learning-disabled children is quite subtle and diffuse, the cause of this damage cannot, in most cases, be determined for certain. Parents should be discouraged then from dwelling on "what went wrong," as determination of the precise etiology of the disorders is not usually possible nor requisite in their treatment.

Discussion of Prognosis of Disorders

Parents almost always want to know "Will my child get better?" The answer to this question can almost always be answered affirmatively, because the child will continue to develop and make academic progress. (The exception to this rule would be the child whose self-concept and attitude toward school have been damaged beyond recovery.)

However, if the question is phrased "Will my child be normal?" the answer cannot be as reassuring. The neurological damage or dysfunction believed to underlie learning disabilities and concomitant conditions will not disappear. It is known, however, that certain areas of the brain can compensate for damage that has occurred in other areas. In addition, learning-disabled children (especially those who are bright) will learn strategies to compensate for areas of weakness. Unfortunately, it is not possible to determine the extent to which compensation will occur and it is, therefore, not possible to determine to what extent functions will eventually appear normal. Parents are often told that their children will "outgrow" the primary handicapping conditions, especially ADD, around the time of puberty. The case manager should caution parents that this expectation is usually unrealistic.

Despite the fact that the neurological damage or dysfunction underlying primary handicapping conditions cannot be changed, parents should not be left with the idea that remedial efforts are worthless. Special education teachers can help learning-disabled children develop strategies for compensating or working around their learning handicaps. Counselors can sometimes help children with ADD apply strategies for controlling their impulsivity. Occupational or physical therapists may be able to help the child find easier methods for accomplishing difficult motor tasks. Despite "specialists'" claims to the contrary and parents' desire for a "normal" child, the current level of understanding of learning disabilities and concomitant conditions does not permit a "cure," and parents should not expect special education teachers or therapists to be able to totally remediate the disorders.

Although special education teachers and therapists cannot be expected to completely remediate learning disabilities and concomitant conditions, they do play a very important role in determining how the child learns to accept and handle his or her disabilities. As we have emphasized several times, prevention or remediation of secondary handicapping conditions, especially inappropriate attention-seeking behaviors and poor self-concept, are vital in determining the learning-disabled child's eventual outcome. Placement in special education classes where the child is presented with materials appropriate to his or her achievement level will allow the child to experience success he or she would be unable to achieve in a regular classroom. Accommodations for poor handwriting, poor organizational skills, or attention problems will allow the child the opportunity to demonstrate what he or she is capable of doing, preventing unnecessary frustration. By implementing these strategies, as well as special techniques for handling secondary handicapping conditions, parents and teachers will be able to ensure the best possible outcome for the learning-disabled child.

PLANNING FOR FOLLOW-UP

Parents should leave the summary conference with the understanding that the interdisciplinary team will monitor implementation of the therapeutic suggestions, conduct regular evaluations of the child's progress, and revise the treatment plan as necessary. If possible, the case manager should outline for the parents any specific tasks they are expected to accomplish (e.g., meeting with the IEP development team, contacting tutors, consulting with the child's pediatrician regarding trial medication for ADD, implementing behavior management strategies). The case manager should, of course, provide as much assistance as necessary to ensure that the parents will be able to accomplish these tasks. In addition, the case manager should outline the tasks to be completed or monitored by the interdisciplinary team (e.g., preparing the IEP, helping the teacher develop a behavior management system, coordinating a medication trial with the school nurse).

The case manager should outline for the parents what types of future evaluations should be conducted (e.g., academic achievement testing only, complete psychoeducational reevaluation, additional testing by allied professionals) and when. Parents should know that the school will automatically conduct evaluations on a regular basis as long as the child receives special education. If the interdisciplinary team feels additional testing is necessary (to be conducted either through the school or privately), arrangements should be made to ensure that this occurs.

Regardless of the case manager's ability to clearly present definitions, data, diagnoses, and recommendations, parents are bound to have further questions and concerns after they leave the conference. Problems often arise as parents, teachers, and therapists experiment with various strategies for dealing with the child's disorders. The case manager should make certain that the parents feel free to contact him or her for further discussion, advice, or assistance.

CONCLUSION

This chapter has addressed the case manager's important role in conveying the results and recommendations of the interdisciplinary team process. It is suggested that the case manager present diagnoses and therapeutic recommendations using a format that clearly distinguishes between primary and secondary handicapping conditions. In order to help parents fully understand their child's disorders, the case manager must clearly define diagnostic terms, present data obtained through the evaluations that are relevant to each diagnosis, integrate the data to explain how each diagnosis was formulated, and describe how the disorders will interfere with normal functioning. Therapeutic recommendations relevant to each specific diagnosis (of both primary and secondary handicapping conditions) are then presented. Common questions regarding the etiology and prognosis of learning disabilities and concomitant conditions are discussed, with special emphasis given to the importance of preventing secondary handicapping conditions. The case manager should make certain that parents leave the summary conference with the assurance that the interdisciplinary team will monitor implementation of the therapeutic recommendations, regularly evaluate the child's progress, and revise the treatment plan as necessary. It is hoped that these procedures will make the parent feel that the interdisciplinary team has worked and will continue to work as the child's advocate in obtaining the support and understanding he or she needs for optimal outcome.

Glossary,
Appendices,
References, and
Reference List of Tests

GLOSSARY

Attention Deficit Disorder   Developmentally inappropriate lack of attention with associated poor impulse control.

Auditory-Figure Ground   The ability to selectively attend to a foreground auditory stimulus in the presence of simultaneous irrelevant auditory stimuli.

Cocontraction   Simultaneous contraction of all the muscles around a joint to stabilize it.

Criterion-Referenced Test   A test designed to determine whether or not the child has mastered specific skills. Unlike scores from norm-referenced tests, scores from criterion-referenced tests do not reflect comparison of the student with peers.

Directionality   Cognitive application of body scheme to external space. Includes cognitive concepts of up, down, in, out, beneath, on top of, beside, between, etc.

Dyscalculia   Discrepancy between arithmetic achievement and cognitive expectation.

Dyseidetic (Dyslexic)   Reading-disabled children who are unable to identify groupings of letters in patterns. They spell and read words by their sounds and consequently read very slowly, as they must sound out each word as they go.

Dysgraphia   Impairment of the ability to express thoughts in writing.

Dyslexia   Difficulty with reading, manifesting as a significant discrepancy between reading achievement and expectations based on cognitive potential.

Dysnomia   Reduced ability to retrieve and recall the names of persons, places, actions, or things.

Dysphonetic (Dyslexic)   Reading-disabled children who are unable to relate symbols to sounds and thus cannot develop phonetic word analysis skills. These children are dependent on their sight word (visually memorized) vocabulary and make bizarre spelling errors unrelated to the sound of the word.

Dyspraxia   Poor praxis or motor planning.

Educational Quotient (EQ)   A score that reflects the expected level of academic achievement. The EQ is based on a measure of intellectual functioning and takes into account the statistical phenomenon known as regression toward the mean.

Environmental Accommodations   Changes made in the home and school environment to minimize or eliminate the effects of primary handicapping conditions, especially attention deficit disorder.

Error of Measurement   An individual's "true score" on a given test is the average of the scores he or she would obtain if the test were given an infinite number of times without any effects from retesting. The error of measurement is the standard deviation of the difference between the true score and the obtained scores. The error of measurement allows the examiner to develop "confidence bands" that indicate a range of scores within which the individual's true score will fall a given percentage of time.

Fine Motor   Movements using hands and fingers for tasks requiring precision.

Gravitational Insecurity   Abnormal anxiety and distress caused by inadequate modulation or inhabition of sensations that arise when the gravity receptors of the vestibular system are stimulated by head position or movement.

Gross Motor   Movements requiring the whole body for appropriate execution. Transfer of body weight and postural adjustment is involved.

Hyperactivity   Excessive motor activity, manifested as excessive running or climbing, difficulty sitting still, or excessive movement in sleep.

Hypertonus   Increased tension in a muscle at rest or when activated; stiffness; a resistance to passive movement.

Hypotonus   Decreased tension in a muscle at rest or when activated; floppiness; exaggerated yielding to passive movement.

IEP   Individualized Educational Plan. A written outline of instructional and therapeutic strategies that will be used for the remediation of a handicapped student in special education.

Impedance Audiometry   Measures the relationship of the change in mobility of the middle ear (ear drum) as air pressure is introduced into the ear canal.

Interdisciplinary   Format of shared communication, trust, openness, respect, and interdependence between professionals in establishing a diagnosis or developing prescriptive plans.

Learning Disability   Condition whereby an individual's academic achievement level (in any specific academic area) is significantly below the level that would be predicted from the level of intellectual ability.

Minimal Brain Dysfunction (MBD)   Subtle brain dysfunction in which a child exhibits a mixture of some or all of the following: learning disabilities, language disabilities, other inconsistencies among various cognitive functions, attention deficit disorder, gross, fine, and oral motor dyscoordinations.

Neurodevelopmental Examination   Examination of the level of development in motor (gross and fine), language (expressive and receptive), visual problem solving, and social adaptive functioning.

Neurodevelopmental History   History of the temporal sequence of development in motor (gross and fine), language (expressive and receptive), visual problem solving, and social adaptive functioning.

Norm-Referenced Test   A test designed to determine how well the child performs on a particular task, in comparison with peers.

Norms   Test scores based on the performance of a representative cross-section of students, usually a national sample.

Nystagmus   An involuntary rapid back and forth eye movement usually elicited by a sudden halt to rotational movement.

Perceptual-Motor Integration   The ability to interpret and respond efficiently to information from those sensory channels concerning vision, touch, and body position.

PL 94-142   The Education for All Handicapped Children Act of 1975, which provides for free appropriate education of all handicapped children, including learning disabled children, in the least restrictive educational environment.

Primary Handicapping Conditions   Handicapping conditions for the learning-disabled child that have a neurological basis, including the learning disability itself, speech-language disabilities, gross and fine motor dyscoordination, and attention deficit disorder.

Proprioception   Conscious or unconscious awareness of body movement (direction and speed), weight, and position in space.

Regression Toward the Mean   A statistical phenomenon whereby students who score higher or lower than the mean on a given test will be expected to score nearer the mean on a subsequent test. Regression toward the mean increases as the correlation between the two tests decreases.

Reliability   The extent to which a test consistently measures what it measures. This can be measured as consistency over time (test-retest reliability), consistency across forms of the test (alternate form reliability), or consistency within the test items themselves (internal reliability).

Secondary Handicapping Conditions   Handicapping conditions that do not have a direct neurological basis, but are the result of primary (neurologically based) conditions that have not been properly managed. The most common are poor self-concept and inappropriate attention-seeking behaviors.

Sensory Integration   The ability to perceive discrete stimuli and to combine them into a meaningful whole generating an appropriate response.

Sensory Integrative Therapy   Treatment involving sensory stimulation (vestibular, proprioceptive, and tactile) with the goal of improving the way a child processes and organizes sensations.

Slow Learner   Term used to describe the child whose learning ability in all areas is delayed in comparison to children of the same chronological age. These children are characterized by low-normal to borderline intelligence, with corresponding slow academic achievement.

Soft Neurological Signs   Neurological findings that are on a developmental continuum, that is, they appear and disappear with development and maturation of the nervous system. Pathology equates with the extent of their presence and the timing of their appearance and disappearance. Mirror movements and syn-kinesias represent the most commonly encountered.

Standard Score   A type of test score that indicates how far an individual's performance deviates from the mean of the standardization sample (the representative sample from which the standard scores were derived). Standard scores for most tests have a mean of 100 and a standard deviation of 15.

Speech Discrimination Scores   Measured in percentages and referring to the person's ability to discriminate among speech sounds or words that are similar.

Speech Reception Thresholds   Measured in decibels and referring to the level at which a person can repeat words or understand conversational speech.

Synkinesis   Overflow or overshooting of muscle movements into surrounding muscle groups when a request is made for movement of an isolated muscle group.

Tactile Defensiveness   Aversive or hypersensitive response to tactile stimuli.

Validity   The extent to which a test actually measures what it purports to measure. A test's validity is determined by how well it samples from the domain of behaviors it was designed to measure (content validity), how well the test correlates with other measures of the same or similar construct (concurrent validity), how well the test predicts the child's future performance (performance validity), and how helpful the test is in understanding the construct measured (construct validity).

Vestibular System   The sensory system that responds to the position of the head in relation to gravity and accelerated or decelerated movement.

Word-Attack Skills   A child's ability to decode unknown words, based on application of phonic skills (making grapheme-phoneme equivalences) and structural analysis skills (identifying word 'parts," including root words, suffixes, and prefixes.

APPENDIX A

Parent Interview Form

Child's Name _____

Interviewee _____

1. Primary concerns: _____

2. Source of referral: _____

3. Current grade: _____

   school: _____

   teacher: _____

   special education services: _____

   type of class: _____

4. School history:

   preschool?

Grade	School	Services	Repeated?	Problems
K	_____	_____	_____	_____
1	_____	_____	_____	_____
2	_____	_____	_____	_____
3	_____	_____	_____	_____
4	_____	_____	_____	_____
5	_____	_____	_____	_____
6	_____	_____	_____	_____
7	_____	_____	_____	_____
8	_____	_____	_____	_____
9	_____	_____	_____	_____

5. Current school grades: _____

6. Teachers' complaints: _____ hyperactive

   _____ distractible

   _____ short attention span

   _____ won't stay in seat

   _____ shy/withdrawn

   _____ sloppy/disorganized

   _____ frustrated easily

   _____ talks out of turn

   _____ fails to complete assignments

183

      _____ destructive

      _____ disruptive

7. Specific weaknesses: _____ reading

      _____ arithmetic

      _____ spelling

      _____ handwriting

      _____ speech

      _____ fine motor skills

      _____ gross motor skills

      _____ hearing/vision

8. Family: _____ father   _____ mother   _____ brothers (ages: _____)

    sisters (ages: _____)   _____ other:

    parents separated? _____   how long? _____

    contact with noncustodial parent? _____

9. Language other than English at home? _____

10. Behavior problems at home?

    _____ fails to listen to and follow instructions

    _____ refuses to obey

    _____ temper tantrums

    _____ lies

    _____ steals

    _____ other

11. Chores required? _____

    type: _____

    problems: _____

12. Homework:

    How much time spent each night? _____

    How much time should be spent? _____

    Supervision required? _____

    Problems? _____

13. Many friends? _____

    Interaction with peers? _____

14. Relationship with siblings? _____

15. Extracurricular activities:

    What does the child like to do? _____

    Organized teams/groups? _____

16. Any unusual fears? _____

    Sleeping problems? _____

    Eating problems? _____

    Separation problems? _____

17. Self-concept? _____

18. Previous testing? _____

19. Family history of learning problems?

    Mother: _____

    Father: _____

    Siblings: _____

    Other family members: _____

20. Medication for attention deficit disorder?

    Started: _____   Stopped: _____   Current dosage: _____

    Schooldays/evenings/weekends/summers: _____

    Effectiveness: _____

    Problems: _____

    On medication today? _____   Time taken: _____

    Any other medications/health issues that might affect testing? _____

    _____

    _____

21. Other concerns? _____

    _____

    _____

APPENDIX B

Description of the WISC-R and WPPSI

This brief description of the WISC-R and WPPSI is intended only to give those professionals who are unfamiliar with the test an idea of the types of tasks presented. The reader who wishes further information regarding the test's statistical properties, norming samples, rationale, or administration should review the manual, preferably with the assistance of a psychologist trained to use the WISC-R with the learning-disabled population.

WISC-R

The WISC-R is designed for use with children aged 6 years 0 months through 16 years 11 months. (Other Wechsler tests are available for preschoolers and adults.) The WISC-R provides three "IQ"s[1]—a Verbal IQ (VIQ), which reflects overall language abilities, a Performance IQ (PIQ), which is associated primarily with visual-spatial perceptual skills, and a Full Scale IQ, which is a composite (but not necessarily an average) of the Verbal and Performance IQs.

VERBAL SUBTESTS. The six Verbal subtests are all presented orally and require oral responses. Only the Arithmetic subtest limits the time available for each response. Each subtest is described briefly:

Information. General information questions, such as "How many inches make a foot?" or "Who was Frank Lloyd Wright?"

Similarities. Asks the student to tell how two concepts are alike (e.g., "How are an hour and a day alike?").

Arithmetic. Word problems (e.g., "Bill made a dozen cookies and ate three of them. How many were left?" or "If Mary runs at an average rate of four miles an hour, how long would it take her to run one-half mile?").

Vocabulary. Requires the student to define a word presented by the examiner. "What is a rodeo?" "What does *fundamental* mean?"

Comprehension. Requires the student to demonstrate understanding of a social situation or everyday phenomenon (e.g., "Why should people wear seat belts when riding in a car?" "Why do children go to school?").

Digit Span. Requires the student to repeat series of digits forward and backward. (Forward series range from 3 to 9 digits; backward series range from 2 to 8 digits).

PERFORMANCE SUBTESTS. Each of the six Performance tests employs visual stimuli or materials manipulated by the student. Only the Picture Completion subtest requires a verbal response (the subject can respond to some of the items,

---

[1]The term IQ or Intelligence Quotient is derived from older tests in which the subject's cognitive abilities were summarized in a score obtained by dividing Mental Age by Chronological Age, and multiplying by 100. The term *IQ* has been retained, despite the fact that no quotient is directly calculated.

however, by pointing to missing parts of pictures). All subtests have time limits. Each subtest is described briefly:

Picture Completion. Requires the student to identify (verbally or by pointing) the part of a picture that is missing.

Picture Arrangement. Requires the student to arrange a series of pictures in order to "tell a story that makes sense."

Block Design. Requires the student to arrange the red and white cubes in a pattern to match the examiner's model or a picture of a model.

Object Assembly. Requires the student to complete six- to eight-piece picture puzzles of common objects.

Mazes. A paper-and-pencil task requiring the student to follow a path from the inside to the outside of increasingly difficult mazes.

Coding. A paper-and-pencil task in which the student is provided with a series of 93 boxes, each with a numeral, ranging from 1 to 9, in the top portion of the box. The student is provided with a code that shows what symbol is associated with each numeral. For each box, the student must write the symbol that corresponds to the number. The student completes as many boxes as possible in 2 minutes. A similar simplified version is administered to children under 8 years.

Some of the subtests have different starting points, depending on the age of the student. All subtests, except Coding and Object Assembly, are discontinued after a specified number of items are failed consecutively. On some subtests, the student is given one point for each item completed (Information, Arithmetic, Digit Span, Picture Completion, Coding). On others, the examiner must determine the quality of responses and assign 0, 1, or 2 points for each item, based on detailed scoring guidelines (Vocabulary, Similarities, and Comprehension). On the remaining subtests, points are assigned according to the speed with which items are successfully completed (Picture Arrangement, Block Design, Object Assembly), or according to the number of errors made (Mazes and Object Assembly items that are not totally correct).

For each subtest, the student's raw score is compared to performance of other children of the same age and assigned a "scaled score" between 1 and 19. For each subtest, the average scaled score is 10, with a standard deviation of 3. Five verbal subtest scaled scores (Information, Similarities, Arithmetic, Vocabulary, and Comprehension) are totalled and converted to a VIQ, using a table provided in the manual.[2] Similarly, five Performance subtest scaled scores (Picture Completion, Picture Arrangement, Block Design, Object Assembly, and Coding) are used to obtain a PIQ. The five Verbal and five Performance scaled scores are totalled and converted to a Full Scale IQ. VIQs, PIQs, and Full Scale IQs are standard scores with a mean of 100 and a standard deviation of 15. They can be converted to percentile scores for easier interpretation by those unfamiliar with standard scores. Functional levels are defined as follows:

---

[2]Although VIQs, PIQs, and Full Scale IQs are calculated from the scaled scores on five Verbal subtests and five Performance subtests, it is recommended that all twelve WISC-R subtests be administered. The amount of time required for the additional two subtests is quite small, and the information obtained from the supplemental tests, especially Digit Span, can be quite useful in understanding the nature of the child's learning difficulties.

130 and above:	Very superior
120–129:	Superior
110–119:	High average (bright)
90–109:	Average
80–89:	Low average (dull)
70–79:	Borderline
69 and below:	Mentally deficient

WPPSI

Like the WISC-R, the WPPSI provides a Verbal IQ, a Performance IQ, and a Full Scale IQ. The WPPSI includes many of the same subtests as the WISC-R, with items designed for a younger population. These subtests include Information, Vocabulary, Arithmetic, Similarities, Comprehension, Picture Completion, Mazes, and Block Design. Digit Span is replaced by Sentences, a sentence repetition task. Coding is replaced by Animal House, a timed task that requires the child to match colored pegs with animal pictures, according to a model presented. Object Assembly and Picture Arrangement subtests are omitted. Geometric Design, a paper-and-pencil figure-copying test, is added.

APPENDIX C

Description of the K-ABC[1]

This brief description of the K-ABC is intended only to give those professionals who are unfamiliar with the test an idea of the types of tasks presented. The reader who wishes further information regarding the test's statistical properties, norming samples, rationale, or administration should review the manual, preferably with the assistance of a psychologist trained to use the K-ABC with the learning-disabled population. Only the Mental Processing portion of the K-ABC is described here. (See Chapter 4 for discussion of the K-ABC Achievement Subtests.)

The K-ABC is designed for use with children aged 2.5 through 12.5 years of age. The K-ABC defines intelligence as the "ability to process information effectively as a means of solving unfamiliar problems" (Kaufman, 1983, p. 206). Three "Global Scores" (or standard scores) are calculated: One for the Sequential Processing Scale, which "measures a child's ability to solve problems by mentally manipulating the stimuli in serial order" (Kaufman, 1983, p. 206); one for the Simultaneous Processing Scale, which "measures problem-solving skill whereby many stimuli have to be organized and integrated in parallel or simultaneous fashion" (Kaufman, 1983, p. 206); and the Mental Processing Composite, which is based on a combination of the Sequential and Simultaneous subtests. (A Global Score for Achievement is also obtained if the achievement subtests are administered. A Nonverbal Global Score can be derived for children who are hearing-impaired, have serious speech-language disorders, or do not speak English.)

Sequential Processing Scale

The three Sequential Processing subtests are described briefly, with the age ranges to which they are administered:

Hand Movements (ages 2 years 6 months through 12 years 5 months)—Performing a series of hand movements in the same sequence as the examiner performed them.

Number Recall (ages 2 years 6 months through 12 years 5 months)—Repeating a series of digits in the same sequence as the examiner said them.

Word Order (ages 4 years 0 months through 12 years 5 months)—Touching a series of silhouettes of common objects in the same sequence as the examiner said the names of the objects. (More difficult items include an interference task between the stimulus and response.)

---

[1]Descriptions of K-ABC subtests are quoted, with permission, from Kaufman, A., and Kaufman, N. (1983). *Kaufman Assessment Battery for Children Interpretive Manual*. Circle Pines, MN: American Guidance Service.

Simultaneous Processing Scale

The seven Simultaneous Processing subtests are described briefly, with the age ranges to which they are administered. All of the subtests are presented on pages of the K-ABC "Easel-Kits" except for Magic Window, Triangles, and Photo Series. The Triangles subtest allows the child to manipulate plastic triangles, and the Photo Series subtest requires the child to arrange cards in order. The Triangles subtest is the only one that limits the amount of time the child is given to arrive at a correct response.

Magic Window (ages 2 years 6 months through 4 years 11 months)— Identifying a picture that the examiner exposes by slowly moving it behind a narrow window, making the picture only partially visible at any one time.

Face Recognition (ages 2 years 6 months through 4 years 11 months)— Selecting from a group photograph the one or two faces that were exposed briefly on the preceding page.

Gestalt Closure (ages 2 years 6 months through 12 years 5 months)— Naming an object or scene pictured in a partially completed "inkblot" drawing.

Triangles (ages 4 years 0 months through 12 years 5 months)— Assembling several identical triangles into an abstract pattern to match a model.

Matrix Analogies (ages 5 years 0 months through 12 years 5 months)— Selecting the meaningful picture or abstract design that best completes a visual analogy.

Spatial Memory (ages 5 years 0 months through 12 years 5 months)— Recalling the placement of pictures on a page that was exposed briefly.

Photo Series (ages 6 years 0 months through 12 years 5 months)— Placing photographs of an event in chronological order.

As indicated by the age ranges, some tests are administered only to younger children, some only to older children, and some to all children. The ratio of Simultaneous to Sequential subtests is 3:2 at ages 2.5 and 3; 4:3 at ages 4 and 5; and 5:3 at ages 6 through 12.5. Most subtests have different starting points, depending on the age of the child. Stopping points for each age group are also indicated, although a child who performs especially well can be given items beyond the normal stopping point for his or her age. All items are scored as either correct (1 point) or incorrect (0 points).

For each subtest, a raw score is calculated that is the total of correct responses. The child's raw score is compared to performance of other children of the same age and assigned a "scaled score" between 1 and 19. Like scaled scores on the WISC-R, the average score is 10, with a standard deviation of 3. Three to five Simultaneous subtest scaled scores (depending on the age of the child) are totalled and converted to a Global Scale score for Simultaneous Processing. Similarly, two or three Sequential subtest scaled scores (depending on the age of the child) are totalled and converted to a Global Scale score for Sequential Processing. All subtest scaled scores are totalled and converted to a Global Scale for Mental Processing Composite. Each of the Global Scale scores has a mean of 100, and a standard deviation of 15, just as the WISC-R VIQ, PIQ, and Full Scale IQ. The K-ABC Manual also provides instructions for obtaining "confidence intervals" (a statistically derived range of scores within which the student's "true score" can be expected to fall), and percentile scores based on both national norms and special norms for various sociocultural groups. Stanines and age-equivalent scores can also be obtained. Verbal descriptions for commonly used standard score ranges are as follows:

130 and above:	Upper extreme
120–129:	Well above average
110–119:	Above average
90–109:	Average
80–89:	Below average
70–79:	Well below average
69 and below:	Lower extreme

Occupational and Physical Therapy Remedial Services

School Program

The following is an "ideal" schedule for planning school-based occupational and physical therapy services for learning-disabled children who demonstrate significant motor deficits. School therapists will modify such a schedule in accordance with limitations on their time, and will work primarily through teachers via consultation and in-service instruction. Given available remedial services including physical and occupational therapy, therapy assistants and aides, and an adaptive physical education program, the following schedule of ancillary services might be arranged for a learning-disabled first grader who demonstrates significant motor deficits. Daily gross motor activities are provided, and individual sessions are scheduled at the suggestion of the therapists and with the teacher's consent.

Monday: Adaptive Behavior Education (30 minutes) with monthly consultation from physical and occupational therapy.

Tuesday: Individual Occupational Therapy (30 to 45 minutes)/Mainstreamed Gym Class (if appropriate) if not, adaptive physical education group.

Wednesday: Individual Physical Therapy (30 minutes).

Thursday: Mainstreamed Gym Class (if appropriate) with twice monthly consultation from physical therapy.

Friday: Sensory/Motor Group with occupational and/or physical therapist (30 minutes)/Individual Therapy (physical therapy/occupational therapy) as indicated (30 minutes)

Home Program

Parents should be scheduled to attend individual treatment sessions at regular intervals for six to eight weeks at which time they would discuss their observations and concerns, participate in short-term goal setting, and receive instruction in and guidelines for correct implementation of a home program designed to support the program goals. A home program might entail a weekly trip to the community park or playground where supervised climbing on ladders, slides, and a jungle gym would be encouraged (within the limits of successful execution). Home programs should be fun and family oriented, and designed to ensure that the child retains control over his or her own body during each activity, and that any assistance he or she receives is offered only as guidance or to reduce anxiety.

Publications Offering Applicable Suggestions for Programming

Stretching, by Bob Anderson, Shelter Publication, Inc., Box 279, Bolinas, California, 94924. These activities can be adapted to address variations in muscle tone, and are useful in home programs and in adapting the warm-up exercises and stretches used in mainstreamed gym class.

Sensory-Motor Integration: An Activities Curricula, by Barbara Fink, OTR, 1328 NW Avenue, Vicksburg, Michigan, 49097; 1977. This is an extensive compilation of suggested activities grouped according to treatment goals.

For ideas on therapeutic dance, see *Clinical Management in Physical Therapy*, 1985, Vol. 5, No. 6, November/December, p. 20.

The Clumsy Child (Arnheim and Sinclair, 1979) offers ideas for motor programming and for employing a trampoline to achieve reflex goals.

REFERENCES

American Psychiatric Association. (1980). *Diagnostic and statistical manual of mental disorders* (3rd ed.). Washington, DC: Author.

Arnheim, D.D., and Sinclair, W.A. (1979). *The clumsy child: A program of motor therapy.* St. Louis: The C.V. Mosby Co.

Ayres, A.J. (1964). Tactile functions: Their relation to hyperactive and perceptual motor behavior. *American Journal of Occupational Therapy, 18,* 6-11.

Ayres, A.J. (1972a). *Sensory integration and learning disorders.* Los Angeles: Western Psychological Services.

Ayres, A.J. (1972b). *Southern California sensory integration tests.* Los Angeles: Western Psychological Services.

Ayres, A.J. (1972c). Improving academic scores through sensory integration. *Journal of Learning Disabilities, 5,* 338-343.

Ayres, A.J. (1975). *Southern California Postrotary Nystagmus Test.* Los Angeles: Western Psychological Services.

Ayres, A.J. (1976). *The effect of sensory integrative therapy on learning disabled children: The final report of a research project.* Los Angeles: Center for the Study of Sensory Integrative Dysfunction.

Ayres, A.J. (1978). Learning disabilities and the vestibular system. *Journal of Learning Disabilities, 11*(1), 18-29.

Ayres, A.J. (1979). *Sensory integration and the child.* Los Angeles, Western Psychological Services.

Ayres, A.J. (1981). Aspects of the somato-motor adaptive response and praxis (Audio Tape). Pasadena: Center for the Study of Sensory Integrative Dysfunction.

Ayres, A.J. (1986). *Sensory Integration and praxis tests-administration manual.* Los Angeles: Western Psychological Services.

Bender, L. (1957). Specific reading disability as a maturational lag. *Bulletin of the Orton Society, 7,* 9-18.

Bender, M.L. (1976). *Bender-Purdue reflex test and training manual.* San Rafael, CA: Academic Therapy Publications.

Berk, R. (1984). *Screening and diagnosis of children with learning disabilities.* Springfield, IL: Charles C. Thomas.

Butler, K.G., Oakland, T., and Bannatyne, A. (1978). Goldman-Fristoe-Woodcock auditory skills battery. In O.K. Buros (Ed.), *The eighth mental measurements yearbook,* (Vol. II, pp. 935-939). Highland Park, NJ: Gryphon Press.

Camp, B., Blom, G., Herbert, F., and Van Doornenck, W. (1977). "Think aloud": A program for developing self-control in young aggressive boys. *Journal of Abnormal Psychology, 5,* 157-169.

Campbell, D., and Stanley, J. (1963). *Experimental and quasi-experimental designs for research.* Chicago: Rand McNally & Co.

Cermak, S.A., and Henderson, A. (1985). Learning disabilities. In D. Umphred (Ed.), *Neurological rehabilitation* (pp. 209-237). St. Louis: The C.V. Mosby Co.

Clark, F., Mailloux, Z., and Parham, D. (1985). Sensory integration and children with learning disabilities. In P.N. Clark and A.S. Allen (Eds.), *Occupational therapy for children* (pp. 359-405). St. Louis: C.V. Mosby Co.

Connolly, B. (1984). Learning disabilities. In S.K. Campbell (Ed.), *Pediatric neurologic physical therapy* (pp. 317-352). New York: Churchill Livingston.

Cratty, B.J., and Martin, M. (1969). *Perceptual-motor efficiency in children.* Philadelphia: Lea & Febiger.

Critchley, M. (1970). *The dyslexic child.* Springfield, IL: Charles Thomas.

DeQuiros, J., and Schrager, O. (1979). *Neuropsychological fundamentals in learning disabilities.* San Rafael, CA: Academic Therapy Publications.

Dunn, W. (1981). *A guide to testing clinical observations.* Rockland, MD: American Occupational Therapy Association.

Embrey, D., Endicott, J., Glenn, T., and Jaeger, D. LaVonne (1983). Developing better postural tone in grade school children. *Clinical Management in Physical Therapy, 3*(3), 6-10.

Frankenburg, W.K, and Dodds, J.B. (1967). The Denver developmental screening test. *Journal of Pediatrics, 71,* 181.

Guilford, J.P. (1967). *The nature of human intelligence.* New York: McGraw-Hill.

Harrington, R. (1984). Assessment of learning disabled children. In S.J. Weaver (Ed.), *Testing children.* Kansas City, MO: Test Corporation of America.

Hessler, G. (1982). *Use and interpretation of the Woodcock-Johnson Psycho-Educational Battery.* Hingham, MA: Teaching Resources Corp.

Hinshelwood, J. (1917). *Congenital word-blindness.* London: Lewis.

Johnson, C. (1981). *The diagnosis of learning disabilities.* Boulder, CO: Pruett Publishing Co.

Kalish, R., and Presseller, S. (1980). Physical and occupational therapy. *Journal of School Health, 50,* 264-267.

Kaufman, A. (1976a). Verbal-Performance IQ discrepancies on the WISC-R. *Journal of Consulting and Clinical Psychology, 44,* 739-744.

Kaufman, A. (1976b). A new approach to the interpretation of test scatter on the WISC-R. *Journal of Learning Disabilities, 9,* 160-168.

Kaufman, A. (1979). *Intelligent testing with the WISC-R.* New York: John Wiley & Sons.

Kaufman, A. (1983). Some questions and answers about the Kaufman Assessment Battery for Children (K-ABC). *Journal of Psychoeducational Assessment, 4,* 205-218.

Kaufman, A. (1985). Review of Woodcock-Johnson Psycho-Educational Battery. In J. Mitchell (Ed.), *The ninth mental measurements yearbook.* Lincoln, NE: University of Nebraska Press.

Kaufman, A., and Doppelt, J. (1976). Analysis of WISC-R standardization data in terms of the stratification variables. *Child Development, 47,* 165-171.

Kaufman, A. and Kaufman, N. (1983). *Kaufman Assessment Battery for Children Interpretive Manual.* Circle Pines, MN: American Guidance Service.

Keith, R.W. (Ed.). (1981). *Central auditory processing and language disorders in children.* Houston, TX: College Hill.

Kendall, P., and Finch, A. (1979). Developing nonimpulsive behavior in children: Cognitive-behavioral strategies for self-control. In P. Kendall and S. Hollon (Eds.), *Cognitive-behavioral interventions: Theory, research, and procedures.* New York: Plenum Press.

Keyser, D., and Sweetland, R. (1985) *Test critiques.* Kansas City, MO: Test Corporation of America.

Kinsbourne, M. (1975). The ontogeny of cerebral dominance. *Annals of the New York Academy of Sciences, 263,* 244-250.

Kirk, S. (1962). *Educating exceptional children*. Boston: Houghton Mifflin.

Klasen, E. (1972). *The syndrome of specific dyslexia*. Baltimore: University Park Press.

Knickerbocker, B. (1980). *A holistic approach to the treatment of learning disorders*. Thoroface, NJ: Charles B. Slack.

Levine, M., Brooks, R., and Shonkoff, J. (1980). *A pediatric approach to learning disorders*. New York: John Wiley & Sons.

Marsh, G., Gearhart, C., and Gearhart, B. (1978). *The learning-disabled student: Program alternative in the secondary school*. St. Louis, MO: C.V. Mosby Co.

McKeever, W., and VanDeventer, A. (1975). Dyslexic adolescents: Evidence of impaired visual and auditory languge processing associated with normal lateralization and visual responsivity. *Cortex, 11*, 361–378.

McLeod, J. (1979). Educational underachievement: Toward a defensible psychometric definition. *Journal of Learning Disabilities, 12*, 322–330.

Meier, J.H. (1971). Prevalence and characteristics of learning disabilities found in second grade children. *Journal of Learning Disabilities, 4*, 1–16.

Mitchell, J. (Ed.). (1985). *The ninth mental measurements yearbook*. Lincoln, NE: University of Nebraska Press.

National Joint Committee for Learning Disabilities. (1981). *Learning disabilities: Issues on definition*. Unpublished position paper. (Available from Drake Duane, NJCLD Chairperson, c/o The Orton Dyslexia Society, 8415 Bellona Lane, Towson, MD 21204).

Newby, H.A. (1972). *Audiology* (3rd Ed.). Englewood Cliffs, NJ: Prentice Hall.

Parmenter, C. (1975). The asymmetrical tonic neck reflex in normal first and third grade children. *American Journal of Occupational Therapy, 29*, 463–468.

Parr, C., Routh, D.K., Byrd, M.T., and McMillan, J. (1974). A developmental study of the asymmetrical tonic neck reflex. *Developmental Medicine and Child Neurology, 16*, 329–335.

Phye, G. and Reschly, D. (1979). *School psychology: Perspectives and issues*. New York: Academic Press.

Position statement on language learning disorders. (1982). *American Speech and Hearing Association Journal, 24*(11), 937–944.

Public Law 94-142. (1975). Education for All Handicapped Children Act, S.6, 94th Congress [Sec. 613 (a) (4)]. Report No. 94–168.

Reynolds, C. (1984-1985). Critical measurement issues in learning disabilities. *Journal of Special Education, 18*, 451–476.

Roth, F.R., and Spekman, N.J. (1986). Narrative discourse: Spontaneously generated stories of learning-disabled and normally achieving students. *Journal of speech and hearing disorders, 51*(2), 8–23.

Rourke, B.P. (1985). *Neuropsychology of learning disabilities: Essentials of subtype analysis*. New York: The Guilford Press.

Safer, D., and Allen, R. (1976). *Hyperactive children: Diagnosis and management*. Baltimore: University Park Press.

Sanger, D.D. (1985). Clinical evaluation of language functions-Diagnostic battery. In J.V. Mitchell, Jr. (Ed.), *Mental measurements yearbook* (Vol. 1, pp. 341–342). Lincoln, NE: University of Nebraska Press.

Silver, S. (1952). Psychologic aspects of pediatrics: Postural and righting responses in children, *Pediatrics, 41*, 493.

U.S. Office of Education. (1977). Assistance to states for education for handicapped children: Procedures for evaluating specific learning disabilities. *Federal Register*, 42(250), 62082–62085.

Wiig, E.H., and Semel, E.M. (1976). *Language disabilities in children and adolescents*. Columbus, OH: Charles E. Merrill.

Wiig, E.H. and Semel, E.M. (1980). *Language assessment and intervention for the learning disabled*. Columbus, OH: Charles E. Merrill.

Wiig, E.H. and Semel, E.M. (1984). *Language assessment and intervention for the learning disabled* (2nd ed.). Columbus, OH: Charles E. Merrill.

Witelson, S. (1977). Neural and cognitive correlates of developmental dyslexia: Age and sex differences. In C. Shagaes, S. Gershon, and A. Friedhoff (Eds.), *Psychopathology and brain dysfunction*. New York: Raven Press.

REFERENCE LIST OF TESTS

Tests included in this list are not necessarily endorsed by the authors. A number of these tests are discussed in the text and are referenced in the index.

Auditory Discrimination Test (1973)
Joseph M. Wepman
Western Psychological Services
12031 Wilshire Boulevard, Los Angeles, CA 90025

Bender Visual Motor Gestalt Test (1946)
Lauretta Bender
American Orthopsychiatric Association
49 Sheridan Ave., Albany, NY 12210

Benton Revised Visual Retention Test (1974)
Arthur Benton
The Psychological Corporation
555 Academic Ct., San Antonio, TX 78204

Boehm Test of Basic Concepts (1971)
Ann E. Boehm
The Psychological Corporation
555 Academic Ct., San Antonio, TX 78204

Brigance Diagnostic Comprehensive Inventory of Basic Skills (1983)
Albert H. Brigance
Curriculum Associates, Inc.
5 Esquire Rd., North Billerica, MA 01862-2589

Bruininks-Oseretsky Test of Motor Proficiency (1978)
Robert H. Bruininks
American Guidance Service
Publisher's Building, Circle Pines, MN 55014

Carrow Elicited Language Inventory (1974)
Learning Concepts
Allen, TX 75002

Children's Apperception Test (1980)
Leopold Bellak and Sonya Sorel Bellak
C. P. S., Inc.
Box 83, Larchmont, NY 10538

Clinical Evaluation of Language Functions-Diagnostic Battery (1980)
Charles E. Merrill
Columbus, OH 43216

Cognitive Abilities Test (1983)
Robert L. Thorndike and Elizabeth Hagen
Riverside Publishing Co.
8420 Bryn Mawr Ave., Chicago, IL 60631

Denver Developmental Screening Test (1981)
William K. Frankenburg
Ladoca Publishing Foundation
511 Lincoln St., Denver, CO 80216

Detroit Tests of Learning Aptitude (1975)
Harry J. Baker and Bernice Leland
Bobbs-Merrill Educational Publishing
4300 West 62nd St., P.O. Box 7080, Indianapolis, IN 46206

Developmental Sentence Analysis (1974)
Northwestern University Press
Evanston, IL

Developmental Test of Visual-Motor Integration (1983)
Keith E. Beery and Norman A. Buktenica
Modern Curriculum Press, Inc.
13900 Prospect Road, Cleveland, OH 44136

Durrell Analysis of Reading Difficulty (1980)
Donald D. Durrell and Jane H. Catterson
The Psychological Corporation
555 Academic Ct., San Antonio, TX 78204

Frostig Developmental Test of Visual Perception (1961)
Marianne Frostig and Associates
Consulting Psychologists Press, Inc.
577 College Avenue, P.O. Box 60070, Palo Alto, CA 94306

Full Range Picture Vocabulary Test (1948)
R.B. Ammons and H.S. Ammons
Psychological Test Specialists
Box 9229, Missoula, MT 59807

**Goldman-Fristoe-Woodcock Auditory
Skills Test Battery (1976)**
Ronald Goldman, Macalyne Fristoe,
and Richard W. Woodcock
American Guidance Service
Publisher's Building, Circle Pines, MN
55014

Gray Oral Reading Test (1967)
Helen Robinson
Western Psychological Services
12031 Wilshire Boulevard, Los Angeles,
CA 90025

House-Tree-Person Technique (1981)
John N. Buck
Western Psychological Services
12031 Wilshire Boulevard, Los Angeles,
CA 90025

**Illinois Test of Psycholinguistic
Abilities (1968)**
Samuel A. Kirk, James J. McCarthy,
and Winifred D. Kirk
University of Illinois Press
54 E. Gregory Dr., Box 5081, Station A,
Champaign, IL 61820

**Kaufman Assessment Battery for
Children (1983)**
Alan S. Kaufman and Nadeen L. Kaufman
American Guidance Service
Publisher's Building, Circle Pines, MN
55014

**Kaufman Test of Educational
Achievement (1985)**
Alan S. Kaufman and Nadeen L. Kaufman
American Guidance Service
Publisher's Building, Circle Pines, MN
55014

**KeyMath Diagnostic Arithmetic Test
(1976)**
Austin Connolly, William Nachtman,
and E.M. Pritchett
American Guidance Service
Publisher's Building, Circle Pines, MN
55014

Memory for Designs Test (1960)
Frances K. Graham and Barbara S.
Kendall
Psychological Test Specialists
Box 9229, Missoula, MT 59807

Metropolitan Readiness Tests (1976)
Joanne R. Nurss and Mary E.
McGauvran
The Psychological Corporation
555 Academic Ct., San Antonio, TX
78204

**Motor-Free Visual Perception Test
(1972)**
Ronald R. Colarusso and Donald D.
Hammill
Academic Therapy Publications
20 Commercial Boulevard, Novato, CA
94947

Otis-Lennon Mental Ability Test (1982)
Arthur S. Otis and Roger T. Lennon
The Psychological Corporation
555 Academic Ct., San Antonio, TX
78204

**Peabody Individual Achievement Test
(1970)**
Lloyd M. Dunn and Fredrick C.
Markwardt, Jr.
American Guidance Service
Publisher's Building, Circle Pines, MN
55014

**Peabody Picture Vocabulary Test—
Revised (1981)**
Lloyd M. Dunn and Leota M. Dunn
American Guidance Service
Publisher's Building, Circle Pines, MN
55014

Progressive Matrices Test (1983)
J.C. Raven
H.K. Lewis & Co., Ltd.
U.S. Distributor: The Psychological
Corporation
555 Academic Ct., San Antonio, TX
78204

Quick Test (1962)
R.B. Ammons and C.H. Ammons
Psychological Test Specialists
Box 9229, Missoula, MT 59807

Rorschach Psychodiagnostic Test (1981)
Hermann Rorschach
Hans Huber
Distributed by Grune & Stratton
111 Fifth Ave., New York, NY 10003

Sensory Integration and Praxis Tests (1986)
A. Jean Ayres
Western Psychological Services
12031 Wilshire Boulevard, Los Angeles, CA 90025

Slosson Intelligence Test (1981)
Richard L. Slosson
Slosson Educational Publications, Inc.
P.O. Box 280, East Aurora, NY 14052

Southern California Postrotary Nystagmus Test (1975)
A. Jean Ayres
Western Psychological Services
12031 Wilshire Boulevard, Los Angeles, CA 90025

Southern California Sensory Integration Tests (1972)
A. Jean Ayres
Western Psychological Services
12031 Wilshire Boulevard, Los Angeles, CA 90025

Stanford-Binet Intelligence Scale (1986)
R.L. Thorndike, E.P. Hagen, and J.M. Sattler
The Riverside Publishing Co.
8420 Bryn Mawr Ave., Chicago, IL 60631

Stanford Diagnostic Reading Test (1976)
Bjorn Karlsen, Richard Madden, and Eric F. Gardner
The Psychological Corporation
555 Academic Ct., San Antonio, TX 78204

Test for Auditory Comprehension of Language—Revised (1985)
DLM Teaching Resources
Allen, TX

Test of Adolescent Language (1980)
PRO-ED
5341 Industrial Oaks Boulevard, Austin, Texas 78735

Test of Language Development— Intermediate (1982)
PRO-ED
5341 Industrial Oaks Boulevard, Austin, Texas 78735

Test of Language Development— Primary (1982)
PRO-ED
5341 Industrial Oaks Boulevard, Austin, Texas 78735

Test of Written Language (1983)
Donald D. Hammill and Stephen C. Larsen
PRO-ED
5341 Industrial Oaks Boulevard, Austin, Texas 78735

Test of Written Spelling (1976)
Stephen C. Larsen and Donald D. Hammill
PRO-ED
5341 Industrial Oaks Boulevard, Austin, TX 78735

Thematic Apperception Test (1943)
Henry Alexander Murray
Harvard University Press
79 Garden Street, Cambridge, MA 02138

Wechsler Adult Intelligence Scale— Revised (1981)
David Wechsler
The Psychological Corporation
555 Academic Ct., San Antonio, TX 78204

Wechsler Intelligence Scale for Children—Revised (1974)
David Wechsler
The Psychological Corporation
555 Academic Ct., San Antonio, TX 78204

Wechsler Preschool and Primary Scale of Intelligence (1967)
David Wechsler
The Psychological Corporation
555 Academic Ct., San Antonio, TX 78204

Wide Range Achievement Test—Revised (1984)
Sarah Jastak and Gary S. Wilkinson
Jastak Associates, Inc.
1526 Gilpin Avenue, Wilmington, DE 19806

Woodcock-Johnson Psycho-Educational Battery (1977)
Richard W. Woodcock and Mary Bonner Johnson
DLM Teaching Resources
One DLM Park, Allen, TX 75002

Woodcock Reading Mastery Test (1973)
Richard W. Woodcock
American Guidance Service
Publisher's Building, Circle Pines, MN 55014

Subject Index

Italic page numbers refer to tables and figures.

B

Basic Motor Abilities Test-Revised, 107–108
Behavioral problems, 124
    management system, 158–164
        home-based system, *160*
        rewards, 161–164
        school-based system, *161*
    psychotherapy, 164
Bender Visual Motor Gestalt Test, 56
Benton Visual Retention Test, 56
Boehm Test of Basic Concepts, 76
Brain damage. *See* Primary handicapping conditions.
Bruininks-Oseretsky Test of Motor Proficiency, 107, 141

C

Carrow Elicited Language Inventory, 92–93
Children's Apperception Test, 57
Classroom observation, in educational evaluation, 64–66
Classroom placement considerations, 133–135, *134*
Clinical Evaluation of Language Functions-Diagnostic
Battery, 91, 94–95
Criterion-referenced tests, 76–77

D

Denver Developmental Screening Test, 20
Detroit Tests of Learning Aptitude, 56
Developmental dyspraxia, 101–102
Developmental Sentence Scores, *92–93*
Developmental Test of Visual-Motor Integration, 56
Durrell Analysis of Reading Difficulty, 73–74
Dyscalculia. *See* Mathematics disability.
Dysgraphia. *See* Written language disability.
Dyslexia. *See* Reading disability.

E

Education for All Handicapped Children Act. *See* Public Law 94-142.
Educational history,
    classroom observation, 64–66
    educational quotient, 111-113, *112*
    educational testing. *See* Academic achievement testing.
    parent interview, 66–67
    school record review, 59–61
    teacher interview, 61–64

Neurological irregularities, in learning disabilities, 7–8
Neurologically based handicapping conditions. *See* Primary handicapping
    conditions.

O

Occupational therapy evaluation,
    clinical observations, 100–101
    history-taking, 96, 98
        sensorimotor history, *96–97*
    interpretation of results, 101–103
        developmental dyspraxia, 101–102
        generalized dysfunction, 102
        gravitational insecurity, 102–103
        intolerance to movement, 102–103
        tactile defensiveness, 103
        vestibular integration dysfunction, 102
    testing, 98–100
        Sensory Integration and Praxis Test, 98–100
    therapy approaches, 139–141
        program implementation, 140–141
Organizational and study skills problems, 120–121
Orton-Gillingham educational approach, 136

P

Parent interview,
    in educational evaluation, 66–67
    in neurodevelopmental evaluation, 16-19
    in occupational evaluation, 96-98
    in physical evaluation, 104
    in psychological evaluation, 33-34
    in speech-language evaluation, 84, *85–86*
Peabody Individual Achievement Test, 72
Peabody Picture Vocabulary Test-Revised, 24, 42, *92–93*
Physical therapy evaluation, 103–104
    clinical observations, 104–107
    history-taking, 104
    testing, 107–108
        Basic Motor Abilities Test-Revised, 107–108
        Bruininks-Oseretsky Test of Motor Proficiency, 107
    therapy approaches, 139–140
        program implementation, 141–143
Preschool-aged children,
    appropriate tests, 42
    neurodevelopmental examination, 20

S